A Black Jurist in a Slave Society

A book in the series Latin America in Translation /
en Traducción / em Tradução

This book was sponsored by the Consortium in Latin American and
Caribbean Studies at the University of North Carolina at Chapel Hill
and Duke University.

A Black Jurist in a Slave Society

Antonio Pereira Rebouças and the
Trials of Brazilian Citizenship

. . . .

KEILA GRINBERG

Translated by KRISTIN M. McGUIRE

Foreword by BARBARA WEINSTEIN

The University of North Carolina Press Chapel Hill

Translation of the books in the series Latin America in Translation /
en Traducción / em Tradução, a collaboration between the Consortium
in Latin American and Caribbean Studies at the University of North
Carolina at Chapel Hill and Duke University and the university presses
of the University of North Carolina and Duke, is supported by a grant
from the Andrew W. Mellon Foundation.

Library of Congress Cataloging-in-Publication Data
Names: Grinberg, Keila, author. | McGuire, Kristin, translator. | Weinstein,
    Barbara, writer of foreword.
Title: A black jurist in a slave society : Antonio Pereira Rebouças and the
    trials of Brazilian citizenship / Keila Grinberg ; translated by Kristin M.
    McGuire ; foreword by Barbara Weinstein.
Other titles: Fiador dos brasileiros. English | Latin America in translation/
    en traduccion/em traducao.
Description: Chapel Hill : University of North Carolina Press, [2019] |
    Series: Latin America in translation / en traduccion / em traducao |
    Translation of: O fiador dos brasileiros : cidadania, escravidao e direito
    civil no tempo de Antonio Pereira Rebouças / Keila Grinberg. Rio de
    Janeiro : Civilizacao Brasileira, 2002. | Includes bibliographical
    references and index.
Identifiers: LCCN 2019004290| ISBN 9781469652764 (cloth : alk. paper) |
    ISBN 9781469652771 (pbk : alk. paper) | ISBN 9781469652788 (ebook)
Subjects: LCSH: Rebouças, Antonio Pereira, 1798–1880. | Lawyers—
    Brazil—Biography. | Slavery—Law and legislation—Brazil—History—
    19th century. | Citizenship—Brazil—History—19th century. | Civil
    rights—Brazil—History—19th century. | Brazil—Politics and
    government—1822–1889.
Classification: LCC KHD304.R43 G7513 2019 | DDC 340.092 [B]—dc23
    LC record available at https://lccn.loc.gov/2019004290.

Cover illustration: "O sr Antonio Pereira Rebouças," *O Novo Mundo*
(newspaper), 22 February 1875, 1. Brazil National Library.

It is impossible to consider the Brazil of Dom Pedro I, Dom Pedro II, and Princess Isabel, the Brazil of the campaign for the abolition of slavery and for the agitation for the republic, and too, of the courtships between a young lady on the verandah speaking the language of love with her fan, flower, or handkerchief and a young gent on the corner in high hat and frock coat, without taking into account two great forces that are new and triumphant, and sometimes conjoined in one: the man of letters and the mulatto.

—Gilberto Freyre, *Sobrados e Mucambos* (The Mansions and the Shanties), 354

Contents

Graph and Table

Graph

Table

Foreword

One of the central goals of historians inspired by the social movements of the past half-century—movements organized around race, gender, sexuality—has been to rescue from historical oblivion the lives and significance of individuals who were not white, male, and upper class. More recently, historians have sought to go beyond what some have critically called a "salvage operation" to consider how the writings and deeds of these previously forgotten individuals impel us to rethink our notions of the past and of the very identities that made us interested in our research subjects in the first place. Keila Grinberg's magisterial study of Antonio Pereira Rebouças and the political and juridical worlds that he inhabited and shaped is a stellar example of a work that both restores a remarkable individual to his rightful place as a historically significant figure and goes far beyond a simple act of recuperation to illuminate the tensions and contradictions of the Brazilian nation-building project.

At first glance, it seems incredible that Antonio Pereira Rebouças would have been in need of "rescue" at all since he was undoubtedly one of the most visible and influential men of acknowledged African descent in any slave society in the Americas. He was an eminent jurist, an advisor to the emperor, an elected legislator; to identify a "man of color" of similar prominence in the nineteenth-century United States, we would have to cite someone such as Frederick Douglass, a familiar figure to anyone with even a passing interest in African American history. But perhaps the juxtaposition of Rebouças and Douglass can help us understand why the former languished in relative obscurity until the publication of Keila Grinberg's book, as well as why his son, the noted engineer and celebrated abolitionist André Rebouças, is much better known to students of Brazilian history than his father. While Douglass was himself a man of great complexity and occasional contradictions, he undeniably corresponds to some of our principal expectations with regard to prominent black historical actors, having escaped from bondage and then become an implacable foe of slavery and a crusader for the rights of African Americans and women. Whatever his particular idiosyncrasies, Frederick Douglass certainly qualifies as a champion of the oppressed.

Antonio Pereira Rebouças, on the other hand, presents a genuine challenge to our standard expectations, as Keila Grinberg's study makes evident. Not only was he never a slave (which was true of many Afro-descendants in early nineteenth-century Brazil), but he never spoke out against slavery, regarding it as a property relation protected by the liberal legal precepts that he held dear. What he did oppose, consistently and vociferously, was a racialized justification for slavery, and any form of bias or disadvantage based on racial difference. Throughout his career as a lawyer, writer, and politician, he championed the claims of both descendants of slaves and ex-slaves to full citizenship. Yet even though he himself suffered various political attacks and personal slights because of his color, and clearly spoke from his position as a racialized person, he insisted on divorcing the problem of race from the problem of slavery, or at least attempted to do so. Furthermore, he collaborated in the repression of popular political revolts and defended the rights of slaveholders to their human property. In other words, it would be difficult to venerate Antonio Pereira Rebouças as a champion of the oppressed. Fortunately, the historian who took on the crucial task of exploring his role in Brazil's political and legal construction did so not to create a transcendent hero, but to consider how his ideas and actions and his personal trajectory reflected a central problem of the new Brazilian nation—the tension between liberalism and the persistence of human enslavement.

Given Rebouças's insistence on the irrelevance of race in the allocation of rights, one can appreciate why liberalism, with its promise of equality before the law, appealed to him, but also why, given his precarious position in Brazilian circles of prestige and authority, he felt compelled to defend liberalism in all its connotations. Thus, even as he opposed the transatlantic slave trade and supported legal protections for slaves who sought to purchase their freedom, he never challenged the sanctity of private property, including in human flesh.

In drawing this contrast between Antonio Pereira Rebouças and Frederick Douglass, my intention is certainly not to reproduce the persistent but problematic notion that Afro-descendant Brazilians lagged behind their North American counterparts in terms of militancy or race consciousness. For one thing, there were a number of black Brazilian abolitionists, such as Rebouças's semi-contemporary, Luiz Gama, whose political trajectories closely resembled that of Frederick Douglass. But what is especially worthy of note is the degree to which Rebouças's particular profile—as an eminent man of color, an important jurist and political advisor, and one who consistently disputed any attempt to use race as a means to diminish the rights of free Afrodescendants—may well be unimaginable in any other slave society.

The general trend in the recent literature on enslavement and emancipation in the Americas, particularly the studies produced by scholars of what has become known as the "Second Slavery," has been to foreground the similarities in the various nineteenth-century slave regimes. By and large, this has been a welcome antidote to the previous tendency to overstate the differences between slavery in North America and Latin America. Still, it is important to keep in mind the specificities of the Brazilian slave regime, including the very large population of free people of color—a much larger percentage of the Afro-descendant population than was the case in the United States—as well as the much wider distribution of slave ownership in Brazilian society, and the much greater presence of slaves and freedpersons of African birth. Each of these features of life under slavery in Brazil contributed to the opportunities and the constraints that made the career of Antonio Pereira Rebouças possible and that shaped his political worldview. The dilemmas that he faced in simultaneously championing the rights of Afro-descendants and supporting the existing politico-legal order surely tell us much about the era in which he lived; in certain ways, moreover, they also resonate with the political challenges of our own time. It is the rare book that so powerfully illuminates both the past and the present, and that does justice to a historical figure of such great complexity. For all of these reasons and more, we are very fortunate to have a fine translation of Keila Grinberg's remarkable book available to the English-reading public.

Barbara Weinstein
New York University

Preface to the English-Language Edition

Since this book was originally published in Portuguese in 2002, several studies have considered the role of Afro-Brazilian intellectuals in the tensions between liberalism, concepts of citizenship, and racial identities and politics in nineteenth-century Brazil.[1] In many ways, these works deal with what historian Hebe Mattos has defined as a "racial silence," probably one of the country's most enduring legal legacies of slavery.[2] Unlike in the United States, where institutionalized segregation and racial terror created distinct patterns of racism and shaped African American ideas of identity, respectability, and moral obligation, in Brazil race was rarely acknowledged at the level of legislation. Even during the period of slavery, there were very few references to race in the Brazilian legal code; while enslaved and freedpersons remained socially stigmatized, free Afro-descendants in Brazil experienced a formal equality unusual in most slave societies. This unique position helps to explain why nineteenth-century Afro-Brazilian intellectuals—who were involved in the movements of culture described by Paul Gilroy in *The Black Atlantic* and more recently by Achille Mbembe in *Critique of Black Reason*—fought stridently for their own inclusion in society, but also complicitly embraced an ethic of silence on race as a broader topic.[3]

For many free Afro-descendants—Antonio Pereira Rebouças among them—this silence was crucial to the project of defining spaces of social mobility and respectability regardless of their race. It was also stifling, however, and played an important role in quelling any potential political mobilization that might have been based on racial identity. Rebouças's trajectory as a liberal, yet conservative, public man offers a quintessential example of this contradiction: even though he rejected movements that were grounded in racial political mobilization and was against any political identification based on race, he was, throughout his whole political career, treated as potentially dangerous for the single fact that he was of African origin.

After slavery ended, the formalization of equal civil rights and an institutionalized silence about race in official records often obscured the everyday practices of racism and the development of racial inequalities. It is only recently, 130 years after the abolition of slavery in Brazil, that this silence has been broken, primarily due to the determined actions of a growing black social movement. It is important to keep in mind, however, that the legal inheritances of this silence remain.

· · · · · ·

This book was originally written over twenty years ago. It began as a PhD dissertation, developed in part during a yearlong fellowship at the University of Maryland at College Park. I defended the dissertation at the Universidade Federal Fluminense in 2000. Although I have updated some references and edited the text with non-Brazilianists in mind, the argument remains the same. I have kept the nineteenth-century racial terminology in Portuguese.[4] *Preto*, literally "black," usually referred to an enslaved person, whether born in Brazil or Africa.[5] *Pardo* ("brown") most often meant a nonwhite person born free, although it was also used to describe enslaved mulattoes. A *mulatto* was almost always a free person of mixed race. *Cabra*, formally a child of a *preto* and a *pardo*, was most commonly used to describe a dark mulatto. And *negro* almost always signified an enslaved person.

Spending the Spring 2018 semester at New York University as the Andres Bello Chair in Latin American Cultures and Civilizations at the King Juan Carlos I of Spain Center gave me the essential workspace to focus on this translated edition of the book. I thank Kristin McGuire for everything, including being such a careful reader of this book and a skilled, creative writer.

Reading the acknowledgments from the Brazilian edition, it is gratifying that I would still thank the same people for their contributions to this work: Ana Mauad, Sheila de Castro Faria, Gladys S. Ribeiro, Ronaldo Vainfas, and Virgínia Fontes, my former professors at Universidade Federal Fluminense; Ira Berlin and Leslie Rowland, my professors at the University of Maryland at College Park; Wanderley Guilherme dos Santos, Sidney Chalhoub, João José Reis, Martha Abreu, and Hebe Mattos, the members of my dissertation committee; and Daryle Williams, Stephan Palmie, Rebecca Lord, Jonathan Shurberg, Linda Noel, Sueann Caulfield, Bebete Martins, Brodie Fischer, and Emilio Kouri, all deeply valued friends and colleagues who eased and enhanced my early academic life in the United States. My godmother, Sultana Levy Rosenblatt, and Maria Almeida revised the Brazilian edition of this book. I continue to appreciate the presence of many dear friends, some of them now colleagues, in both my personal and academic life: Adriana Morgado, Alexandre Valuzuela, Ana Nogueira, Anita Almeida, Beatriz Mamigonian, Claudia Santos, Daniela Uziel, Patrícia Sampaio, Ivana Stolze Lima, José Antonio Ribas Soares, Karen Klajman, Lucia Grinberg, Maria Correa, Marcia Chuva, Marcia Ladeira, Mariana Muaze, Marta Fidlarczyk, Miriam Lahtermaher, Ricardo Salles, Sheila Bazilewsky, Simone Intrator, and Simone Raitzik. My family supported me in all possible ways, especially my grandfather Leo Epstein, my brother Alexandre Grinberg, and my sister-in-law Rachel Platenik. My parents, Piedade and Túlio Grinberg, deserve a special thank-you for always encouraging me in my projects.

It has been a gift in my academic career that my colleagues are also my good friends. I am proud to have been advised by Hebe Mattos, who remains both a mentor and an academic partner. In the United States, Paulina Alberto, Sueann Caulfield, Brodie Fischer, and Daryle Williams have been my interlocutors since my graduate student days. They have pushed my thinking on these subjects, but more, their friendship has brought joy and pleasure to our shared commitment to the field of history. And then there is Barbara Weinstein. This translated version of my book would not exist without her encouragement and support. I am deeply appreciative of her friendship.

In my own life, there have been additions and losses, and I am grateful for the love and support of those around me, especially Flavio Limoncic. I know that my dad would have been proud to see this English-language edition. My daughters, Tatiana and Carolina, were not yet born when I wrote this book, and I wish I could tell them that racism and all forms of prejudice are stains of the past. But *a luta continua*, and I am happy to witness the two of you growing as passionate (but ever kind) fighters.

Rebecca Lord and Jonathan Shurberg participated in every phase of researching and writing the original version of this book. It seems terribly unfair that they are not here to celebrate together this English version—one they could actually read!—with an abundance of food, drink, and good cheer, as was their way. Rebecca and Jon left this world far too early—you are highly missed, my dear friends.

Preface to the Portuguese-Language Edition

It is a great pleasure to write the preface to Keila Grinberg's second book. During our ten years of knowing each other, starting out as student and advisor, we have developed a unique friendship and academic partnership. While I was conducting my own doctoral research, Keila was an undergraduate, joyfully discovering the National Archives. Poking around the documents one day, she came across over 400 freedom lawsuits from the late 1800s that had gone to the Court of Appeals. I had looked at a handful of lawsuits myself when studying cases of people moving from slavery to freedom in the mid-nineteenth century, but clearly this trove of legal documents raised a whole new level of questions. The lawsuits called for someone to delve into a study of the history of law and liberal ideas in the context of slavery in nineteenth-century Brazil. I suggested to Keila that she might be the one to pursue this, and that work resulted in her well-received first book, *Liberata: A lei da ambiguidade* (1994).

Keila continued to research and reflect on the relationship between civil law, liberalism, and slavery in nineteenth-century Brazil, while my own research became increasingly focused on processes of building racial identities in Brazil after the abolition of slavery. Our exchanges grew ever more rich as we found that these two issues were closely related, and they eventually came together more concretely in the study of a figure who was unique to understanding the relations between civil law, liberalism, and slavery in nineteenth-century Brazil, as well as the processes of racialization in this same period: Antonio Pereira Rebouças.

In this short preface, rather than reporting on Keila's many contributions to the historiography or praising the literary qualities of her prose, I will share how much I have learned from Keila's approach to our old acquaintance, Rebouças. I also want to suggest that at this present moment, when the question of adopting affirmative action policies to combat racism in Brazil places the issue of racial identities at the center of public debate, a better understanding about the meanings of being *preto* or *pardo* in nineteenth-century Brazil under slavery is crucial to the current question of who is black and what that means in contemporary Brazil.

Central to this discussion about blackness is an understanding that black racial identities in the Americas developed in conjunction with the emergence of modern racism. Europeans increasingly relied on concepts of race to justify African slavery, and later to justify the restriction of civil rights of Afro-descendant populations. Thus, during the eighteenth and nineteenth centuries when the values of freedom and equality of Western modernity were emerging and being diffused, there was also a growing ethos of racialization that supported a social hierarchy based on race.

In this context of the progressive racialization of slavery and struggles for abolition, a new social subject developed: the black intellectual trained in the framework of modern Western culture. Rebouças is a paradigmatic example of this figure. Rebouças's entire intellectual and political career, as well as his worldviews, grew from the new possibilities opened by the principles of equality and freedom that were revolutionizing the Atlantic world. For many years, he climbed the social ladder and was a successful politician and lawyer, and yet, the continued existence of slavery and the individual and daily experience of racism never let him forget his condition as a *pardo*.

Keila Grinberg offers us a comprehensive reading of the multiple meanings of Reboucas's thoughts—liberal and antiracist, although not antislavery. Her introduction opens with an excerpt published by Rebouças in his own newspaper, *O Bahiano*, in 1829, which refers to the equality of law between "citizens of all classes and status" and to his "cause": the "Cause of Justice," "of the human race," and "of all the rational beings who expect from the protection of laws . . . their fortune, their security, their happiness."

In the last lines of her conclusion, Grinberg reasserts that "Rebouças spent his life insisting in the Assembly and in the courts on the principles of equality, arguing that what was then called race did not matter. Or, at least, should not matter." One of the main indirect conclusions to be drawn from Grinberg's important work is that a man who spent his life denying race as a justification for the legal continuity of slavery—with which he agreed—or as a reason to restrict civil and political rights of new Brazilian citizens, himself spoke, thought, and acted always first and foremost as a racialized person.

This is not a biography of Rebouças. Rather, Grinberg has considered the life story of this enigmatic figure as a key to understanding the dilemmas of nineteenth-century Brazilian modernity, especially in the field of law and its role in the continued presence of slavery. In doing so, her text sheds light not only on the fundamental dilemma in nineteenth-century Brazil of how to create a liberal government in the context of a slave society, but also on the social identity of this man who was deeply involved in these debates—and who refused to view political or legal rights via the lens of race, but was himself racialized throughout his life.

Rebouças is a guiding thread in Grinberg's study of slavery, liberalism, and civil rights, and we follow his story through three parts. Part 1, "Civil Rights," presents the world of Rebouças from an Atlantic perspective. In Salvador, Rio de Janeiro, Baltimore, or New Orleans, since the late eighteenth century, many Afro-descendants moved from slavery to freedom—yet, even as free individuals, they continued to be marked by racial stigma. These men and women, either having been enslaved themselves or having lived close to slavery, faced daily conflicts about the meanings of this freedom, in the most essential or basic terms in which the notion of civil rights can be experienced. By considering this Atlantic dimension of the dilemma between modernity and slavery in the nineteenth century, Grinberg highlights the specificity of the Brazilian situation, with its Iberian cultural bias and the presence of an unprecedented number of Africans of various ethnicities.

In Brazil, as in all of Afro-America, the experience of racism and the movement of liberal revolutions with their promises of civil equality and freedom produced black intellectuals torn apart by a double consciousness—in the case of Rebouças, a *pardo* and a citizen of Brazil. In the broader context, however, the simultaneous conservatism and vanguardism of Rebouças's thinking was specifically Brazilian, given the dramatic increase of manumission rates throughout the nineteenth century and the formation of a significant population of free blacks. He defended the legality of slavery in the name of property rights, but he fought against the African slave trade (although not against the entry of Africans as "free" settlers) and supported the legalization of enslaved persons' rights to buy their own freedom and civil equality among all Brazilian citizens. "Any *pardo* or *preto* can be a general," the title of chapter 2, was one of the main sentences attributed to Rebouças and emblematic of his philosophy.

The second part of the book, "Civil Rights and Liberalism," reconsiders the classic debates about nation building in nineteenth-century Brazil from the perspective of a black jurist and intellectual. Grinberg analyzes the liberalism of the generation who fought for Brazilian independence, looking in particular at the limitations of their political strategies. The political ostracism of Rebouças allows us to consider the events of the 1830s—when the conservatives came to power—and the actions that followed beyond the usual dichotomies of public versus private, and centralization versus decentralization. The rise of the conservatives and the defeat of liberal ideas are essential to understanding the thoughts of other nonwhite nineteenth-century Brazilian intellectuals at this time, such as the lawyer Luiz Gama or the writer Machado de Assis.

In part 3, "Civil Rights and Civil Law," Grinberg returns to the topic of nineteenth-century Brazilian modernity, particularly with regard to the law and its greatest challenge, the institution of slavery. Her work comes full circle here: having begun her academic career with a study of the freedom lawsuit of Liberata, in this final section of the book she analyzes a number of freedom suits to consider the conflicts between modern ideals of equality and property and the institution of slavery. In this section, Grinberg takes up the well-known difficulties of codifying civil law in Brazil. In addition to deepening our understanding of that drawn-out process, she shows how the civil code that finally emerged was constructed around the omission of the slave past—an omission that ensured a racialized social hierarchy. As can be seen in the writings of leading jurists of the late nineteenth and early twentieth centuries, even with the formal guarantee of equal rights after abolition, the term "pardo"—much to the despair of Rebouças—continued to be loaded with hierarchical significance associated with the stigma of slavery.

I invite the reader to follow Keila Grinberg as she traces the life of this man who saw himself as "the guarantor of the Brazilians"—an educated, successful black man to be viewed as assurance that blacks could indeed be upstanding citizens—and became a specialist in civil law in a country where citizens and slaves coexisted. The most fundamental rights, such as the right to physical integrity, to freedom of movement, and to the possession of property, had specific meaning for those who were enslaved or lived close to slavery. Rebouças was betting on the promises of legal equality and liberalism as he built his identity as a black Brazilian citizen. Following his trajectory, Grinberg captures new dimensions, from both the social and political point of view, of the problems posed by the codification of civil law in nineteenth-century Brazil.

Hebe Mattos
Professor of History
Universidade Federal Fluminense

A Black Jurist in a Slave Society

Introduction

· ·

No one should serve despotism and inequity. . . . My Cause is the Cause of
Justice, it is the Cause that the Emperor swore; and that every Nation has
sworn; this Cause belongs to Citizens of all Classes and Status—this Cause is
of the human race—of all the rational beings who expect from the protection
of Laws, and from their fulfillment and observance, their fortune, their
security, their happiness, the happiness of their Sons, their Daughters, their
Brothers, and those close to them.

—Antonio Pereira Rebouças, *O Bahiano*[1]

In May 1829, imprisoned in the Fortress of São Pedro, in Salvador, Bahia,
Antonio Pereira Rebouças sent these words to *O Bahiano*, the newspaper
he published in Salvador, the second largest city of Brazil at the time.[2] Thirty
years old and one of the few practicing black lawyers in Brazil, Rebouças
was a prominent public figure, particularly known for his participation in
the fight for independence in the early 1820s and for his roles as Secretary
of the province of Sergipe and member of the General Council of the province of Bahia. In his letter to the paper, he complained that he had been
subject to political persecution and an abuse of authority. As there had only
been a verbal command for his arrest and never an official order, he claimed
he was the victim of a conspiracy by those who supported Portuguese colo-
nialism and were fighting against the consolidation of independence and
the establishment of the liberal order in Brazil.

Rebouças had plenty of enemies among the important people of the city
of Salvador. Since the proclamation of Brazil's independence in 1822, he had
been at the center of disputes over Bahia's political hegemony, and he was
well known for his support of the Constitution and his rejection of the restoration of Portuguese colonial rule—positions that made him quite unpopular among the great landowners of the Brazilian northeast. The message
he published in *O Bahiano*, however, was not merely a response to his imprisonment, but a reflection on what would become his lifelong political and
professional commitments. Rebouças was a member of the General Assembly for multiple terms in the 1830s and 1840s, and his speeches there

expressed his commitment to the constitutional order and to the principles of political freedom. The significant role he played in the repression of popular social movements in the 1830s also reaffirmed his belief in the Brazilian liberal monarchy founded in 1822, defined in opposition to everything that hinted of despotism. In his later work—as a member of commissions for judicial reform and the drafting of civil laws, as a legal defender of those who had their properties confiscated during the war of independence in Bahia, and as a lawyer of the Council of State and Counselor of the Emperor—Rebouças was always on the side of guaranteeing individual rights. He consistently advocated for ideals that understood law as the maintenance of the property and security of "citizens of all classes and status."

The story of Rebouças's convictions and political positions offers a unique lens through which to consider slavery, race, law, and politics in nineteenth-century Brazil. By following the remarkable life of this Afro-Brazilian intellectual, statesman, and lawyer, whose son, engineer André Rebouças (1838–1898), later became one of Brazil's main abolitionists, I analyze the ways in which slavery and race shaped the concepts of law, citizenship, and liberalism in post-independence Brazil.

· · · · · ·

Born in the Bahian hinterlands to a white Portuguese father and a free black mother, Antonio Pereira Rebouças was a self-taught lawyer who earned the right to practice law alongside the sons of the elite, who at that time were educated in Portugal. In the early 1820s, he joined the Brazilian forces in the struggle for independence, earning respect as an intellectual, politician, and orator, even while being constantly subjected to racism. Throughout his career as a politician and a lawyer, he argued in favor of equal citizenship rights for all Brazilians, regardless of race, while ardently defending the law, including laws that supported the rights of slave owners. His political attitudes and views about liberalism and property rights (including slaves as property) help us understand how the liberal, independent Brazilian state coexisted with slavery and how Afro-Brazilians experienced social mobility while also facing clear limitations because of racist beliefs and attitudes. Moreover, we gain insight into how this deeply liberal, intellectual Afro-Brazilian experienced and made sense of racial identity and racial discrimination.

Although Rebouças was among the prominent lawyers and deputies who became heroes of Brazilian independence, he is more often remembered as the father of André Rebouças, one of Brazil's most important abolitionists.[3]

André and his brother Antonio Pereira Rebouças Filho (1839–1874) were the first black engineers in the country, and their work continues to be recognized and honored as seen in the tunnels, avenues, and roads that carry their names. While André's work has been widely documented and analyzed in a variety of contexts, the political and legal contributions of his father have largely been forgotten or underestimated. Most scholarly mentions of Antonio Pereira Rebouças appear in regional accounts of independence and Bahian history in the 1830s. Rebouças figures in the studies of Luiz Henrique Dias Tavares, Maria Thetis Nunes, and Felisbelo Freire, for example, as an important activist for independence,[4] and in João José Reis's study about the popular revolts in Salvador between 1835 and 1837.[5]

There are some works, however, that refer to Rebouças as an important Afro-Brazilian politician of his time. Joaquim Nabuco, for example, in his 1899 masterpiece on the Brazilian Empire, *Um estadista do Império* (A Statesman of the Brazilian Empire), details Rebouças's political-parliamentary activity, describing him as a true "representative of the old historical liberalism," someone "who combined aristocratic respectability with the spirit of equality."[6] Nabuco suggests that Rebouças had a reputation in the Chamber of Deputies for defending greater participation of free blacks in Brazilian public life simply because he was Afro-Brazilian himself. More recently, Bahian anthropologist Luiz Mott and U.S. historian Leo Spitzer have considered Rebouças's approach to politics and justice. Mott, analyzing the effects of the Haitian Revolution in Brazil's northeast region, argues that Rebouças was a conspirator who joined others to celebrate the independence of Haiti and foment revolts against the local landowners.[7] There is no evidence that Rebouças actually played such a role. Spitzer, in a broader study of assimilation and social integration after enslavement, analyzes Rebouças's participation in the battles for independence and in the political movements in the 1830s as motivated primarily by his desire for social mobility, as this participation was one of the few possibilities of social integration for Afro-Brazilians in early nineteenth-century Brazil.[8]

From different perspectives, each of these works seeks to understand how a poor Afro-Brazilian at the beginning of the nineteenth century could manage to ascend socially and occupy prestigious political and judicial positions in the Brazilian Empire—in other words, how this self-educated lawyer was able to establish himself among the elite of the Empire's capital. Rebouças originally caught my attention for similar reasons. I came across Antonio Pereira Rebouças for the first time when I was reading nineteenth-century freedom lawsuits that had reached the Court of

Appeals of Rio de Janeiro.[9] It interested me that this famous name—even though made famous by his abolitionist son—appeared in such a considerable number of cases. Although I had never heard of this Rebouças, as soon as I focused my attention on him, he was everywhere. Papers, books, and images related to Rebouças were sitting in various archives, waiting for someone to notice them—in the manuscript section of the National Library, the National Archives, the Brazilian Historic and Geographic Institute, the Brazilian Lawyers Institute, the Cachoeira Chamber of Deputies, and the Library of Congress in Washington, D.C.[10] It was quickly clear to me that Antonio Pereira Rebouças was a fascinating character. His life story was so compelling that I changed the course of my original project and reoriented it toward tracing his social and political trajectory. At the risk of disappointing my readers, I must say at the outset that although his life is indeed intriguing and remarkable, I have not written a biography of Rebouças. Rather, I have used the figure of Rebouças to guide me through a study of citizenship, civil law, and slavery in the early decades of modern Brazil.

Rebouças was viewed by his peers as skilled and knowledgeable, climbing the social ladder based on his merits, despite his social origins and his race. As we will see, on more than one occasion he had to prove that he was a free citizen. And yet, he became a well-known politician and a successful lawyer, concerned with civil law, property rights, and the protection of individual freedoms. In this sense, he was indeed an exemplary representative of historical liberalism as portrayed by Joaquim Nabuco. But Antonio Pereira Rebouças was also an exceptional person who pushed the boundaries of his time, stretching the fabric of historical possibilities. Precisely because of this, his story is a gateway to understanding the world of nineteenth-century lawyers and their juridical and political universe, as well as their connection to politics and to the foremost debates of this era, including discussions that were directly related to Rebouças's personal destiny: citizenship, the end of slavery in Brazil, and the establishment of civil rights for Afro-Brazilians.

These themes are crucial to understanding nineteenth-century Brazil, and indeed they have been widely debated in Brazilian social thought. One classic line of argument suggests that, because the post-independence monarchy in Brazil maintained and even expanded slavery, it was not possible to conceive of the existence of citizenship in the country until after abolition in 1888.[11] As civil rights presuppose the existence of a body of free citizens, a country whose population was largely made up of slaves could not seriously be considered liberal. Therefore, as many concluded, discussing citizenship and civil rights in the imperial period made no logical sense. This argument is the basis of the well-known discussion about the dual character of Brazilian liberalism: liberalism, so the argument goes, was imported as a model from Europe and applied only superficially to the Brazilian reality of the nineteenth century, without really changing patriarchalism, the very essence of that society. Brazilian liberalism was thus "out of place," nothing more than a veneer of civil rights, which did not correspond to the reality of forced labor in the country. This understanding of liberalism in Brazil has been a fundamental aspect of Brazilian social thought since at least the beginning of the twentieth century, and in the 1970s, Roberto Schwarz laid out the argument in more concrete terms in his influential article "Misplaced Ideas"—and this line of reasoning continues to echo, even in more recent texts.[12]

Jurists allow for an interesting perspective on these debates about the nature of liberalism in post-independence Brazil. Indeed, when we include jurists among the intellectuals who consolidated a certain interpretation of Brazilian society starting at the end of the nineteenth century, we see that from early on in the process of elaborating a civil code—one of the great liberal projects of the Brazilian Empire (1822–1889) only finished in 1916—liberalism was understood as a set of European ideas that, disconnected from Brazilian reality, would be able to perfect it, freeing Brazil from its slave past. For these jurists, the construction of the new nation required the regulation of the law, which depended on a codification of civil law. Law was the gateway to civilization, they believed, and it was critical that Brazilian civilization not be tainted with any former colonial elements. These scholars envisioned liberalism as necessarily directing the country toward the rationalization of laws and the promotion of free trade, and established a conception of liberalism that was incompatible with the existence of slavery. For them, and for most nineteenth-century liberal politicians and lawmakers, slavery was a vestige of the colonial past, a temporary necessity to keep the coffee economy growing, but fated to be extinguished.

One of the strongest voices in this conception of liberalism was that of the jurist Francisco Cavalcanti Pontes de Miranda (1892–1979), a prominent civil law expert in the 1920s. As Pontes de Miranda wrote in *Fontes e evolução do direito civil brasileiro* (Sources and Development of the Brazilian Civil Law) in 1928, "The liberalism of the Brazilian Civil Code is the liberalism of a people who have built a constitutional, rational, quasi-secular Empire, and the scientific aspirations and 'idealistic justice' which ground it must necessarily be reflected in the laws."[13] Understanding the codification of civil law as a key step in the construction of a liberal state and society, Pontes de Miranda reinforced the idea that liberalism was incompatible with slavery. He argued that the decision to keep slavery after independence had actually stunted the development of Brazilian liberalism: "What characterizes Brazilian law? Tolerance and kindness, imbued, however, with patriarchal and capitalist tones. Tolerance and kindness have a good side, which is the human capacity to adapt to different situations and overall less despotism, and they have a bad side, which is not resisting pernicious elements and being too benevolent, sometimes indifferent to rights themselves."[14] In Pontes de Miranda's view, legal benevolence had become a defining feature of Brazilian law, hampering the country's path toward "democratic evolution." This approach to the law was a remnant of colonial paternalism, he argued, believing that this was due to the incorporation of large numbers of Africans into the Brazilian population.

Pontes de Miranda is considered the last of a lineage of great jurists from the late nineteenth and early twentieth centuries who were trained at the Escola de Recife, one of the oldest law schools in Brazil. He adhered to a positivist framework that conceived of law as science, leading to his most important works: *O sistema de ciência positiva do direito* (The System of Positive Science as Law) and *Tratado de direito privado* (Treatise of Private Law).[15] Further, like Tobias Barreto,[16] Silvio Romero, and Clóvis Beviláqua, who preceded him, Pontes de Miranda believed that the so-called racial question was crucial to unraveling several of the nation's problems.[17]

Pontes de Miranda's thoughts were directly influenced by the work of jurist Clóvis Beviláqua (1859–1944), who drafted the civil code in the early 1900s and first applied the term "legal benevolence" to the Brazilian context. He believed that Beviláqua had correctly identified the presence of Africans and their descendants as the element in Brazilian culture that led to the ethos of tolerance, but, unlike Pontes de Miranda, Beviláqua viewed tolerance as a positive force in the law. Beviláqua also believed that with the abolition of slavery and the promulgation of the republican constitution in 1891, the racial question had ceased to exist. In his view, from the moment of granting citizenship rights to all Brazilians and integrating all citizens into the new society, race was no longer a relevant category in understanding Brazilian society.[18] Believing in the integration of society through legal order, Beviláqua dissociated slavery from the process of drafting the civil code. In his view, there was no legal difference between citizens, and thus it made no sense to talk about an Afro-Brazilian presence per se in the law:

> Precisely because it entered the formation of the Brazilian people in the capacity of slavery, that is, without personality, without legal condition beyond those that can radiate from a cargo of goods, race only appears in our legislation with regard to the exception of the regime of slavery, the effects of which we still see today. Studying the laws of slavery as enacted in our country . . . , we encounter an African element, but without question there is nothing specific about their presence.
>
> He is a slave. What does the color of the granulations of his skin pigment matter? And his ethnic background, what does it matter?
>
> With the elimination of the slave regime, blacks were incorporated into Brazilian society. . . . They can no longer be the object of a special study by the historian or legal scholar.[19]

Beviláqua was thus among those who fought for an understanding of Brazilian liberalism as separate from slavery. In his view, any mention of race in the civil law would effectively be allowing the slave past to taint the new liberal institutions of the country.

This conception of liberalism, civil law, and civil rights has deep roots in Brazilian social thought. The dichotomy between liberalism and slavery permeated studies on the nineteenth century and the formation of contemporary Brazilian society, whether by those who viewed slavery as the limits of the liberalism of independence or those who believed that liberalism was a foreign formulation unsuited to the Brazilian reality.[20] There are very few studies on citizenship and civil rights during the imperial period, despite the recognition that civil and political rights for the free population of Brazil were first defined by the 1824 Constitution. Further, of those few works, most emphasize the absence of these rights in everyday practice and argue that there was no pressure to obtain them. It was only in the late 1990s that a new wave of studies on race, slavery, and citizenship in nineteenth-century Brazil, of which this book is part, highlighted the role of Brazilian social groups in pressing for the expansion of citizenship rights.[21]

The pioneering work of historian José Murilo de Carvalho on nineteenth-century Brazil remains central to that discussion. In a seminal article, "Brasileiro: Cidadão?" (Brazilian: Citizen?), Carvalho argues that "the poor, uneducated person lacks sufficient knowledge of his civil rights, and both the intellectual and material conditions to ensure those rights."[22] This is due to the lack of Brazilian civic culture, Carvalho suggests, which he viewed as "one of the legacies of slavery, this antithesis of the spirit of freedom. . . . The values of slavery permeated everything, all social classes. Within our citizenship, the mentality of master and slave remained alive."[23]

Carvalho bases his analysis on T. H. Marshall's classic schema of the development of citizenship in Western Europe, which posits a sequence of civil, political, and social rights as an explanatory model for the constitution of citizenship in England. This model does not work for Brazil, Carvalho argues, because it does not take into account the informal mechanisms of popular representation and expression.[24] In his view, the difference in Brazil was the role of the state's "top down" initiative in creating a culture of citizenship, which was part of the process of secularization, organization, and bureaucratization common to the modern Western states.[25] Thus, the fact that the population had refused certain measures implemented by the state should be understood as a refusal to allow regulation from above, which failed to take into account the population's traditional or, as it were, customary rights. In conclusion, he argues that "the population found the face of the state unattractive. . . . The legal reforms and the new civic duties introduced changes into everyday life that were not understood."[26]

I propose starting from a slightly different perspective. I take it as given that slavery had a profound effect on Brazilian society, and that the persistence of the slave regime during the Brazilian Empire laid deep roots in the organization of the state and in the configuration of national society. And yet, I argue here that the Brazilian population, and especially Afro-Brazilians, sometimes viewed the "face of the state" as quite attractive. With independence, various sectors of Brazilian society began to exert pressure for the recognition of their rights to citizenship, movements led in particular by individuals who had experienced slavery directly or through their ancestors.

Moreover, although this process did not occur in the exact way as in some Western European countries, it did resemble the trajectory of several countries in the Americas—primarily in the fact that Afro-Brazilians, some still enslaved, and others freed and free, took actions to claim the legal and practical extension of the civil rights that had been established in the Imperial Constitution of 1824. Indeed, ever since the thirteen American colonies began the movement that resulted in the independence of the United States of America, the question of the emancipation of the enslaved in the Americas was closely linked to each newly founded country's process of nation building. This was a time of deciding who would be part of the body of individuals—from then on called citizens—who would form the new nations. This question definitively changed how political leaders addressed the issues of manumission and emancipation of the slaves, as it had become necessary to decide if these individuals and their descendants, now free, would also be considered citizens.[27] Thus, although with different circumstances, countries such as the United States and Brazil and colonies such as Cuba and Jamaica were all eventually forced to discuss the issue of citizenship with an ultimate vision of the emancipation of slaves.

This was true even when the controversy was defined negatively. In the United States, citizenship rights were gradually withdrawn from freedpersons and their descendants following the failure during Reconstruction to integrate them into U.S. society. In this case, the Afro-descendant population only conquered full civil rights in the mid-1960s, a full century after the Civil War that ended slavery in the United States.[28] In Cuba, the rebellion against the Spanish colonial government, which came to an end in the late nineteenth century, was only possible once the issue of the emancipation of slaves was resolved; in this case, the promises of freedom and equity for all Cubans in the future independent nation became central to the formation of the idea of Cuban nationality.[29]

In Brazil, civil and political rights, with no specific reference to race, were defined in the early 1820s, as the new independent regime decided to maintain slavery and continue to bring enslaved Africans to the country. It is this nexus—the tensions around disputes about the concept of citizenship and the permanence of slave labor—that I will analyze here, specifically through the process of the codification of civil law in nineteenth-century Brazil.

· · · · · ·

Following the life story of Antonio Pereira Rebouças, I have divided this book into three parts. In the first part, which follows the years of Rebouças's education, I look at the process of fighting for civil rights in Brazil during the decade of independence. Tracing Antonio Pereira Rebouças's experiences in Bahia, his subsequent visit to Rio de Janeiro, his time as Secretary of the province of Sergipe in 1824, and the investigation against him in Bahia, I examine his efforts to be recognized as a citizen and the difficulties he encountered. Analyzing Rebouças's actions and the responses of his peers, we start to see the conflicts and problems faced by those who, even with successful positions in politics and the law, crossed the border that separated noncitizens from citizens in this period.

Part 2 shows a more mature Rebouças, focused on political-parliamentary work and concerned about the extension of citizenship rights to all free Brazilians, especially mulattoes, whom he believed were disadvantaged in the new order. In discussions on the status of citizens that occurred during the meetings of the Constitutional Assembly of 1823, Rebouças proposed changes to the bill on purchasing manumission, seeking to normalize the movement from slavery to freedom and to guarantee rights of citizenship to those who, according to his logic, met the necessary conditions. This is the key paradox. While Rebouças sought to consolidate himself as an important political leader in Bahia, highlighting how he played an important role in repressing popular revolts, his peers viewed his discourse as radical because of his views on equal citizenship for all free Brazilians. In his political attitudes, Rebouças was the symbol of moderation, as he consistently emphasized a discourse of order and refused to enforce illegal actions, even if he considered them socially legitimate. As a parliamentarian, however, he was viewed as increasingly radical because he did not believe in allowing nuances in a liberalism that he believed should be for everyone. By looking at the premature end of Antonio Pereira Rebouças's political-parliamentary career, I seek to unravel how the conservative politics of the Brazilian Empire, in place since the late 1830s, restricted the possibilities of access to citizenship rights.

In the third part of the book, I focus on the effort by jurists and politicians of Rebouças's generation to write legal codes that corresponded to the new social relations that emerged after Brazil's independence. In this sense, the goal of legal experts like Rebouças was to defend a certain conception of civil rights, and to consolidate this interpretation in the civil legislation, which they saw as essential for the modernization of the country. I analyze this relationship between civil rights and civil law, which was elaborated through the writing of the civil code. For Rebouças and his contemporaries, the code was the final step for the necessary formalization of access to citizenship in Brazil. The work of drafting the civil code was so complex, however, that it was not finalized during the nineteenth century, reaffirming how complicated this process of defining civil rights and citizenship was in Brazil—a process that perhaps remains unfinished to this day.

Part I **Civil Rights**

· ·

1   The World of Antonio Pereira Rebouças

Antonio Pereira Rebouças was born in Bahia at the time of an unprecedented economic boom. In the late eighteenth century, especially following the 1791 slave revolution in the French colony of Saint-Domingue (Haiti),
the international price of sugar spiked dramatically, creating a thriving market for the sugar plantations in Bahia's fertile Recôncavo region.[1] Access to
world markets through the sugar economy led to increased demand for
other products as well, such as cotton, *cachaça* (distilled cane liquor), and
tobacco. The prosperity from one realm trickled steadily into others, leading to higher production needs throughout the region—and thus also to
greater numbers of enslaved Africans who were brought to the area to work
in the mills and on the plantations.[2] It was a period of thriving trade and
general economic well-being for the wealthiest rung of society. For others,
however, these were extremely challenging times. Sugarcane plantations
displaced the growth of basic foodstuffs; and manioc, for example, became
so expensive that it disappeared as a mainstay of the local diet. Multiple
years of drought in the backlands (*sertão*) added to the hardship, driving
up the price of meat until it was prohibitive for most people. The well-known
professor of Greek, Luís dos Santos Vilhena, witnessing the scene, observed
that the inhabitants of Bahia—with the exception of the traders and some
ostentatious plantation owners—had become "a congregation of the poor."[3]

Brazil had an estimated 1.5 million inhabitants at this time, with nearly
one-fifth living in Bahia, almost all concentrated in Salvador and in the
small towns and plantations of the Recôncavo. Salvador alone had close to
60,000 residents, and after Lisbon it was the second largest city in the Portuguese Empire. Although it is difficult to know exactly how many people
lived in the region as a whole, estimates range around 150,000 inhabitants.
Of these, at least two-thirds would have been considered *pretos* or *pardos*,
including enslaved people as well as free people, who worked as servants
or small-time agriculturists, some having been only recently manumitted.
The region's population overall was growing, and the increase in the number of people of African origin was dramatic: between 1775 and 1807, the
nonwhite population grew from 64 percent to 72 percent of the regional

total.[4] Those who didn't live in the city of Salvador tended to spread out across the Recôncavo, a region that was attractive both for its proximity to the capital and for its abundant sources of water.

Perhaps it was the development of small urban centers, with their promise of opportunities for upward social and economic mobility, that led Gaspar Pereira Rebouças and Rita Brasília dos Santos—Antonio Pereira Rebouças's parents—to move from Salvador to the village of Maragogipe, on the opposite side of the bay, at the end of the 1780s.[5] At the time, Maragogipe had some 5,000 inhabitants, most of whom made their living from the sale of manioc and shellfish, both regionally and overseas. Like many craftsmen of this era, Gaspar, a tailor, had come from the north of Portugal to try his luck in the colony. Having married Rita dos Santos, a free parda from Salvador, he moved to Maragogipe in search of stability, and it was there that the couple established their family. According to his son, Gaspar was "a Master craftsman, exercised great influence on the village and enjoyed the general esteem of the local big shots."[6] The tailor never amassed any substantial wealth, however, and did not have the means to educate his four sons and five daughters, all born after the couple moved from Salvador. Antonio Pereira Rebouças, born in August 1798, was the youngest of those nine children.

There was nothing unusual about Gaspar Rebouças's migration to Brazil, nor about his marriage or the move from Salvador. For many Portuguese, especially after an earthquake devastated entire regions of Portugal in the mid-eighteenth century, the Brazilian colony presented the possibility of a better life. The increase in sugarcane cultivation in regions such as the north of the province of Rio de Janeiro and the Bahian Recôncavo had led to new urban centers, with small-time commercial activities and a demand for subsidiary agricultural production. The vastness of Brazil's territories also offered refuge for anyone fleeing the metropole's justice system or needing to free their names of past stains.[7] Although we don't know the specific motivations that led to Gaspar's departure from Portugal, we know that he arrived in the late 1780s in Salvador with his brother, Pedro—both men certainly with minimal worldly goods, eager to make a new life.

The trajectory of Rita Brasília dos Santos, although totally different from her husband's, was no less typical of the time. We know little about her family's history of enslavement, as there are no records indicating who had been enslaved. The only reference to her skin color is in the baptismal records of Antonio Pereira Rebouças and his brother José, and as the mother, she is described as pardo. In this context, that description connects her directly to a slave past, but signals that she is of African origin, born free.[8] In any case, it is not surprising that she was born in Salvador. A large number of free and freed persons of African origin lived in the cities, where there was greater employment opportunity as well as the ability to interact more regularly with other free people. Urban areas often afforded the conditions to create distance from a slave past, marriage being one route to this distancing. Although we cannot know for sure whether Rita Brasília dos Santos was making this strategic calculation, her marriage to a white man surely improved her social condition, and at the least would have protected her against any attempts of illegal reenslavement.[9]

The couple's move from Salvador to a smaller town in the Recôncavo was also quite a common practice among free and freed persons of African origin. Although social mobility was widespread in all segments of society, studies on the mobility of free and freed persons suggest that, in addition to having their freedom to come and go, many sought to free themselves from their slave past by establishing new social relations. Integrating into free society, even through marriage, often took many years, and being in an unfamiliar place could make the reference to color, or to social status, disappear much more quickly. We will likely never know for certain whether Antonio Pereira Rebouças's parents moved with the specific intention to cut a connection to slavery. But even if this was not a deliberate strategy, it seems, from what we know, that their children and grandchildren distanced themselves from any such past.[10]

· · · · · ·

It's very possible that it was raining and windy on the August day when Rebouças came into the world. Trade winds from the southeast were common in Bahia during these months, bringing the rains that made the local flora turn a lush green. But other storms were also brewing. Before Antonio Pereira Rebouças was even aware of his own existence, major events were shaking Bahia and the Atlantic world. Only two days after his birth, in Salvador and some cities in the Recôncavo, the famous Revolt of the Tailors broke out. Rebouças's father, a tailor himself, took no part in the uprising. Even so, this was an auspicious beginning to Rebouças's life, as the revolt was in many ways emblematic of the changes that came to define Rebouças's work and political commitments.

Despite its name, tailors were not the only participants in the uprising. The records of those imprisoned for their participation include landowners, enslaved, soldiers, and craftsmen, some of whom were pretos or pardos.

Although a number of social movements challenged the colonial order in the last decade of the eighteenth century, the Revolt of the Tailors was unique in creating this type of alliance between members of different social groups. Distributing pamphlets in the streets of Salvador and spreading their ideas through *Avisos ao Povo Bahianense* (Notices to the People of Bahia), the rebels publicized their immediate goals, which included protesting trade limitations and tax levies and addressing the needs of the troops through higher wages and increased participation in decision making. The movement's broader proposals were all related to the ideal of freedom. They rejected the repressive government of Fernando José de Portugal (who had been in power in Bahia since 1788) and called for national independence, the formation of a republican regime, full equality of citizens before the law, the end of racial discrimination, the establishment of industries, the opening of new mines, and a revised relationship of church and state.[11]

Of course not all members agreed on the stated goals. For the enslaved, the word "freedom" meant liberation from the yoke of slavery; for others it was the guarantee of rights to ownership and the things that come with that, such as free trade and equal rights for free men, with no thought to other forms of equality or legal equality for all. And this discrepancy in interests between the owners and the enslaved was no greater than the differences between the enslaved and the free pretos and pardos. Abolition was not necessarily in the interest of the latter, as the end of slavery would leave them socially and legally on par with those who had hitherto been enslaved.

Freedpersons and free people of African origin, as citizens, sought to eliminate the racial differences between whites and themselves, pardos and pretos, especially those serving as soldiers, who believed that after the revolution they would have full equal rights.[12] Almost ten years after the proclamation of the Declaration of the Rights of Man and of the Citizen in France, these rebels were not using the word "citizen" casually. This was a purposeful reference to the idea that all who had equal natural rights should also have civil rights, which would make them citizens, both de facto and de jure. Citizenship, in this view, had nothing to do with criteria of birth. If citizenship were based on status and education rather than family origins, then these men too would be considered equal citizens. Free pardos and pretos thus sought to expand the meanings of the words "freedom" and "equality" so as to encompass their own demands, pushing for their own inclusion. They sought to belong to this society, not to transform it.

Divergent political interests did not negate the basic fact that in the Revolt of the Tailors, men of different conditions held basic ideas in common and disregarded their own inequalities, at least inside the group itself, for the duration of the revolt. Although the uprising had no major practical impacts, the authorities clearly felt threatened by the events, as reflected in the punishments of the convicted rebels: some were imprisoned, others were banished to Africa, and those with the worst luck were hanged. The revolt terrified the authorities because pretos and pardos, African-born and Brazilian-born, slaves and freedpersons, had come together to voice their demands. As Vilhena warned, this was a "fearsome fellowship worthy of close attention": "[It should not be] tolerated that in the streets and the yards of the city these crowds of blacks, from both sexes, hold their barbaric rounds, to the beat of *batuques*, dancing lasciviously, and singing Gentile songs, speaking different languages, and this with such horrendous, dissonant cries that it causes fear and anxiety even for the most bold when judging the consequences of what might be to come."[13] There were in fact good reasons for the authorities to be wary: if the explicit reference to the influence of French revolutionary ideals was not enough, there was also the recent and very visible example of Saint-Domingue.

Although it began as a rebellion against slavery and French slave owners, the 1791 revolution of the French colony of Saint-Domingue quickly expanded into wider political contours. This had been one of the richest colonies in the Western Hemisphere, with sugar production that far surpassed that of any competitors on the continent, and a population of 40,000 whites, 28,000 mixed-race and free Afro-descendants, and 450,000 enslaved persons. The rebellion took place during the French Revolution, when the power of the colonial elite was crumbling and great divisions separated those who supported the new groups in power and those who rejected them. Freedpersons, free Afro-descendants, and enslaved joined together in Saint-Domingue to lead a revolt that destroyed plantations, drove away the white owners, and, after thirteen years and the defeat imposed on French, Spanish, and British armies, ended in the proclamation of independence of the country that became Haiti. The uprising ultimately helped to lead to the end of France's colonial ambitions in the Americas. Soon after the proclamation, France sold the vast Louisiana territory to the United States, disconnecting itself almost entirely from the region. The revolt of Saint-Domingue, which grew out of a unique combination of colonial war and revolution, was the most violent uprising the region had seen, and had the most significant repercussions. It turned out to be a very particular case in the history of the Americas, but of course at the time, no one knew how singular this event would be.

Rumors circulated throughout the 1790s that the revolution that had brought about the independence of Haiti might well reach other Caribbean slave societies of the Americas. Groups of freed and free Afro-descendants who were merchants in the region, as well as owners who had left the island after the uprising and migrated toward the Antilles and Louisiana, spread stories about the conflicts. And like a rock thrown in the water that creates increasingly larger circles, these rumors provoked ever-larger hopes—or fears—about the future. It's not that there had never been rebellions and revolts of this kind before, but the ideals of the French Revolution, which were particularly inspiring to those in the French territories of the Caribbean, gave these events a different meaning. Although not initially questioning slavery or defending racial equality, by challenging the institutions of the Old Regime, the revolutionaries of Paris made the colonies feel included in the new projects of the French nation. Thus, even though the influences came more from abolitionist ideals than from the Revolution itself, the rebellious Caribbean interpreted the French Revolution as antislavery, and the proposed reforms in Saint-Domingue were then more radical than they were in France.[14]

As many historians have argued, insurrections in the Americas in the 1790s became increasingly politicized and took on greater significance than ever before.[15] In addition to the role of the French Revolution, studies also show that the American Declaration of Independence and the subsequent abolition of slavery in some U.S. states influenced how masters and enslaved persons throughout slave societies in the Americas understood the concept of freedom. Many of the masters who freed their slaves were imbued with the revolutionary spirit and inspired by Thomas Paine's invocation of the principle of universal equality; others viewed manumission as a way of expressing the divine reasoning in the ideology of independence, which rendered the enslaved and the masters equal before God.[16] Enslaved persons seized the moment to achieve freedom, whether by participating directly in wars of independence or demanding the right to purchase their own manumission, threatening escape or rebellion if not granted the request. Increased reform efforts—particularly by English abolitionists who sought to end trafficking and to change the culture of work in the colonies—also contributed to gradually destabilizing the slave regime. Although these reforms were for the most part unsuccessful, they were an important factor in fostering certain expectations. Rumors about possible emancipatory decrees led to high hopes on the part of both enslaved and free people, who believed that, once implemented, these measures would bring emancipation and the end of racial discrimination.[17]

The enslaved individuals of the Atlantic world suffered great frustration at the turn of the nineteenth century as they realized that there were no further reforms, let alone freedom. At the same time, masters were obsessed with the possibility that the specter of Haiti could reach their own domains. While it's difficult to determine if the events of the Saint-Domingue rebellion were responsible for other uprisings, one can safely say that the rumors helped to spark a number of events that disturbed slave owners throughout the Americas. These tensions were at play in the rebellion of Denmark Vesey, who in 1822, after buying his freedom, revolted against the continued enslavement of his family and led a major uprising in Charleston, South Carolina, involving two to three thousand slaves, with plans to annihilate whites and burn the city. Charleston was full of enslaved persons brought from Saint-Domingue by their supposed owners, who were fleeing the revolution. Their presence heightened the anxiety of the South Carolina masters, many of whom believed that freed people like Vesey helped to spread these revolutionary ideas.[18] Another example occurred in the English colony of Demerara-Essequibo, Guyana, where nearly 12,000 slaves rebelled in 1823. Both the masters and the colonial authorities were preoccupied that the phenomena leading to the formation of Haiti would be repeated, even though those involved in the uprising never created any kind of platform from those events.[19]

The rumors that circulated also included false promises of increased freedoms. In Port Salut and Dominica, for example, a story spread that enslaved persons would be entitled to three free days a week, and it then caught hold in Saint-Domingue and Martinique as well. These rumors probably derived from a French abolitionist treaty of 1789, which was often referenced by activist freedpersons throughout the Caribbean islands. Other riots were triggered by the suspicion that colonial rulers had been informed of emancipatory measures, but were refusing to implement them. In Demerara, the rumor that documents had arrived from England proclaiming freedom for the enslaved brought discontent and chaos on both sides: among the colonists, who revolted against what they considered an improper intervention by the British government, and among the enslaved, who were convinced that the mere reference to "new laws" was sufficient evidence for their emancipation. David Geggus estimates that one-third of the uprisings that took place in the Caribbean in these years had their origins in such rumors, and this was a decade that registered an average of four riots a year, a dozen of which involved more than a hundred slaves.[20]

In this context, it is not surprising that the authorities in Bahia were alarmed by the Revolt of the Tailors. They feared an uprising of the enslaved, and even more, an alliance between the enslaved and the freedpersons, as happened in Saint-Domingue, which would bring greater instability to a population that was already difficult to control. In the end, both masters and enslaved came to understand, from the events in Bahia in 1798, that ideas of freedom and revolt had different social and racial meanings for different sectors of the population.[21] The revolt of Saint-Domingue caused even those who advocated for the "equality of men" to be more cautious. As Manuel José Novais de Almeida, a member of the Literary Society of Rio de Janeiro, had already written in 1792: "I am very concerned with the Americas. . . . What happened there [in Saint-Domingue] demonstrates what could one day come to pass with us, and God willing I never have to see it. . . . Sell the slaves that you have, generously grant them freedom and you will have fewer enemies."[22]

Until this point, in eighteenth-century political uprisings in Brazil, the word "freedom" had either a specific political meaning (upheld by the elite of Minas Gerais in a revolt in 1789) or an economic meaning (expressed in the defense of free trade and justified by Brazil's prosperity in sugar production, as Saint-Domingue was withdrawing from the world market). These were anticolonialist ideas that grew, in part, from the influence of the American Revolution, which, for more than two decades, had managed to carry out political transformation without any commitment to changes in social structures. Once the term "freedom" became connected to the events in Saint-Domingue, however, the colonial and metropolitan elite turned themselves against the "abominable and destructive principles of freedom," which they saw as the cause of this "fire of revolt, this insurrection that made the slaves of the island of Saint-Domingue rise up in a civil war" and realize the "fatal revolution."[23] It was precisely this radical interpretation upheld by the Bahian conspirators of 1798—an understanding of freedom based in social and racial equality that promoted equal opportunity and the end of racial discrimination—that transformed the notions of freedom and equality of men into what, for the owners, were "abominable and destructive principles."

For the masters in Bahia, especially after the events of 1798, any movement, any song or drumming, was taken as a warning that people might, at any moment, break out in rebellion, like the rebels in the Caribbean uprisings. And, in these years at the turn of the eighteenth century, there was no shortage of songs or drumming in the city of Salvador. Quilombos (Maroon communities) abounded in the rural areas around the Recôncavo, some close to Salvador, many of them created by recently arrived Africans to Bahia who had seized an opportunity and escaped enslavement. Contrary to what the authorities believed, it is possible that many of the African and Brazilian-born enslaved involved in movements against colonial society were not aware of the slave uprisings throughout the Atlantic world. They represented such a significant threat, however, that the authorities responded with violent repression even to everyday cultural practices.

It is difficult to know how the mulatto Antonio Pereira Rebouças experienced these events. Rebouças was the youngest of nine children and born free, with financial resources sufficient to keep him from joining the masses of workers in the Recôncavo or the capital, but not enough for him to pursue his studies, as he had intended. We can be almost certain that he was aware of the revolts led by freedmen and free Afro-descendants, although here we are in the sticky territory of historical conjecture, as there is no direct mention of this in the documents. However, he was almost eleven when the municipal judge of Maragogipe passed an ordinance that established curfews and forbade drumming and any meetings of enslaved people with freed people, allowing the use of force on anyone who refused to cooperate. And he was sixteen when he decided, in 1814, to travel from Maragogipe to Salvador to try to continue his studies. This was precisely the moment when the enslaved African Hausas in Salvador were planning a conspiracy in the region, putting the authorities on high alert and increasing their suspicions of any slaves or freedmen traveling in the area.[24]

Although there is no information on how Rebouças moved from one city to another—if he was alone or with someone, if he traveled by land or by sea—the preparations for the trip must have been done with great care. The roads around the Recôncavo were considered dangerous at the time, especially as the town of Cachoeira had put out a warning about a possible uprising that would bring together the enslaved of the sugar plantations, the Hausas, and the freedmen of Salvador. Even though it was rare for the enslaved born in Brazil to unite in revolt with those born in Africa, the authorities feared that such a revolt could quickly escalate out of control. An uprising did actually occur in February that year, followed by a conspiracy in May, led by escravos "ao ganho" (urban enslaved who had been hired out),[25] who seemed to move freely around the city. When Antonio Pereira Rebouças arrived in Salvador, safe and sound by all indications, the city was surely still suffering the effects of the uprising, whose repression, according to the residents, was insufficient for reestablishing order. In a letter to the King of Portugal, one resident complained that they were "surrounded by a sea of blacks," in a ratio of almost twenty to one of pardos and pretos to whites, and unless the governor resolved to take strong action to contain the revolts, it would be better if he were removed.[26]

The city most likely seemed disorganized and chaotic to Rebouças, as it was a place where social hierarchies and rules had become jumbled, as Vilhena, a defender of well-defined social categories, had noted. Vilhena believed that a person's place in society should be based on rights and privileges, and distinct categories should differentiate those who had both (the nobles), those who had only rights (the free in general), and those who had neither (the enslaved). At this time in Salvador, these categories had indeed become more malleable, with the overlapping of roles by free Afro-descendants, freedpersons, and enslaved, as well as the growth of new groups, primarily of freed slaves. There was an increasing number of enslaved being manumitted each year, many having purchased freedom themselves, which was another sign of an autonomy that was easier to come by in the city than in the rural areas. Increasingly, whites began to view the city as ungovernable. As Vilhena reported, Salvador had become "populated by slaves, barbarians as ferocious as beasts." He noted a general fear that freedpersons were a dangerous influence on the enslaved: those already free "want to show those still enslaved the difference between freedom and captivity, and so they indulge in the vices of idleness." He lamented a society where "almost all the mulattos want to look as if they were noblemen, very arrogant and haughty, and friends with neither the whites nor the blacks."[27]

In these respects, there was nothing that differentiated Salvador from the other major cities of the Americas, such as Rio de Janeiro, Lima, Baltimore, and New Orleans, to name a few. These cities were economic centers with vibrant ports, ample trading of regional products, and concentrations of wealthy families; they offered opportunities for employment and for those with undefined social and legal status to mix into a large contingent of the population. Cities were preferred destinations for freedpersons and free persons of African origin, as well as for the enslaved. With some astuteness, an enslaved person could pass for free, or could be employed and then save the money to buy freedom. Whoever was freed could then join one of the networks of solidarity, and thus start to integrate into society, through paid jobs or savings from income. This occurred not only in cities that were experiencing economic growth and an expansion in the population, such as Baltimore, but also in more depressed cities such as Lima, which suffered from a significant economic downturn and political instability in this period.[28]

Regardless of the specific location, from the late eighteenth century to the mid-nineteenth century, the significant difference in the life of the enslaved in any urban environment was the very fact of living in a city, with access to everything that urban life provided. To a greater or lesser extent, it was possible in all of the urban areas of the Americas to achieve freedom, particularly by buying manumission, although in some places in the United States, states restricted the number of manumissions that masters could grant. Authorities there feared that the growing population of freedpersons would bring disorder and loss of control over the region. Nonetheless, beginning with the Declaration of Independence of the United States, followed by the revolution of Saint-Domingue, and taking into account the far-reaching effects of the French Revolution as well as the anticolonial movements in the colonies of Spain and Portugal, this was truly a period in which slaves, freedpersons, and others of African origin could sometimes change their living conditions, by taking advantage of new economic situations and of the ideals of equality and freedom that were in circulation.[29] It was a time of great changes, and it seems that everyone—whether with optimism or pessimism, hope or fear—was swept up in this, including the young Antonio Pereira Rebouças.

In the end what united people of African origin and their generations of descendants was a general social exclusion, but as we have seen, the experience of this exclusion differed depending on location and situation. Individual action, with some good fortune, is what made it possible for some to move out of their given position in society. While paths to social mobility existed, there was of course no easy or safe route, and while many tried, there was no promise of a good outcome. Changes in social status faced great resistance from those who saw the movement as a threat to their own social position.

Still, the unfolding situation at the turn of the nineteenth century included increasing fluidity in the meanings of many social norms and practices—which, in Brazil by the 1820s, created an opening for changes in legal status and social mobility. When deciding to make Salvador his home in 1814, Rebouças very likely took into account that the pervasive social uncertainties there might work in his favor. He certainly saw Salvador as a city where enslaved, freed, and free persons mixed, and where many individuals found ways to reverse the social conditions they were born into.

The World of Antonio Pereira Rebouças   23

There was no lack of people seeking to expand their opportunities, and Antonio Pereira Rebouças was one of them: people who sought to distance themselves from their own slave origins, either by entering the world of freedpersons, or, like Rebouças, seeking a different social position via education. Having departed Maragogipe to pursue further studies, Rebouças was surely aware that an education could open the way for an improved situation in the social hierarchy of Salvador.

2   Any *Pardo* or *Preto* Can Be a General

. . . .

By 1820, Antonio Pereira Rebouças was beginning to reap the rewards of his time in Bahia's capital. It had been six years since his arrival in the city, when everything had seemed so new, and he had used those years to educate himself in politics, law, and jurisprudence. After working as a clerk in the notary office of Francisco Alves de Albergaria and João Carneiro da Silva Rego, where he quickly learned the tools of the trade, Rebouças petitioned the court for permission to practice law. Even with no formal law degree, he received permission to work as an attorney on cases related to Bahia.[1] Having no financial or social resources, Rebouças was counting on education, in this case his self-education, to secure his place in the social hierarchy.

Antonio Pereira, at this point, was no different from any of the Rebouças brothers—after completing primary school, each had to find his own way to continue his education. It was probably not a coincidence that all four worked first as clerk assistants, although only one, Manoel Pereira, stayed in this position for the rest of his life. José Pereira, the eldest, after working for some years in a notary office in Cachoeira, went on to serve in the military, while also pursuing piano and violin. He left Bahia in 1828 to study music in Paris, and later received a master's degree in harmony and counterpoint from the Bologna Conservatory. An accomplished violinist, José even played his Stradivarius once in the Imperial Palace, and upon his return to Bahia, he became conductor of the Theatre Orchestra in Salvador.[2] The third brother, Manoel Maurício, also served in the Brazilian army, volunteering in the Battalion of the Periquitos.[3] In 1824 he set sail for Paris, where he received a bachelor's degree in arts and sciences and completed his medical studies. After returning to Bahia in 1832, Manoel Maurício devoted himself to clinical and academic work, caring for patients who were victims of common epidemics such as yellow fever and cholera. From 1833 to 1858, he was chair of the Botany and Zoology Department of the Salvador Medical School and devoted himself to the field of medical education. He published a number of articles and books, including the *Treaty on Domestic and Public Education*, in which he insisted that the improvement of humanity and society depended on both the education of the body through hygiene and the mind through instruction.[4]

It is perhaps not surprising that two of the brothers, Manoel Maurício and Antonio Pereira, wrote about education, as they likely sought to encourage poor young *pardos* like themselves to pursue paths of learning. The success of three of the brothers was partly due to the prominence of professions that required expertise, which at the time could offset the lack of a title or famous surname. Education—whether a formal education in Europe, or self-education like Antonio Pereira's—was possibly as valuable as birth title in the early 1800s, as the Brazilian state was in such extreme need of employees. But there is another important element to note in the story of the Rebouças brothers: the three who rose in life served in the military or participated in battles for Brazilian independence, which seems not to be true for Manoel Pereira, the one brother who stalled early on in his career path. José Pereira was a member of the military for a short time, and both Manoel Maurício and Antonio Pereira gained recognition in the resistance movement against the Portuguese in the town of Cachoeira, in the Bahian Recôncavo.[5]

Antonio Pereira Rebouças was already in the thick of politics when he received permission to practice law in Bahia in 1821. A year earlier, revolution had broken out in Portugal with demands that King João VI and the Portuguese Court return from Brazil, where they had fled in 1808 during the Napoleonic Wars. The revolution also resulted in the writing of a Portuguese Constitution, debated by deputies in Lisbon and ratified in September 1822. In Brazil, which had been administratively autonomous since 1815,[6] many believed that João VI's departure meant the country's return to previous conditions of colonization. When the intentions of the Portuguese Court became known in Bahia, an opposition movement formed immediately—and quickly intensified with the appointment in February 1822 of a military governor, whose powers would be directly connected to Lisbon. Rebouças joined those who called for the dismissal of the appointed government. They sought to elect a government of *Brazilians*—one that would recognize his son Pedro as the Regent of Brazil, making him Pedro I—and to form a constitutional state independent from Portugal.

Rebouças's commitment to legal solutions for these conflicts reflected an approach that would characterize his entire political career: adamantly against deposing the government by force, Rebouças argued for electing a new governing body that would replace the old one with greater legitimacy. His strategy did not prevail, and in his memoirs, Rebouças laments that no one had taken him seriously because of his lack of "prestige through family and wealth, . . . being only a simple lawyer."[7] At the time, however, this worked in his favor, as he was spared being sent to Fortaleza do Mar, where the rebels were imprisoned, some of whom were then sent on to Lisbon.[8] Rebouças remained active in the movement in Salvador until February 1822, when the inauguration of a new military governor from Lisbon, Madeira de Mello, led to more violence and bloodshed. At that point, with panic already gripping the local elite, Rebouças boarded the only boat willing to enter the Paraguaçu River and headed toward Cachoeira, where two of the most important episodes of the fight for independence would unfold.

After getting settled and establishing himself professionally, Rebouças joined those organizing the resistance in the Recôncavo. They proclaimed their support of the Brazilian government of Pedro I, providing that he reject the new Constitution of Portugal. Rebouças became a member of the Provisional Governing Board, and was named secretary in June 1822.[9]

The months that followed were formative and probably life-defining for this young man, barely twenty-three years old. In his vast writings about his life—both in published texts and in hand-written documents—he always highlighted the Cachoeira events of 1822. Rebouças never tired of narrating what he described as heroic acts, always placing himself in the center of the action. On the night of June 28, the Brazilians had a key victory over the Portuguese, who had attacked Cachoeira from the town of São José on the other side of the Paraguaçu River. According to his own account, Rebouças played a central role in strategizing how to liberate the Paraguaçu River, and he figured importantly in how the Brazilian troops confiscated a Portuguese gunboat and the artillery of the garrison. As these incidents unfolded and news of the victory traveled, proclamations of support for Cachoeira spread throughout the region, in the towns of Maragogipe, Nazareth, and Jaguaripe. And so Antonio Pereira Rebouças turned himself into a hero of independence. Thereafter, his portrait was included in all the laudatory albums and commemorative editions celebrating Brazil's independence, and his name was among the great personalities listed in the chronicles of Brazilian history of the time.[10]

After this military victory, the rebels moved to form a government that would address the civil and military issues in towns throughout the Recôncavo and fight the Portuguese, who were still in power in Salvador. Although Rebouças considered himself an obvious candidate to represent the town of Cachoeira, his colleagues—who did not share Rebouças's view of his own role—elected Francisco Gê Acaiaba de Montezuma,[11] a newcomer to the provincial capital. Rebouças feigned indifference, claiming that he would not have accepted the position anyway because autonomy was so crucial to a patriot. As he later emphasized in his memoirs, anyone committed to the nation's independence should "not accept government jobs if he lacks income or family wealth sufficient to maintain his living."[12] Rebouças also recalled that he had declined a similar position in the town of Pedra Branca in order to return to practicing law. Even with these claims, however, Rebouças could not disguise his disappointment, evident in his vitriolic criticism of the Interim Governing Council and their methods of selecting representatives, which ended up excluding people like his friend João Dantas from Itapicuru, who had been an important figure in the independence movement. Writing later in his life about what he considered to be a great injustice, "incompatible with the dominant patriotic ideas of today," Rebouças reported that he "turned the assembly into general disorder by way of actions that resulted in bruises and scratches on some, torn clothes on others, until they managed to quell the chaos."[13]

This was such a major brawl that our attorney thought it best to disappear for a while. Together with João Dantas, who was also defeated, he went to breathe some clearer air in Rio de Janeiro, the capital seat. Even after sneaking away, Rebouças did not let go of the fight: at the first opportunity, he wrote and published a long petition to the Emperor, claiming that electoral fraud had led to the election of Montezuma as Bahia's representative to the Assembly of 1823.[14] He brought his complaints as far as the Constitutional Committee of the Constituent Assembly, which declined to hear them because of lack of sufficient information.[15]

Rebouças's emphasis on his important role in the fight for independence surely reflects his awareness, as he looked back on his life, that his participation in this movement had been key to the successful political and legal career he went on to build for himself.[16] After all, this was precisely the moment when Emperor Pedro I declared freedom for enslaved persons who had participated in defending the province. This moment of independence had created opportunities for social and political mobility for those who succeeded in seizing the chance—although, while there were many who pursued freedom, not all achieved it. The political disorder made it possible for some to reach a status previously unthinkable for pardos such as Rebouças or Montezuma, but they fought tooth and nail for it.[17] Indeed, it is impossible to consider these new opportunities for social mobility without noting how limited they were. As we have seen during the elections of Cachoeira, when new groups of power were being formed, even those who had gained prestige by participating in the battle against the Portuguese were often blocked from getting an official government position. It is not surprising that Rebouças, excluded from power in Cachoeira, decided to try his luck in Rio de Janeiro—he was surely optimistic that in Rio, the seat of the new Brazilian Empire, he might successfully convert his symbolic capital gained in the fight for independence into a real political position.

The journey from Bahia to Rio, via land and sea, was full of adventures and chance encounters. Rebouças traveled through Maragogipe, Nazaré, Morro de São Paulo, Valença, Barra do Rio das Contas, Ilhéus, Porto Seguro, Vitória, Guarapari, and Campos, meeting with local people in influential positions—he crossed paths with Colonel Manoel Gonçalves Bittencourt, a previous member of the Government Council of the province of Bahia; Chichorro da Gama, father of the future High Court Judge of Appeals of Chichorro, Pinto da Gama; and Silvestre Rebello, who would be named the chief administrator of the Emperor's household and who told Rebouças "not to forget to look for him in Rio de Janeiro."[18] But things were not always easy, and Rebouças clearly encountered a number of challenges along the way. He was confronted in Porto Seguro, for example, and could only pass once he persuaded people of his identity by sharing stories of the independence battles and helping the local judge with his knowledge of criminal law. Once he convinced the local authorities about his origins and his history, they welcomed him and offered him a sponge cake in appreciation. Although Rebouças did not specify what led to the misunderstanding, he may easily have been mistaken for another person with an inferior situation and status, such as a freedman. In other words, if he had just been any mulatto, without the recognition from recent events, Rebouças possibly would not have been able to pass the border of the province, at least not at that time, when revolts of slaves, freedpersons, and other Afro-descendants frightened the owners of the region's sugar plantations. To differentiate himself from others, Rebouças took advantage of the only two resources available to him: his legal profession and his participation in the fight for Brazilian independence.

These resources were the very same ones that helped Rebouças make the most of his stay in Rio. He made contacts, came to know the Andradas brothers,[19] kissed the hand of the Emperor and then talked with him at a second audience, managed to be named secretary of the province of Sergipe, and, moreover, received the honor of Knight of the Imperial Order of the Cross. Rebouças later emphasized that he received that honor even without requesting it, and as a person who would normally be considered too poor for that title.[20] It was also in Rio, however, that Rebouças realized the extent to which his success did not render the color of his skin invisible. The first time that he references his skin color in his memoirs is during an episode that took place in these years. He and João Dantas were visiting Deputy Araújo Gondim, from Pernambuco, and Rebouças quickly came to understand that he was not welcome to stay for dinner:

> It was the house located on the left side of the entrance to São Cristóvão,[21] and gathered there were the Vicar of Rio Pardo . . . , Miguel and Antonio Calmon and Col. Villasboas, and the future Baron of Maragogipe. They were about to head to the table for dinner. Rebouças then noticed that Dep. Gondim went to Col. Villasboas and asked if he could, after all, invite him to dine with them, even though he knew that as a mulatto, Rebouças ultimately was an embarrassment for Dep. Gondim at the table with his white and noble guests. From what Rebouças observed from the gesticulations and the movement of the arms and hands, it seemed to him that [Villasboas] indicated that [Gondim] was in his house and he could do what he wanted. The owner of the house then talked to João Dantas and it seemed to Rebouças . . . that Gondim was excusing himself for not inviting him to dinner because he would have to invite his companion to the displeasure of his other guests.[22]

Rebouças went away angry, less with the discrimination itself and more with the fact that it had happened to him, emphasizing that his status was equivalent to others at Gondim's house that day. After all, he wrote, he was "a lawyer by profession, and in politics he had served as a member of the government before the others, and in that capacity he had given orders to people who were at the same level or even higher in the hierarchy as the people present."[23] The wound must have been deep, indeed so deep that Rebouças never mentions such episodes again in his diaries, even though they certainly continued to occur.[24]

In fact, the snub of the dinner was nothing compared to what happened in 1824, when Rebouças took over as secretary of the province of Sergipe.[25] Uncomfortable with a mulatto at the head of government affairs, the local landowners did everything to remove him, and succeeded within his first year in office. When Manoel Fernandes da Silveira was chosen as the first president of Sergipe, and took Antonio Pereira Rebouças with him as secretary, the political situation in the province was a disaster. The Corcundas—the conservative landowners who supported Portugal—and the liberals were in a violent battle for local power. At the time of the November 1823 elections for the governing board, twenty-three Corcunda landowners were in prison, swearing vengeance on the Brazilians who had arrested them.[26] The arrival of Silveira and Rebouças did not ease any tensions. The liberals, who had been in power until that time, resented the appointment of Silveira as president—although born in Sergipe, he was already in his seventies and had lived for many years in Bahia.[27] And to make matters worse, the troops were unable to maintain security. The local battalion had practically no officers, as many were among "the declared enemies of the holy cause" of independence; furthermore, the battalion created by the Provisional Committee to fight against the Portuguese included only low-ranking officials and was ineffective, while consuming the province's revenue.[28]

At this same time, the so-called Confederação do Equador, a republican revolt against the highly centralized government of Pedro I, had broken out in Pernambuco and was spreading to the northeastern provinces of Paraíba, Rio Grande do Norte, and Ceará. News of these events soon reached Laranjeiras, then the main town of Sergipe, where free blacks and freedpersons as well as the largest group of Portuguese in the province had established themselves. The fear—or the hope—that the revolts would encompass Sergipe and ultimately lead to a republic independent from the Brazilian Empire only fueled the tensions in the city.[29] Daily conflicts broke out, and a general sense prevailed that no one could subdue the violence and chaos.

In this hostile setting, one can imagine Silveira's reception when he arrived in March 1824, especially when people saw that he had brought a mulatto as secretary, the terrible "grandson of Queen Njinga," as people called Rebouças.[30] Further, the president seemed to listen to Rebouças more than to anyone else. Their problems started right away: as early as April, the troops rebelled against the new government because they were not receiving wages, and they took over the barracks. The Corcundas took advantage of the situation to win the sympathies of the troops, encouraging them to join their rebellion against Silveira. They developed a plan to overthrow the president on the very day that the six elected members from the province took office, none of whom were members of the Liberal Party.[31] Rebouças, alerted about the conspiracy, took action. He and President Silveira left Sergipe in the middle of the night, after writing a proclamation to the soldiers, begging them to renounce the rebellious officers and join them. Ultimately, the Corcundas failed. Without a president, the representatives never took their seats, and there was no government to overthrow. Silveira and Rebouças returned to great celebration and were empowered to arrest the officers and dissolve the disloyal battalion.[32]

Even after that victory, however, the challenges continued. Local landowners blamed Rebouças, in particular, for sabotaging their plans and for continuing to provoke dissent. The situation reached a crisis in June, when Rebouças swore his loyalty to Brazil before the Constitution, a ceremony that took place on certain Sundays at a local church.[33] In a show of his abiding support of Brazil, Rebouças took the text from the parish vicar, a native of Portugal, in order to read the oath aloud himself. At the end of the service, after the public made the regular cheers, one of the lieutenant colonels of the Battalion of Henriques—a battalion made up only of mulattoes—yelled, "Death to all of the Portugal supporters."[34] This call set off a rampage of persecution against the Portuguese, who took refuge in the woods, only coming out when Chief Commander Manoel da Silva Daltro, appointed to pacify the northeast region, arrived in Sergipe. In this incident, Rebouças presumably was considered as identifying with the Battalion of the Henriques simply because he too was mulatto.

After this outbreak, landowners complained daily to Daltro about Rebouças. He was accused of everything: belonging to the "Gregorian Society" which sought to seize power for the blacks, inciting the general population against the whites, being republican, and, worst of all, supporting the Haitian Revolution. Reports also suggested that Rebouças had exaggerated the chaos of the conspiracy just to be seen as having thwarted it.[35] But of all the accusations, perhaps the gravest centered around events in Laranjeiras on the night of June 25, when a group, "accompanied by a *zabumba*[36] and other instruments," had run through the city yelling, "Live blacks and mulattoes, die Portuguese and whites"[37] and posting fliers with the same slogan. In a complaint made to the Military Commander, Rebouças is portrayed as the leader of the movement:

Governor of Arms. ALERT. A small spark makes a big fire. The fire is already spreading. In a dinner in Laranjeiras, three toasts were made against the "Mata Caiados": the first was to the extinction of all the Portuguese, calling them the "marotos"; the second against all whites in Brazil, call[ing] them "caiporas"; the third to the equality of blood and rights. Stay alert and very alert. The young R . . . . . brother of another young guy, uttered praises to the King of Haiti, and because they did not understand him, he spoke more clearly: Saint-Domingue, the great Saint-Domingue. This was no stunt. Your

Ex. must take care. Good men trust in Your Ex. They only want Religion, Throne, and the Government sworn in on June 6. Caution. Caution. Act while there is time. Laranjeiras, June 26, 1824. Anonymous.[38]

The denunciation—unsigned, but presented in the name of the good citizen—invokes the very event that was bound to lead to a conviction: the independence of Haiti. And the strategy worked. One month later, Chief Commander Daltro sent a representative to the Emperor to report on the situation in the province, stating that the person responsible for all of it was Secretary Antonio Pereira Rebouças, who was "protecting bad men, and overthrowing the wealthy and virtuous owners for not following his wild fancies."[39]

President Silveira wrote a defense on behalf of Rebouças, but even that was not enough. Although he argued that Daltro was behaving "out of the lines of duty," Silveira's meetings with the representatives of the province to try to block the accusations were unsuccessful. In December, the president and his loyal secretary were dismissed. Daltro also left Sergipe at this time, claiming that he was unwell. A formal charge was made against Rebouças, holding him responsible for all of the disturbances of that year, and even accusing him of heading a new rebellion in Laranjeiras that month that involved the enslaved.[40] In February 1825 he traveled to Salvador with his mother and sisters, his two slaves, and two "servants"[41] in order to make his own defense in the inquiry, which had reached the Court of Appeals in Bahia. In the end, he was acquitted for lack of evidence.

It is difficult to know to what extent Rebouças was actually involved in the events that he was accused of leading. The various accounts presented to Captain Daltro make it clear that the presence of a pardo secretary bothered many people, but it is not always clear which of the reports were based on actual events and which were pure invention, meant to incriminate him. It seems preposterous, for example, to imagine that Rebouças really "cheered the Haitians," as was suggested.[42] Furthermore, only five of the twenty-one witnesses—all white landowners—claimed that Rebouças had participated in the riots at all. And if he had really been a leader of uprisings for equality, surely Rebouças would have been more proud of his participation. In his memoirs, where he devotes many pages to less important details, he doesn't mention these events a single time. It is easier to imagine the young Rebouças defending the equality of rights with the phrase that made him famous in those days: "Any pardo or preto can be a general."[43] Even

Rebouças's enemies knew that he never tired of repeating this slogan to anyone willing to listen.

Whether or not he was a leader, Rebouças served as an example for various groups: owners saw him as a bad example for the pardos, who might actually start to believe that "the pardo was equal to the white." For Afro-descendants, by contrast, he symbolized how far a person of Rebouças's background might rise in the new Brazilian regime after independence. For pardos such as Sebastião Soares, who sought to convince the enslaved and freedpersons from nearby plantations to join a Christmas revolt, Rebouças was held up to convince others that "they would soon be happy and that the wealth of the white was on this earth for them."[44]

Regardless of how he was perceived and portrayed, Rebouças certainly was not interested in serving as an example. Both when he defended himself in front of the court in Salvador and when he suffered the exclusion from the dinner in Rio, he viewed his personal problems from an individualistic standpoint. Refusing to politicize his skin color, Rebouças developed beliefs that came to define his lifelong philosophy: as established in the 1824 Constitution, citizens should be distinguished only by their merits and qualifications, and not by their color. Perhaps the most grievous accusation that Rebouças suffered during his unfortunate stay in Sergipe had nothing to do with being a troublemaker, but rather with his disqualification as a voter: "Rebouças, only present in this town and municipality as of March 5 . . . , *dared* to vote in the Local Elections that took place last June 27, insisting, though they tried to prevent him; he couldn't possibly know the people that he should vote for, so on that occasion he chose ones who were not qualified for the job."[45]

For the local elite, Rebouças had no right to vote—he was not from there and, worse, he voted for the wrong people: a pardo of course would not know how best to vote. It was precisely this type of accusation that Rebouças fought against, being compared with any other nonqualified pardo who hadn't achieved the status of elector.[46] In basing his claim to rights on his qualifications and distancing himself from the question of color, Rebouças was not necessarily undertaking a "deliberate strategy" of whitening, as historian Leo Spitzer argues in his book, *Lives in Between*.[47] I would argue, instead, that he was acting in the same manner as many of his peers from Brazil and other parts of the Americas, seeking a higher social status by distinguishing himself from the majority of pardos, who had fewer merits.

At a time when there was no concrete definition of civil rights, social groups competed for increased liberties that would guarantee certain basic rights. Those who were enslaved sought to purchase manumission or bring freedom lawsuits against the masters, while those who were poor Portuguese or free pardos fought for jobs and opportunities for social mobility. In a similar spirit, Rebouças sought to achieve the highest social position possible, believing that this would guarantee him full rights of citizenship. In an era that Eric Hobsbawm famously referred to as the Age of Revolution, it is not a coincidence that the pressure exerted by enslaved persons, freedpersons, and free blacks to be recognized as full and legitimate members of society was part of the revolutionizing force.[48] This pressure, which of course took different forms for different social groups, was one of the things that made the period so significant. Even though the experience of social mobility was different for different individuals—an urban enslaved person certainly had different aspirations from Rebouças, for example—at all levels people sought a guarantee of basic civil rights, such as the rights of freedom and property.

Because there was no concept of equal rights for all, pressure for social change was almost never exerted by different groups acting together. The granting of civil rights to one group almost always implied the exculsion of another group from those same rights, as the law that rendered citizenship to some ended up circumscribing and limiting the daily existence of others. When we talk about "others" in this scenario, we are talking about Africans and also Portuguese, who suddenly had the status of foreigners after independence, and who, in different ways, saw their access to citizenship questioned.[49]

Rebouças, in this context, was not so much a symbolic figure, but rather an individual who sought to maintain the civil rights he had achieved with independence. He never took seriously Sebastião Soares's request that he support the Christmas revolt, for this was not Rebouças's main concern. What he cared about, in addition to the framework of law and order, was solidifying his own superior status in relation to other pardos who were less qualified. In this, Rebouças was typical of his time. Like others, he reinforced hierarchy as the organizing social principle, and privileged distinct criteria for exercising the rights of citizenship, criteria that he believed he easily met. It is in this sense that his phrase "any pardo or preto can be a general" needs to be understood. Anyone who has pursued opportunities of literacy and education can become a general, but of course not everyone actually will. Indeed, as Rebouças would fiercely argue, not everyone *should* attain this status, otherwise it would subvert the ideal ordering of society.

That's why, upon returning to Salvador in February 1825, Rebouças dedicated himself primarily to defending the civil rights guaranteed by the Constitution of 1824—basically the rights to free speech and property. He soon created a name for himself, in particular by defending a landowner who had not been compensated by the imperial government for property and wealth lost during the battle of independence in Bahia.[50] To ensure his own freedom to express his views, Rebouças purchased the newspaper *O Bahiano* in 1828. He believed it was important to make public how often the conflicts between the representatives of Portuguese interests and Brazilian interests—both the conservatives and the liberals—still threatened the political scene, and how constitutional rights then tended to be disregarded. As an upholder of the Constitution, Rebouças defended "freedom that is compatible with the law," and not, like the "radical" rebels of Pernambuco, that "which degenerates and brings about anarchy, the worst of all political evils."[51] These were the civil rights that interested him, the very ones he had not yet been able to secure for himself: access to property and freedom of expression.

As Rebouças was often in the middle of these conflicts between Portuguese and Brazilians, which were particularly intense in Bahia, the political instability meant that his problems were far from over. Active in the liberal press, he also became involved in a number of polemical debates, especially in response to criticisms about the authoritarian attitudes of Pedro I. In 1828, his political opponents in the Conservative Party once again attacked him, using a strategy similar to Daltro's in 1825 and accusing Rebouças of a radical past. In a letter to the newspaper *O Soldado da Tarimba*, an anonymous contributor accused Rebouças of being "the persecutor of honorable residents, especially those who, with their purity of blood, wealth, or civil or military representation, obfuscated his character, which is jealous, turbulent, and an enemy of good order"; he was also accused, once again, of "being the head of the revolt of the blacks, and slaves, whose object was the general massacre of the whites, and the dreadful system of the Island of Saint-Domingue." The author goes on to write that such a "dangerous individual" should be watched "with the greatest caution and vigilance."[52]

The article, signed simply as "Citizen," was printed together with part of the charge from 1825 made against Rebouças, to show what a dangerous person Rebouças was and to alert the authorities, who had improperly acquitted him. The author sent only those excerpts that were against Rebouças, as he notes himself at the end of the transcription. Disgusted with the articles that Rebouças had been publishing in the newspapers, but unable to charge him with any crime, the anonymous author claimed that Rebouças was an enemy to those, like himself presumably, who had "purity of blood, wealth, or civil or military representation." The author purposefully ignored the fact that according to the Portuguese law of 1821, purity of blood was no longer considered a condition for citizenship, and that Rebouças was, himself, an elected representative. He thus assumed a definition of citizenship far from the one that had taken hold in Brazil—indeed, a definition from which Rebouças would have been excluded.

This portrayal of Rebouças seems to have been taken seriously, as he landed soon after in prison, at the Fortress of São Pedro. It later became clear through correspondence published in *O Bahiano* that the denunciator was the Portuguese Francisco das Chagas de Oliveira Castilho, former editor of *Soldado da Tarimba*. Castilho was a known supporter of the Portuguese colonial government, and in 1822, when Brazilian independence was proclaimed in Rio, he fled to Lisbon, returning only in 1827. He often accused political opponents such as Rebouças of abusing the right of a free press. In response to these accusations of undermining public safety by supporting the Constitution in May 1829, Rebouças ranted against those who refused to understand that their cause was "the Cause of Justice," which "belongs to Citizens of all Classes and Status."[53]

Despite making these claims, Rebouças knew very well that the cause of justice did not belong to all citizens, and that there was no consensus about what made up citizenship and civil rights. If nothing else, he knew this as a lawyer. After all, he had been involved in many lawsuits that revolved around these very topics: the granting of civil rights, the concept of citizenship, and the characteristics and limits of property rights. However, contrary to sudden changes produced by revolutions, he argued that this process was long and slow, and would only be complete with the writing of the civil code, which he saw as the only real guarantee of citizens' rights. This was an argument he had voiced some years earlier in an article about the French Revolution, when he suggested that even more important than "going right from being a slave to being free . . . is, rather, instructing the People of their rights. . . . Without literacy, Peoples of Brazil, nothing will ever be: the proclaimed freedom which is only ephemeral will be replaced by the most insolent despotism and arbitrariness; without literacy the efforts of the friends of Humanity to assure us a civil code will be for nothing."[54]

Part II   **Civil Rights and Liberalism**

3   Defining the Brazilian Citizen

. . . .

The word citizen does not automatically mean equal rights.

—Deputy Araújo Lima, 1823

Deputy Antonio Pereira Rebouças must have been furious as he left the session of the Legislative Assembly on August 25, 1832. After a heated debate about the criteria for appointing officers to the National Guard,[1] including Rebouças's own compelling speech, his position had been narrowly defeated. The conflict centered around two amendments that had recently been brought to the floor, calling to allow only electors to be nominated to the Guard. As defined in the Constitution of 1824, Brazilian electors were male citizens over twenty-five years of age with a net annual income of more than 200,000 réis in property, industry, trade, or employment; with few exceptions, electors could not be servants, cloistered religious, criminals, or freedmen. The proposed bills clearly intended to set the maximum number of restrictions on who could belong to the Brazilian National Guard.

Overall, Rebouças was not bothered by the restrictions—except for the clause concerning freedmen, which was an exclusion that incensed him. He contested the first proposal immediately and with such vehemence that its author, Baptista Caetano, the representative from the province of Minas Gerais, withdrew the amendment before it was even put to debate. In the very next session, however, the Bahian representative Miguel Calmon du Pin e Almeida put forward a similar amendment that read: "Only a citizen who is an elector can be appointed officer of the National Guard."[2] Rebouças took this second proposal as a personal offense. It was painful, he noted in his response, that after the withdrawal by the representative of Minas Gerais, the very same language could be proposed by a deputy from Bahia, where, according to Rebouças, feelings of "equality and justice, unity and freedom" were widespread. He himself was the proof, he claimed, stating: "The example, gentlemen, you can find always in me."[3]

Rebouças did not elaborate on how he exemplified the egalitarian character of the Bahians, but rather went on to explain why he considered the amendment "unjust, incendiary, impolitic, and unconstitutional." Excluding the freedmen was unjust, he argued, because these men had fought in the country's war of independence with the same determination and courage as any others, as had happened in "the whole civilized world." Further, it was incendiary because by denying full rights of citizenship to a segment of the population that had won those rights in the 1824 Constitution, the Assembly was certainly inciting revolt. He compared the Brazilian situation with France before the Revolution, suggesting that the treatment of the freedmen had swayed those events: "If the freedmen of the French colonies had been included among the citizens of France, the world would not have seen such horrific scenes and atrocities . . . but, as all the conciliatory attempts were ignored, the planters, the clergy, and the noble, unwilling to compromise anything, ended up with nothing."[4] Rebouças knew that the comparison was particularly powerful: the French Assembly, reunited in 1790 and 1791, yielded to pressure by the white planters of the Caribbean and excluded free blacks from rights of citizenship, thus provoking their alliance with the enslaved persons, which resulted in the famous rebellion of Saint-Domingue.[5]

The amendment was also impolitic, he continued, because it denied many citizens a status they had already obtained, such as "meritorious officers, clergymen, and the decorated, who enjoyed the greatest esteem of their fellow citizens." Lastly and most importantly, he viewed it as unconstitutional, because according to the Constitution, Brazilian citizens who were born as *ingênuos*[6] were only excluded "from being a parish elector, provincial councilor, deputy, senator, state councilor; this exception establishes the general rule, which, in accordance with the principles enshrined in the same constitution, is that all citizens are obliged to take up arms in defense of the country, and are eligible for all positions with no distinction other than of their skills and virtue."[7]

This debate was not new in the parliamentary forum, as Rebouças was well aware. Two years before, in 1830, discussing this same topic, the representative from Rio Grande do Norte, Paulino de Albuquerque, had argued that there would be too few members in the National Guard if freedmen were not admitted, and he warned: "If we want good order, let us make an example of that class of citizens who are not as dangerous as we sometimes like to think. I often remind people of this, and have already drafted a bill for all Brazilian citizens to be soldiers [of the National Guard]."[8] The discussion had not been fruitful, as can be seen from the law of June 5, 1831, whose tenth article authorized the government to enlist, arm, and employ only electorate citizens to constitute the National Guard.[9]

Harking back to those earlier discussions about the standards, Rebouças once again asked the Assembly, "Would it not be sufficient for the desired officers to qualify, as I have proposed and supported, on the income of more than 300 réis, and for soldiers 200 réis?"[10] Rebouças referred specifically to the "individual and political rights of the citizen" in his speech, signaling, in fact, his own commitment to the defense of order, public safety, and property. His peers, however, clearly did not hear his words in the same way. While Rebouças considered it a danger to deny certain citizens the responsibility of fighting for the country's order, which, he argued, would eventually incite them to disorder, other deputies thought it imprudent to arm what they called the "dangerous class of citizens." Rebouças viewed property as the "holy foundation" of the Constitution and believed that the introduction of criteria other than income was an attack on property rights. After all, if property was truly absolute and inviolable, as everyone preached, how could someone who possessed 200 or 300 réis be denied the right to be a National Guard officer?

Criteria for the National Guard were certainly not the only issue that divided the representatives in the Legislative Assembly. A few months earlier, in July 1832—just over a year after Emperor Pedro I's abdication and return to Portugal[11]—Justice Minister Diogo Antonio Feijó had led a debate about the urgency of maintaining the country's governability. Feijó (1784–1843), a liberal deputy, had opposed the influential Andradas brothers, who were important advisors to the Emperor. Although Feijó had gained power with the Emperor's resignation, he had failed to undermine the authority of the oldest brother, José Bonifácio, whose conservative group represented Portuguese interests in the country. Feijó sought to regain the governability that was lost during the revolts of the *exaltados*, or radical liberals. This had gone wrong because several liberal deputies, including Montezuma and Rebouças himself, had positioned themselves against Feijó's plan, fearing that in addition to removing the conservative *restauradores* from power,[12] it would also lead to an undesired accumulation of power by Feijó.[13]

Debates in the lower house were just as contentious. The radical liberals viewed the authoritarian policies of Pedro I as too centralized, and called for a structure with increased autonomy for the provinces. The moderate liberals, however, pressed for the dissolution of local autonomy in the name of regaining governability. The two sides, deeply divided in their visions for the country, clashed over constitutional reform about the political and administrative structure of the Empire, and over public security, which of course included the important topic of the formation of the National Guard.[14]

In fact, this climate of discontent and insecurity had permeated the mood of the capital since the abdication of Emperor Pedro I, and had not improved with the election of deputies, the selection of ministers, or the establishment of the "Regência trina permanente," the three-person regency elected by the deputies in June 1831.[15] Many Portuguese politicians had retained their positions in public offices and in the army, and as it became more apparent that the restauradores intended to resume their positions in the main offices of government, public confrontations broke out in Rio and in some provincial capitals, such as Recife and Salvador. Every day, newspapers published denunciations of the government's conservative policy. In 1831, the year that Feijó was Minister of Justice, seven revolts broke out—five in Rio de Janeiro, one in Ceará, and one in Pernambuco—as well as smaller conflicts in other provinces. The resignation of the Emperor had not led to the type of reforms that both the people and the leaders of the exaltados had anticipated. Indeed, it was becoming increasingly clear that the new political arrangement led by the liberal moderates was not sufficient to address the demands by the various social agents, such as the military.[16]

Only a few days after the inauguration of Minister Feijó, the Twenty-Sixth Infantry Battalion, crowded into the Monastery of St. Benedict, revolted. The revolt was quickly dissolved, but it initiated a movement that began to gain strength, obtaining expressions of solidarity from military groups throughout Rio de Janeiro, with the exception of the navy, the First Artillery Corps, and part of the Second Artillery Corps. Soon after this event, troops met at the Campo de Santana and formulated demands, which they sent to the government by way of a representative: they sought the deportation of eighty-nine citizens who were known to be loyal to Portugal, including some who were senators, the dismissal of public officials who were considered to be against the national cause, and the suspension of all Portuguese from entering the country for a decade.

Dissatisfaction among the troops had indeed exacerbated the tense atmosphere in the capital. Seen as out of control since the resignation of Emperor Pedro I, the troops were frustrated with the Assembly's substantial reduction of the budget—which had cut promotions, benefits, and salaries— and with the law of July 5, 1831, which had subordinated all armed forces to Minister of Justice Feijó, granting him control over the entire judicial and police apparatus of the Brazilian Empire.[17] The same law had also authorized the government to establish the so-called Municipal Guards, a civil militia made up of electors, while a law on the formation of the National Guard was being debated.[18] The grievances were brought before the permanent session of the Chamber, in conjunction with the Senate, the Ministry, and the Regency, and resulted in a radical reform of the cabinet. Feijó, however, maintained his position as Minister of Justice, and the government continued to take action to control the military, including a suspension of recruitment, the dissolution of some battalions, and the removal of others to far-off parts of the country—all of which contributed to a diminished presence of the military in Rio.

The troops, once seen as the guardian of civil order, were now considered "undisciplined, arrogant, an anarchic body that raised its head as soon as there was a riot."[19] The creation of the National Guard had thus become an urgent debate. Evaristo da Veiga, one of the authors of the bill proposing the creation of the National Guard, was adamant that while he believed in the forces of law and order, "one cannot deny that the security of citizens is never better protected than by the very citizens interested in their own preservation."[20]

The events of July 1831 thus had a direct influence on the passage of the law that established the National Guard. A year later, debating the criteria for choosing its members, the deputies felt this same sense of urgency. After all, one of the main reasons for the fear and suspicion about the regular troops was that they were composed of varied segments of the population, including the dreaded freedmen whom Antonio Pereira Rebouças was defending.[21]

An important part of the debate about eligibility for the National Guard was how different deputies formulated the issue: some viewed this as a matter of public safety, while for others it was primarily a question of defining citizenship. Put in another way, for some deputies, it was impossible to address public security without, at the same time, limiting the guaranteed rights of citizens. And this is what Rebouças protested. The Chamber's behavior on this particular issue is difficult to understand because the vast majority of parliamentarians were liberal, whether moderate or radical. It is therefore hard to imagine a split between the deputies based on their party sympathies. But in fact, whenever Rebouças raised the subject of the freedmen's inclusion in the National Guard, he met opposition from his liberal peers—such as Bernardo Pereira de Vasconcelos (1795–1850)—who were close to the Feijó group and who, in the name of maintaining order, were willing, when necessary, to sacrifice individual freedoms and guarantees.[22]

If we consider the broader political scene of the time, it is possible that our dear lawyer was actually acting with cunning. After all, revolts were popping up throughout the Empire. Especially with the Brazilian defeat in the Cisplatine War,[23] it was unclear whether the military would be capable of maintaining control in the provinces and, further, whether they would actually follow orders to do so. At the same time—as the struggles for independence had already demonstrated—it was impossible to predict what the enslaved and the freedmen who participated in the movements would later demand. This led to the precaution of the majority of the liberal deputies and the formation of a conservative consensus that included both liberal moderates and *exaltados*, a coalition usually attributed to their fear of losing the capacity to govern after the abdication of Emperor Pedro I.[24]

Rebouças, however, in asserting the unconstitutionality of restricting the rights of citizenship for freedmen, showed himself to be abreast of political debates long before he was elected as a representative to the Assembly. Perhaps the main reason for his disappointment on that afternoon in August 1832 was that those who rejected his ideas were the very same men who had espoused similar proposals during the Constituent Assembly, such as the priest Henriques de Rezende—an old liberal and a leader of the Pernambuco revolt against the Portuguese of 1817, who, as Rebouças certainly remembered, participated in the constitutional debates of 1823. In his address, Rebouças asked, were Rezende's "feelings now other," as he had shown himself "quite ready to support the toxic amendment"?[25] He reminded his audience that as a representative of Pernambuco in the Constituent Assembly in 1823, that very same Henriques de Rezende had argued that denying freedmen the privilege of occupying military posts would be a regression, since, even when Brazil was still a colony of Portugal, this was a right they had already enjoyed.[26]

The change of attitude of Henriques de Rezende, who was now willing to support the restrictions, is emblematic of the shifts in the Brazilian political spectrum in the 1820s. Many politicians, particularly in response to the experiences of the First Reign, took a conservative turn after the abdication. Not coincidentally, Rezende's views shifted after a visit to the United States. At that time, there were strict limits on granting manumission to slaves after American independence, and further, freedpersons and free blacks were denied rights of any kind on the grounds that they would be damaging to society. In 1823, this pastor, the former revolutionary, had given an extremely enlightening speech, arguing that freedmen had enjoyed rights before independence, which would have conferred on them a status equivalent to citizen, if that designation had then existed. As far as he was concerned at that point, if they denied citizenship rights to freedmen, then they were in fact more despotic than "during the time of despotism itself."[27]

It is instructive to consider those earlier debates. A draft of the Constitution was presented to all deputies in 1823, and of its 272 articles, 24 were approved before the Chamber was dissolved on November 12, 1823.[28] Two articles, 20 and 21, on the inviolability of the rights of property (with the sole exception of public good, which provided for indemnification for the expropriation of property), were endorsed without any discussion. The others, however, were debated at some length. Article 5, in particular, which defined who was Brazilian, provoked heated and lengthy discussions that took place in eight sessions between September 23 and October 2.

Debate about Article 5 started around the wording of the title, which in the original draft read: "On the members of the society of the Empire of Brazil." Campos Vergueiro proposed that the word "members" (*membros*) be replaced with "citizens" (*cidadãos*) and that the following clause be added: "if we can call all the members of the Empire citizens." This comment set the hall on fire. Some were in agreement, such as Montezuma, who thought it necessary "to dispel the idea that there is a difference between Brazilians and Brazilian citizens; . . . to be Brazilian, is to be a member of *Brazilian society*: therefore, every Brazilian is a Brazilian citizen." Others decried this view, arguing that Montezuma was clearly including indigenous people and the enslaved in his understanding of citizens. Montezuma, who believed that it was important to discuss these issues but hastened to deny this accusation, emphasized that there was a distinction between Brazilians and inhabitants of Brazil: "We must confirm that [Indians and slaves] do not enter the class of citizens, and therefore they are not Brazilians in the proper sense. . . . They are men not to be tyrannized, but . . . while exercising rights in society they are considered a thing, or as the property of someone; the laws treat and recognize them in this manner. Therefore, how to call them Brazilians in the proper sense? How to mention them in the constitution, which we have at our charge? . . . Sirs, the slaves are nothing more than inhabitants of Brazil."[29]

They were thus faced with a clear dilemma. There were inhabitants of Brazil who, even though they were born in the country, could not be considered citizens because they were not members of society. Further, there were those who could not be citizens because, even being Brazilian-born, they were owned by other Brazilians. The problem was far from new. Ever since antiquity, one of the keys to understanding the concept of citizenship was its application only to free men—slaves and foreigners, and of course women, were left out of the social organization.[30] The conflict ensued because not all deputies viewed this restrictive definition of citizenship as self-evident. Although most saw the discussion as only about free individuals—and then specifically about freedmen—some believed it was necessary to address the dilemma of enslaved persons. Deputy Henrique Dias, for example, noted that it was wrong to suggest that only the free have rights, as even enslaved people were "subject to all punishable and criminal laws, as well as protected by the same laws which guarantee their rights, and preserve their existences: therefore they are not things; because things do not have rights and duties."[31]

The situation was indeed ambiguous. First, while slaves did have some legal responsibility and juridical prerogatives, they were, according to civil law, things, the property of someone. Further, there was no consensus even about the meaning of "Brazilian." For example, when Deputy Carvalho e Melo argued that all Brazilians should be "given the title of citizens," and that Brazilian citizens were "all those who were born in Brazil, or who became such by law," it was not clear whether the definition meant the inclusion of the enslaved. Were free Africans included in this definition at the moment they became Brazilians "by law," as the slave trade was still legal? Deputy Almeida e Albuquerque, for one, understood the language to mean that the enslaved were included in the definition, and he shouted the proposal down: "To suggest that all members of society are Brazilian citizens is to purposefully confuse ideas: it would be good if all were citizens, but is this not a true chimera? In a country where there are slaves, where a multitude of blacks uprooted from the coast of Africa and elsewhere enter the domestic sphere and become part of the families, how is it possible that there is no such division? . . . Will we be the ones to devalue the title of Brazilian citizen by indiscriminately giving it to every individual?"[32]

Although after great debate the Assembly did approve Vergueiro's amendment to Article 5, there was no consensus about what it was to be Brazilian nor what it was to be a Brazilian citizen, let alone about the definition of either. Most members of the Constituent Assembly did not even take seriously the idea of granting citizenship rights to the enslaved, but some clearly feared that it was in the realm of possibility, as we can see in the passion of their arguments against the proposal. After all, for some, citizens were any individuals who had rights, and the enslaved did have certain rights, in particular the right to be protected by the state.

If the vast majority agreed that African-born slaves should not have Brazilian citizenship rights, as they were not born in Brazil—few took into account the fact that they had not come from Africa of their own volition—theoretically it was not easy to argue in favor of excluding Brazilian-born slaves from citizenship, since nobody dared to say that they were not persons, and they had clearly been born on Brazilian territory. Following this reasoning, it would be almost impossible to deny citizenship rights to freedpersons, especially to Brazilians, as was clear from the discussion of paragraph 6 of Article 5, which established that "slaves who obtained a letter of manumission" could be citizens. A number of deputies joined Henriques de Rezende in favoring the approval of this item, although there was discussion regarding the extension of these same rights to their African ancestors. Even so, the content of the approved amendment was even broader than the original paragraph: it established that all "freedmen who acquired their freedom by any legitimate title" would be citizens— technically, this allowed for the possibility of an enslaved person to purchase his or her own freedom.[33]

In discussions about extending citizenship to freedmen—and all deputies agreed on this—the representatives of the Constituent Assembly were referring to civil rights, never to political rights, which would make it possible for them to effectively intervene in the destiny of the Empire. This was true even for those who were decidedly on the side of the freedmen, such as Deputy Silva Lisboa, who said, "Why should arbitrary distinctions be made for freedmen, because of their place of birth, and their service and office? Once they acquire the status of citizen they deserve equal protection of the law. . . . To be deemed a Brazilian citizen is, indeed, a designation of honor, but one that gives only *civil rights* and not *political rights*."[34]

This situation was not unique to Brazil. In countries that were models for the Brazilian parliamentarians, such as England, France, and the United States, a large part of the population had no political rights. In England at this time, for example, the right to vote was conditional on the possession of minimum standards of income or property. After the electoral reform of 1832, when the right to vote was extended to leaseholders and tenants with some economic base, which increased the electorate by 57 percent, artisans and dispossessed workers still had no political rights.[35] In France, even though the National Assembly had decided during the revolutionary period that all members of the nation would be free and equal before the law, the subsequent definition of passive and active citizens—the former possessing only the "natural rights" of protection of one's own person, freedom, and property—resulted in only a small number of French nationals possessing voting rights. The group included only white males thirty years of age and older, with an established address, who paid 300 francs a month in direct taxes; running for office required paying 1,000 francs a month in taxes. In the elections of 1827, only 1 of every 360 inhabitants of France was an elector; counting only the population consisting of adult men, there was 1 voter for every 50 or 60 citizens.[36]

The case of the United States, which Brazilian parliamentarians turned to often as an example, was equally exclusive—women, minors, slaves, and those who did not own property could not be citizens. With regard to racial criteria, the policies in the United States were more restrictive than in other countries. In the 1820s, alleging public safety measures, judges from states such as Missouri and Kentucky gradually repealed the civil rights of the vast majority of free and freed blacks, arguing that they could not be considered fully American citizens because they were descendants of Africans. This was more extreme even than the actions in the 1790s, when the specter of the Haitian Revolution was causing such anxiety. In 1820, the year of the Missouri Compromise (which admitted Missouri into the Union as a slave state), as slavery in the North was increasingly being restricted, the constitution of Missouri prevented free blacks even from entering the state.[37]

Thus, to speak of political rights anywhere in the first half of the nineteenth century refers to a very restrictive concept, and Brazil was no different. Even in those countries where citizenship was proclaimed to be universal, political rights were not considered among the rights of citizenship.[38] It was not by chance that deputies often quoted from Benjamin Constant's popular commentary on the French Constitution, *Cours de politique constitutionelle*. Constant explicitly defends the differentiation between civil and political rights, arguing that membership in the political society should be determined not only by criteria of birth and age, but also property. In his view, this was not a preference for hierarchical social structures; on the contrary, the abolition of the nobility as a social mark and the adoption of the criterion of property ownership meant an unprecedented opening, since the status of owner was not for life, while that of a nobleman was. Any citizen could become a property owner, and from there, an elector.[39] In the case of Brazil, the use of Benjamin Constant's theory could be justified even in relation to the enslaved: if they could liberate themselves by buying their own freedom, they could also become citizens and electors. But the members of the Council of State who ended up drafting the Constitution in 1824 did not share Constant's appreciation of liberalism, and the possibility of freedmen becoming electors was duly excluded.

The debate that took place around the definition of civil and political rights is crucial to my argument. The legislative sessions dedicated to discussing the civil rights of freedmen reveal how important the concept of citizenship was for these lawmakers, both because of the "new social pact" in the context of Brazilian independence and as a means to secure public peace. As several representatives emphasized, it was critical to make use of the word "citizen," "because . . . even though the meaning is the same [as "member of society"], there is so much importance currently attached to the word that there would be great jealousy and disgust if a class of Brazilians believed that this title was intended to be exclusive for another class."[40] The word "citizen" required a clear definition, and it was important to use the term itself not only because there was a "class of Brazilians" who wanted to be considered citizens, but because so many attached importance to it, given the social pressures throughout the decade on the meaning of the term. The fact that the deputies regularly invoked the enslaved and freedmen in their speeches demonstrates that they were well aware of the happenings in the streets—and indeed, it was a charged time.

The fear of uprisings, revolts, and social unrest helps to explain the correlation that many deputies constructed between citizenship and public security. In that impassioned speech of August 25, 1832, Rebouças made use of the association himself when he alerted his peers to the incendiary potential of the proposal, apparently intending to frighten them by referencing what could happen to Brazil if they insisted on making the same mistakes as the French in Sainte-Domingue, now Haiti. Seeing it as their responsibility to ensure the well-being and protection of good citizens, the majority of the deputies found it difficult to regard freedmen as de facto citizens—in their view, the freedmen were among the very people responsible for the waves of revolts and discontents that had swept the Empire.

The importance of the debate on civil rights in nineteenth-century Brazil seems clear. As historian José Murilo de Carvalho points out, however, until recently historical analyses focused almost exclusively on elections and electoral participation, translating citizenship as the exercise of political rights even though the definition of civil rights was fundamental in the 1820s and 1830s.[41] Being a citizen was a desired distinction, even if it did not necessarily come with political rights, or even a guarantee of basic rights, such as personal security. Although the prevailing significance of the expression "civil rights" came from recognizing the validity of a previously existing situation—as with the enslaved and freedmen who had fought for independence and therefore deserved the "honorific designation" that

Deputy Henriques de Rezende spoke of in 1823—this did not make the rights less important. After all, as T. H. Marshall asserts in his classic text on the subject, "the story of civil rights in their formative period is one of the gradual addition of new rights to a status that already existed."[42]

These debates and conflicts form the context for understanding Rebouças's concerns about membership in the National Guard on that long afternoon of August 1832. Even after the requirement that all members be born free was revoked in the Senate, and although the Decree of 1832 provided for the admission of freedpersons, the National Assembly remained divided on the subject. And indeed, there was ultimately a reversal of the decision, "again by the difference of only a few votes,"[43] once again excluding freedmen from the National Guard.

In all of this back-and-forth, it was often unclear whether or not freedmen could actually be recruited for the Guard. In 1833, in the newspaper *O Brasileiro Pardo*, a complaint was lodged that "we *pardos*, with the exception of freedmen, have already been reduced to being unable to belong to the National Guard, except those of us who were born free." In a notice of 1835, in response to an inquiry, Minister of Justice Manuel Alves Branco confirmed that freedmen were excluded from enlistment because they were not electors. Three years later, however, in response to another question on the same issue, Minister of Justice Bernardo Pereira de Vasconcelos stated in another notice that freedmen, because of their status as Brazilian citizens, could be enlisted in the National Guard.[44]

What Rebouças was able to see in this issue was an increasing tendency to target freedmen as playing a major role in the political instability of the Brazilian Empire. In his view, the real enemies of the order were those who supported the cause of the restoration, such as José Egídio Gordilho de Barbuda (1787–1830), the Viscount of Camamu and a well-known defender of the interests of Portugal in Bahia. Rebouças had long blamed the Viscount for the persecutions he had suffered in 1824 in Sergipe. Since his arbitrary arrest and imprisonment at the Fortaleza do Mar in 1829, Rebouças had learned his lessons in how easily citizens' rights were suspended on any pretext.[45]

Rebouças's reactions in these debates were less tempestuous than they had been during the episodes of the independence battles in Bahia and the accusations in Sergipe. His life had changed significantly since he had been released from prison three years before; he was now a respected deputy elected to the National Assembly—occupying the last of the thirteen seats of the province of Bahia—and a member of the Council of the Province.[46]

In April 1831, he had married Carolina Pinto, daughter of Anna Joaquina and André Pinto de Silveira, a merchant in Cachoeira. They were married one day before the disturbances in the capital of Bahia that had broken out following the "Noite das Garrafadas" (Night of the Bottle-Blows), a conflict that started on March 13 in Rio, when liberals, exaltados, and restauradores confronted each other in the streets.[47] Rebouças was reportedly interrupted on his honeymoon to meet with local authorities, who sought to take precautions against the alarming state of public unrest, particularly given the uprising of the troops. Fearful of attacks on the president of the province by some "bad-tempered Patriot exaltado," Rebouças, in addition to having voted in favor of the deposition of the Commander of Arms, resolved to remain "vigilant alongside that very President throughout the night until dawn of the 5th of April, which was when he returned to his house and the company of his new wife."[48]

Whether because of a different maturity at age thirty or perhaps the anticipation of marriage, Rebouças had for some time been opposed to violent manifestations against the limitation of guarantees and rights for all, such as the local Portuguese.[49] At this point in his life, he preferred to discuss important matters in the Chamber of Deputies, where he went on April 23 to reassume his position and "demonstrate his monarchical-constitutional principles."[50]

In this moment, everything indicated that Rebouças's personal life was moving toward greater stability due to his improved social position, and yet, he was still not free from old accusations, such as those from 1824 and 1825 in Sergipe and Bahia. Only a short time before, in a debate in the Chamber, Rebouças had noted the need to refute the slander published against him in *Diário do Governo*, where it was said that he had provoked "a revolution of slaves."[51] There is no evidence that Rebouças actually initiated a suit against the paper. Even so, the fact that he was once again addressing these denunciations shows that the office of deputy had not made him immune to unfounded claims against him. Like the freedmen he defended in his speech about the National Guard, it seemed that Rebouças himself was still viewed by many as emblematic and controversial.

Rebouças was committed first and foremost to the inviolability of the Constitution, which included property ownership as a criterion of citizenship. This was an issue for many deputies, who believed that other criteria beyond property should be part of the definition of a citizen. This was an intolerable position as far as Rebouças was concerned, as it had the potential to restrict the exercise of citizenship, which could easily result in abuses carried out in the name of public safety. Rebouças had experienced this very situation in an earlier debate. In refusing a bill that proposed the imprisonment of people with no possibility for bail, claiming that this was an attack on citizens' rights, Rebouças heard in response: "I wouldn't want to violate the constitution; but when citizens are not safe in their homes, because evil is extreme, then a prompt response is necessary."[52] For the parliamentarians whom Rebouças opposed, civil rights were still seen as privileges to which only the few were entitled, and in the end these rights were not always connected to "skills and virtues" enshrined in the Constitution.

It was the irreducibility of civil rights that differentiated Rebouças's ideas: by consistently emphasizing the right of property, Rebouças was demonstrating the truly liberal aspect of his thinking, in the sense formulated by Benjamin Constant. Citizenship should be based on acquired criteria, not on inherited social status. Property was something that anyone could acquire or lose. The fact that it could also be inherited was not part of his consideration. The important point, for Rebouças—as for Constant—was that any individual male, no matter his birthright, could in theory rise to the position of citizen.

After all, although from today's perspective the correlation between citizenship and property is deeply restrictive, at the beginning of the nineteenth century it was exactly the opposite, and for that very reason was seen as the revolutionary character of capitalism. The substitution of property for birthright had allowed people to be incorporated into society without precedent, and Rebouças was convinced of the benefits of this practice, and not only because he himself was one of these beneficiaries. For him, this was most likely the best way of exercising his radicalism while remaining moderate: through an absolute commitment to property and law.

In this sense, the exclusion of the enslaved from the so-called rule of law and the prerogatives of citizenship as laid out in the Constitution did not pose a problem for Rebouças. If enslaved persons were legally defined as *objects* and thus outside the field of civil law, there was nothing that could be done. Rebouças did not entertain the dilemma pointed out by Montezuma in 1823, that there would be people born in Brazil who were not citizens, because for Rebouças, citizenship was only for free people. His issue was what happened at the moment a former slave gained the status of *person*, and thus became part of civil society. As we can see in his statements about the inclusion of freedmen as National Guard officers, his concern was how to incorporate freedpersons into society. But he also understood that this was murky territory because enslaved persons, even those formally owned by others, were often able to accumulate enough money to buy their freedom, and, in this case, he argued, they too should be granted the status of citizen.

This has to be why Rebouças, as late as 1830, put forward a bill to regulate the rights of enslaved persons who sought to buy their own freedom. At the legislative session of May 14, he proposed adapting for Brazil the Ordenações Filipinas (1603) (in particular, book 4, title 11, paragraph 4), which, following the Ordenações Afonsinas (1446–1448) and the Ordenações Manuelinas (1501), legislated the enslaved Moors in Portugal.[53] The original text stated that while "no one should be obliged to sell his inheritance or things against his will," this was not always the case with captives, "because in favor of freedom, many things are granted against the general rules." The main purpose of the law was to enable the exchange of Moorish captives for their Christian counterparts, according to a fair assessment of their value by competent persons. When there was no one to exchange for the Moor, he could be released through payment of his own value increased by 20 percent.[54]

Rebouças suggested using a similar principle in the question of obtaining manumission, proposing that "any slave who deposits the amount of his worth, plus a fifth of that same worth, will be immediately freed even against his master's will."[55] This reflected his belief that anyone who demonstrated the skills and virtues of citizenship belonged to society even though they did not yet belong by law. In his view, the fact that many enslaved persons had enough money to buy their own freedom or the freedom of their relatives should correspond to the right to pay the public deposit in court and guarantee their manumission—which would make them freedmen and therefore citizens. It is important to note that Rebouças maintained the clause established in the Ordenações Filipinas about compensation guaranteed to the master, which had the potential to turn this acquisition of manumission into good business: considering the financial crisis of the late 1820s, a bankrupt master might have had an interest in recovering his investment in a slave plus an additional 20 percent.

Rebouças also added a new aspect to the law, however: any master had the right to accuse the slave of stealing the money presented for his manumission, as long as he could provide evidence. At that time, evidence only required testimony by two people, and thus if a master was able to find two people willing to speak to the court in his favor, he could prevent the granting of freedom. On the one hand, the proposed law challenged the prerogative of the master's control over his slaves, as Rebouças ultimately advocated that even against the master's will, an enslaved person be allowed to purchase his or her own freedom. On the other hand, he also included this ambiguity that made it relatively easy for the owner to deny the manumission. What ultimately counted for Rebouças in legal terms was the possession of the property, whether by the slaves or by the masters.

In this discussion, Rebouças clearly demonstrated his commitment to property as the foundation of social organization. Such a law could even have had a favorable effect on ways in which slaves acquired freedom, but it never would have been approved. In seeking to regulate the Ordenação Filipina, he was proposing a specific interpretation for a law that was already being used, but in extremely broad terms. In freedom lawsuits, lawyers regularly invoked the clause "because in favor of freedom, many things are granted against the general rules" to argue in favor of the manumission of slaves. Indeed, it was the most cited ordinance—and it was invoked by both sides—in the freedom lawsuits at the Court of Appeals of Rio de Janeiro that took place throughout the nineteenth century.[56]

We can take as an example the trial of Felizarda Bernarda, who attempted to regain her freedom in a process that began in 1827 in São João d'El Rei.[57] The daughter of two freedpeople who continued to live with their former master, Felizarda was born free and baptized as such. Her situation changed radically, however, when the master died, and his debts provoked the sequestering of all his possessions. At twelve years of age, Felizarda was included on the list of slaves owned by the family. Her father having died and her mother being a "poor black, with no knowledge of her rights,"[58] Felizarda was left helpless. She was sold and illegally enslaved, and her own children were then also wrongly baptized as slaves. In the first trial, the judge ruled to maintain the woman and her children in slavery. As there was an ex officio appeal in these cases, the proceeding went to the Court of Appeals of Rio de Janeiro in 1830, the same year Rebouças made his proposal to the Chamber.

The lawyer for Felizarda and her children based his argument on the fact that she was born free, and even though she had come to belong to someone, in these cases, he argued, freedom took precedence. He claimed, "Even in less enlightened centuries our legislators have recognized this principle, 'because in favor of freedom, many things are granted against the general rules' (Ordenação book 4, title 11, paragraph 4)." The master's lawyer used the same quote to defend the opposite position: "Although we recognize how favorable the cause of freedom is, and that the Laws sometimes allow for it to be granted against the general rules of law according to the clause in Ord book 4, tit 11, par 4, it is not clear that the inviolability of the citizen's property is in conflict with freedom. That the maintenance of one [property] is not in fact less important than of the other [freedom]."

In addition to the Ordenações being used by both sides to substantiate opposing arguments, neither side took the original meaning of the ordinance into account, instead relying on a later interpretation. It is quite possible that this was precisely the type of case Rebouças sought to avoid, since, with equally invalid arguments on both sides, the final decision could never be based on the letter of the law, but was instead dependent on the interpretation of the judges. In the case of Felizarda, the Court ruled in favor of the owners, but it could also have ruled the other way.

Rebouças's proposal ultimately sought to regulate the enslaved person's ability to purchase his or her manumission, which was an early attempt to legislate the *peculio* (the personal savings of an enslaved person) and the purchase of one's own freedom, a practice so widespread that even travelers like Henry Koster thought it was a law. It is not surprising that Rebouças approached this issue via the only legal terms he considered legitimate: the demonstration of the right to freedom through proof of ownership.[59] We start to see how Rebouças worked simultaneously in two spheres, the legislative realm in Parliament and daily legal practice. Indeed, it was in working at these two levels that he dedicated himself to his preferred political causes: the regulation of laws, the organization of the judicial structure of the Empire, the creation of a justice system endowed with equity, and the constitution of a body of citizens who, based solely on their skills and virtues, were able to overcome the problems faced in the period after independence.

In fact, it would be difficult to dissociate his parliamentary position from his ideas and respect for legal practice, since he understood that, in order to be accepted, legal practice had to be validated by law; for that reason he chose to regulate the norm established in the Ordenações Filipinas, book 4, title 11, paragraph 4 instead of proposing a new law. As a deputy, but also as a lawyer with broad legal experience, he was keenly aware of the calamitous state of the country's laws and the need to reform them. Yet, although many lawmakers shared these concerns about the future of justice in the Brazilian Empire, Rebouças's colleagues did not take his ideas seriously. His views on citizenship were refuted in 1832; in addition, his bill on personal savings and regulating access to freedom by enslaved persons was not granted his request of urgency, but instead was referred to a commission for review, where it remained, unnoticed.[60]

4   A "Guarantor" for the Brazilians

. . . .

The Constitution states explicitly and clearly that everyone has equal
[rights] to the functions and occupations of the Nation, so long as
they have the required skills and virtues. But what we see!
—*Novo Diário da Bahia*, December 26, 1837

Rebouças was certainly aware of the freedom lawsuits that made their way
to the courts throughout the early nineteenth century. Even though he was
not a lawyer in the Court of Appeals in Rio de Janeiro—he was only granted
permission to try cases in that court in 1847, after leaving his position as
deputy—his reputation as a good legal professional had spread through the
Brazilian Empire. Since the early 1830s, he often received letters requesting legal assistance in lawsuits in Rio de Janeiro, and it seems he spent as
much time in the courts as in the Legislative Assembly. It was precisely
because of his experience and reputation that prominent public figures, such
as the Andrada e Silva family, looked to Rebouças when they needed legal
or political assistance.

One such request came from José Bonifácio Andrada e Silva, who, in
April 1835, asked Rebouças to take on the case of a friend. In a letter describing the case, the elderly statesman makes explicit reference to Rebouças's double prestige:

> My friend, whom I so highly esteem. For several weeks I have
> intended to write to you to request that you take interest in the case
> of Countess de Itapagipe and represent her. Your legal ability and
> your integrity assure me that you are still the same Rebouças who
> thundered in 1832. I would be grateful to you, as I am a friend of the
> Countess and she deserves [our help]. I am here in the solitude of
> Paquetá,[1] free of the evil political opponents who have been trying
> to blacken my reputation.[2] Continue, honorable sir, to fight against
> those rogues who infest our disgraced land, like mushrooms in
> rotten wood. D. Maria and my daughter send you their best regards.
> I have the honor of being Your Truest Friend.[3]

Bonifácio is referencing his dismissal, some years earlier, from his position as tutor of the young Emperor Pedro II, which helps to explain his appeal to Rebouças. In 1832, amid the political crises after Pedro I's resignation, Diogo Antonio, then minister of justice, accused Bonifácio of leading a conspiracy against the new government and sought to take away his position as tutor of Pedro II. Rebouças was one of the few to support Bonifácio, arguing that the tutor deserved the right of defense:

> [The] illustrious members . . . think that the Tutor should not be heard; that he should be expelled from the guardianship on a note of disgrace! Yes, gentlemen, on the note of disgrace! . . . And will it be that a law, made by the General Assembly of Brazil, restrains the rights of the Tutor of the Emperor, . . . rights that no man is denied, natural and social rights common to all men, always respected by all legislators? . . . Does not the Imperial Tutor . . . deserve the right of defense, common to every man and every employee? He is a Minister!!![4]

Rebouças argued that Bonifácio, as a deputy, legally could only be removed by the General Assembly, and not by the minister of justice.[5] His efforts were in vain, however: José Bonifácio was removed from his position on December 14, 1833, and imprisoned in his house on Paquetá Island in Guanabara Bay, in Rio. In his place, Manuel Inácio de Andrade Souto Maior Pinto Coelho (1782–1867), later the Marquis de Itanhaém, was nominated to be the Emperor's tutor.[6] Given Bonifácio's exile, Rebouças was likely one of the few lawyers to whom the former tutor could turn. Most likely Rebouças honored the request for help, as—judging from subsequent appeals made by Martim Francisco Ribeiro de Andrada e Silva—his relations with the Andrada e Silva family remained quite friendly.[7]

Rebouças's familiarity with the country's highest authorities, on the one hand, reflects the arrival of his generation—the "generation of Independence"—to power, while, on the other hand, it demonstrates how his career as a deputy and his reputation as a legal expert increasingly won him visibility on the national level, even in areas not directly related to knowledge of the law. From the beginning of the 1840s, for example, he was often asked to review plays for the newly created Brazilian Drama Conservatory, an institution tasked with censoring plays to ensure proper decorum, especially when the imperial family would be present at a performance. Rebouças addressed a wide range of issues, from the correct use of grammar to the depiction of social mores, such as family honor. In his review of *Isabel, the Orphan from Paraná*, for example, he criticized the play for portraying conflicted marital relations in a way that could serve as a bad example for the audience.[8]

It was in the legal world, however, that Rebouças was most well known. There was even talk that he had been considered for the position of minister of justice. As reported in Rebouças's memoirs, Feijó, who had become Regent in 1835 and was in the midst of a political crisis in 1837, asked Rebouças to be minister. Rebouças reportedly preferred to "wait to take part in the administration of the Empire after the Emperor personally assumed control of the government."[9] Even a close look at the sources does not make clear whether Rebouças refused the invitation, not wanting to be identified with a government that had such strong opposition in the Chamber, or whether he accepted and failed to take the office for obscure reasons. An anonymous article published in 1880 in the *Revista do Instituto Histórico e Geográfico Brasileiro* honoring Rebouças right after his death suggests the latter, stating that "the appointment was not made for reasons that will not be discussed here."[10] But there is little evidence that the invitation was actually ever made. In a letter from Feijó to Rebouças in 1842, Feijó appears not even to know Rebouças, as he is not familiar with Rebouças's full name. Feijó writes that he recommended Rebouças to a friend, specifying, "I assured him that I knew only the good reputation of Mr. Rebouças." At the end of the letter, Feijó apologizes, "Forgive me for not using your first name in the opening, as I do not know it."[11]

If Feijó did not know Rebouças in 1842, how would he have invited him to be part of his cabinet in 1837? And yet, as rumors tended to spread more quickly than actual news, Bahia was already aware of the hypothetical invitation even before Rebouças returned to his native province that year. The story sparked the usual animosity in his political opponents, especially Chief of Police Francisco Gonçalves Martins, who had never gotten along with Rebouças. In a meeting in the Provincial Assembly, Martins complained that Rebouças "declared that he had constantly rejected great positions, even that of Minister of Justice, *which had never been offered to him*; he did not stop talking about his autonomy and wealth: factors that led him to reject any subordinate place in Brazil."[12] Rebouças responded with irony, asking: "I declared in the Provincial Assembly that I would not accept a subordinate place in my country? And where would I accept it? In the United States of America? Whether or not I was offered it is something I have no need to discuss."[13] Rebouças had claimed that he was invited in order to integrate the cabinet, and he was not pleased when this statement was challenged—perhaps because he really believed it himself, or perhaps because he sought political gains from the fact that he was important enough to receive such an offer, even if only a proposal. As there is too little documentation to know for certain, we can only do as Rebouças did and refrain from debate on whether the position of minister was actually offered to him or not.

The more important issue here is the political role that Rebouças had come to play, different from his position through the mid-1830s. With the continuous back and forth between Salvador and Rio de Janeiro to attend the National Assembly, especially when he was also a representative in the newly created Provincial Legislative Assembly,[14] Rebouças succeeded in becoming a key figure in the relationship between those in the Empire's capital and colleagues from Bahia. Over the course of a few years, Rebouças had risen in status from being an important local politician to a figure of national prominence, albeit indelibly linked to the affairs of his native province.

The various requests that Rebouças received demonstrate both the extent of clientelism in Brazilian imperial politics and Rebouças's prominence in all affairs concerning Bahia. Regardless of the positions that he defended in Parliament, Rebouças was a key figure in most political affairs and negotiations that involved the province.[15] Even Montezuma, with whom Rebouças had felt offended in the episodes of independence in Cachoeira, had to bow to Rebouças's influence; in a series of letters, Montezuma asked Rebouças to help him with a bureaucratic issue: "If to help me you need some personal sacrifice, be patient: I think I deserve it . . . as I never offended my fellow natives [Bahians]: quite the contrary, my life has been nothing other than vital sacrifices in the cause of [Bahia's] glory, its independence, its liberty. Shouldn't I deserve, then, such a demonstration of friendship?"[16]

Rebouças was well aware that his status as a politician depended on building and maintaining good relations with national authorities, while at the same time preserving his loyalty to the leading political figures in Bahia. This meant responding to requests for favors and information, such as that of Minister of Justice Antonio Paulino Limpo de Abreu, who asked that Rebouças pass on all "information and advice he deemed necessary, especially in regard to this Province," referring to Bahia.[17] The more Rebouças responded to those in power, the more solicitations they sent him, and in turn, he was in a better condition to ask for favors. These friendships with key people in the politics of the Empire increased his prestige in Bahia, which then led to requests for favors from local leaders such as

Montezuma. By responding to these requests, Rebouças attracted the loyalties and the necessary votes to continue being elected deputy by his province.

It is not surprising, then, that Rebouças, when in Bahia, never tired of emphasizing his importance in Rio de Janeiro and his good relations with all sectors of society:

> My relations of friendship and trust are confirmed, increased, and progressively extended to the largest and most distinguished civil servants in Brazil. . . . In the Council of Ministers, in the Supreme Court of Justice, among all secular and regular Ecclesiastical Dignities, in the Supreme Council of War and Justice, in the Chamber of Deputies, in the Court of Commerce, in all scientific and philanthropic organizations, among the Presidencies of the Provinces, in the Diplomatic Corps, in all affairs, in the Corps of the Judiciary in general, among the Secretaries of State, I count on friends, who do not hesitate to correspond with their affection and benevolence. In Bahia—what authority does not treat me with friendship and affection . . . ? Why should I not take pride, as I deserve the trust and friendship of all the noble Brazilians who have known me closely, and know me?[18]

Rebouças did clearly take great pride in his friendships and made them visible for public display in both the national and provincial realms. On the one hand, Rebouças was continually highlighting his position as a prestigious figure in the capital in order to maintain his authority as a provincial leader; on the other hand, he was always trying to show the central authorities that he could defend the interests of the nation in the province by politically supporting the government. This was a complex game involving competing political interests in the province. After all, Rebouças was not the only deputy aspiring to build a successful career in national politics. A considerable number of Bahian politicians were active on the national scene, and to survive politically, Rebouças needed to uphold his own position of strength, usually to the detriment of others.[19] This is, in short, the story of his rivalry with Chief of Police Francisco Gonçalves Martins.

Gonçalves Martins came from what could be called a "new family" in Bahia, who, once poor, had made their way during the economic boom to owning sugar mill plantations in the region. Gonçalves Martins was part of the first generation of his family to study in Portugal and then return to seek a bureaucratic position. After serving as chief of police of Salvador, he was deputy in the General Assembly from 1834 to 1850, and Governor of Bahia from 1848 to 1852, and again from 1868 to 1871. He also served as a senator and in 1852–1853 as Minister of Internal Affairs; at the end of his life he was honored with the title of Viscount of São Lourenço.[20]

Gonçalves Martins thus rose much higher in politics than Rebouças, who never went beyond his position as a deputy in the Legislative Assembly. But back in 1835, Gonçalves Martins was still a local judge aspiring to a political career. His rapid rise was likely to be worrying Rebouças, who, as a veteran of the battles for independence, had greater public prestige.[21] In describing the episodes in Bahia between 1835 and 1837, Rebouças emphasized the unfortunate role of Gonçalves Martins, who lacked the capacity—in the case of the Malê revolt in 1835—and the political will—in the case of the Sabinada in 1837—to protect Salvador from the dangers of that time.

It had been a while since Rebouças, having been the first alternate in the last elections, had returned to reside in Salvador.[22] His family had grown considerably by then. In addition to his already elderly father, who lived with them, there were now two daughters: Anna Rita and Carolina, born in 1832 and 1833. He and his wife soon would have two more children, André and Antonio Pereira, both born in Bahia.[23] His father-in-law, now a widower, also lived in the city and, according to Rebouças, he was the one responsible for alerting the authorities about the Malê revolt.[24] As Rebouças wrote to Gonçalves Martins years later, "You know very well, Sir Chief of Police Gonçalves, that it was to my father-in-law that the African freedwoman revealed the secret of the impending insurrection; that my father-in-law, as soon as he heard this, spread the news to all the people who were with him (as was his custom between seven and ten to eleven o'clock at night); . . . that the District Justice of the Peace heard the African freedwoman in great detail; and, if I'm not mistaken, the Commander of the Police Corps also heard it."[25]

It was Saturday, January 24, 1835, the Feast of Our Lady of Guidance. The day before, in front of the church of Bonfim, rumors had circulated that a group of Africans had spent the whole day welcoming their compatriots, who were arriving from the Recôncavo with plans for the greatest rebellion of Africans that Bahia had ever witnessed. This news reached the African freedwoman Guilhermina Rosa de Souza, who confirmed the rumors with her friend Sabina da Cruz, whose husband, Vitório Sule, was involved in organizing the conspiracy. Guilhermina decided to run to the house of her neighbor and landlord, André Pinto da Silveira, father-in-law of Rebouças, to tell what she knew, arriving there at eight o'clock at night. She came across an enslaved African working for the Silveira family, and insisted that he tell his master about the revolt. He refused, but their raised voices had attracted Silveira's curiosity, and so Guilhermina herself ended up explaining the reason for her visit.[26]

Rebouças clearly did not like Guilhermina, who came often to make demands about the state of her house to Rebouças's father-in-law. Describing her as "very impertinent," Rebouças was likely unhappy that an African woman lived close to his own family members and, further, that she felt entitled to lodge complaints. It was this same Guilhermina who shortly afterwards sent Antonio Pereira Rebouças the message that he should "caution" his slaves, because a group of more than sixty insurrectionaries had gathered in a house near the church of Our Lady of Guadalupe, which was later revealed as the home of Manoel Calafate.

If they did not get along well, why would Guilhermina have immediately told Antonio Pereira Rebouças about the insurrection? Was it because of her relationship with André Silveira, which also was not very good? It's difficult to know. One might suppose that Guilhermina saw Rebouças as someone who could better understand the situation and react accordingly. If true, this implies that his daily contact with the world of Africans and freedpersons was far greater than he depicted in his accounts. Regardless, Rebouças would have gone quickly to the meeting place, where thirty policemen and the leaders of the police had already gathered, along with "many citizens armed and equipped with torches to scour every corner of the house."[27] Everyone seemed to be gathered there, except for Francisco Gonçalves Martins, who was then chief of police.

According to Rebouças's account, Gonçalves Martins was on the slope of the Palace Square, and would surely have seen the thirty policemen and the citizens armed with torches, the Palace Guard with its forty bayonets, the College Guard with more than twenty, and the Third Battalion of the First Line and the National Guard, who were also beginning to approach. Yet even with so many armed people assembled there, Gonçalves Martins left the scene without giving a command. He only moved to suppress the rioters when they arrived at the square where the Cavalry Battalion was stationed.[28]

Earlier, at one o'clock Sunday morning, the plan of the revolt had already been discovered by a justice of the peace, a police officer, and two National Guard officers, who had found the rebels gathering at the house of Manoel Calafate. The Malê rioters took to the streets right away, waking up other Africans and calling them to "war." When they arrived at the neighborhood of Água de Meninos and encountered Gonçalves Martins, they had already passed through Palace Square, where, facing the Guard, they had unsuccessfully attempted to free some prisoners; they had already gone down Ajuda Street and arrived at Teatro Plaza, where they found a large contingent of volunteers waiting for them; they had already passed the Pelourinho toward the lower city. From there, they intended to take the road to Cabrito to meet the Africans coming from the Recôncavo. They did not make it that far. At Água de Meninos, they came face to face with the cavalry of Gonçalves Martins, and the final battle of the dawn broke out. In less than half an hour, the African rebels were defeated, killed, trapped, and scattered, as the chief of police later proudly described.

At this point, it should come as no surprise that for Rebouças, the scandal was the police chief's delay in repressing the rebellion, not the brutality of the repression itself. Although the cavalry headed by Gonçalves Martins killed more than forty people, trapped others, and dispersed the rest, Rebouças argued that "he would have more easily defeated, killed, arrested, and dispersed them in the house where they were in Ladeira da Praça, if he had stayed at the siege for a while longer."[29] He repeated this opinion later in the General Assembly, claiming that the chief of police had not fulfilled his duties during "the insurrection of January 1835, which Brazil would have been grieving forever if it had not been exposed shortly before its outbreak. . . . I am not talking about the lack of knowledge of the plotting of this insurrection, or of the police absolutely ignoring the Islamism [of the Malês] and its propagation among this *brutal race*. I am talking about the poor manner in which the police behaved."[30]

Rebouças depicted Gonçalves Martins as making similar mistakes in 1837 during the federalist revolt known as the Sabinada.[31] Moderate liberals, including Rebouças, were losing political influence at the time. On the one hand, supportive of the monarchical-constitutional project, Rebouças was in favor of the repression of all separatist movements in the Empire in the 1830s, such as the Farroupilha (1835–1845) in the province of Rio Grande do Sul and the Cabanagem (1835–1840) in the province of Pará; on the other hand, he did not look favorably upon the Regresso (1837), a conservative movement led by his friend Bernardo Pereira de Vasconcelos that emphasized centralization and the reinforcement of authority, policies that made Rebouças wary.[32]

Situating himself precisely between centralizing conservatives and radical liberals, Rebouças may also have seen the Sabinada as an opportunity to make clear his commitment to order and to monarchical-constitutional principles. As we will see, he did not play a significant role in repressing the Sabinada, which occupied the capital of Bahia for five months in 1837. Nonetheless, the revolt is featured in his book *Recordações da vida patriótica* (Memories of a Patriotic Life), published in 1870, amid other notable episodes such as the struggle for independence and the defense of the Constitution during the riots that followed the abdication of Emperor Pedro I. Rebouças reports in his memoirs that he was in Bahia in November 1837, after the end of the legislative session. When he heard the rumors on November 7 that a great revolutionary movement was taking place near the fortress of São Pedro, he went to see for himself, and there he encountered Lieutenant Colonel Luiz da França, who had the military force at his disposal, as well as Chief of Police Gonçalves Martins, who at that point was also a judge.[33]

The revolts in the province of Bahia—which had not enjoyed a moment of tranquility from 1831 to 1837—need to be understood in the context of the economic decay that had overtaken its capital, Salvador, since at least 1820, when a rapid economic boom began to give way to depression. After the wars of independence, a shortage of various staple foods, such as cassava, led to extreme price increases, while the uncontrolled production of copper coins triggered unprecedented inflation. The financial situation exacerbated the position of the federalists, who were already disappointed with the direction the nation was taking after independence. Together with the military, whose members were increasingly disillusioned by low salaries, they advocated for greater autonomy for the province, condemned the aristocracy that dominated the country, clamored for liberal legal reforms, and complained against high taxes.[34]

These liberals, the so-called *exaltados*, had been hopeful that the Additional Act of 1834, an amendment to the 1824 Constitution that contributed to the process of decentralization, would lead to important political changes. With greater autonomy for the provinces and, from 1835, with Feijó alone in the Regency, they hoped to pass reforms limiting the power of the landowners whose political and economic interests were connected to the central government. When this failed to happen, the effects were soon felt in several provinces, and a number of federalist revolts broke out, including the Cabanos in Pernambuco (1832–1835), the Cabanagem in Pará (1835–1840), the Farroupilha in Rio Grande do Sul (1835–1845), and, a little later, the Balaiada in Maranhão (1838–1841). In the case of Bahia, the resignation of Feijó gave rise to a group committed to the political strengthening of Rio de Janeiro's government, and signified an end to the hopes of political decentralization and federalist experimentation. In addition, massive military participation in the rebellion demonstrates how many officers disapproved of the military reforms of the 1830s, which created the National Guard and considerably reduced the military budget.[35]

The movement led by Vasconcelos, who put the landowner Pedro de Araújo Lima in power—marking the beginning of the Regresso—was unpopular with all the liberals, both the exaltados and the *moderados*. But the two groups reacted with different strategies. The exaltados viewed Vasconcelos's agenda as grounds for breaking with the government, while the moderados sought a legal approach to counter the threat of the Empire's fragmentation, seen, for example, in the revolt in Bahia.

Antonio Pereira Rebouças was part of the latter group. That is why, from the vicinity of the fortress of São Pedro on that November 7, as soon as he learned that the rebels João Carneiro da Silva Rego and Francisco Sabino Alves da Rocha Vieira had taken over Palace Square and that the president of the province was fleeing via boat through the bay, Rebouças began to contact his cohorts to organize a resistance—as always, originating in the Recôncavo. Rebouças convinced Provincial Vice President Paim to pass via Santo Amaro and from there to assume the interim presidency of the province; he then arranged with the treasurer general, Manoel José de Almeida Couto, to recover as many copper coins as possible from the Treasury; finally, he prevented Antonio Simões da Silva, the vice police chief, from moving the soldiers, so they would stay in the best place to besiege the rebels.[36]

If this last task fell to the vice police chief, the immediate question is what exactly the police chief, Francisco Gonçalves Martins, was doing at that time. Gonçalves Martins had already gone to Santo Amaro, where, even according to Rebouças, he was using all his means to repress the rebellion. Rebouças accused him, however, of acting in response to his own guilt for not having responded more swiftly against the conspiracy when he first learned of it: "The rebellion of November 7 would not have happened if the magistrate concerned here [Gonçalves Martins] had prevented the conspirators from leaving when he observed them at his club. It would have been enough to have them in custody, and make them leave at dawn the next day. Everything would have been discovered; they would take care of apologizing as they could, and the country would not go through the experiment of a revolution that threatened to dissolve and lose the empire!!!"[37]

In fact, Gonçalves Martins and Francisco Sabino Alves da Rocha Vieira, the movement's main leader and spokesman, had a long-standing friendship, and their meeting before the outbreak of the revolt is well known. Gonçalves Martins, like Rebouças and Sabino, had a newspaper in the early

1830s. Sabino had briefly headed *O Bahiano* after Rebouças's move to Rio de Janeiro, but had just founded his own newspaper, *O Investigador*, which was printed at Gonçalves Martins's press, where he published his newspaper *Órgão da Lei*.[38] When Sabino became involved in two crimes in the early 1830s, which involved the death of his wife and the murder of the journalist Moreira, apparently her lover, Gonçalves Martins not only refused to publish any news about the case, but also printed a note by Sabino, in which he defended himself against all accusations.[39]

Sabino went to Gonçalves Martins before the revolt began to inform him of what was about to happen and even to ask for his support. Although he did not actively assist the rebels, Gonçalves Martins did not denounce Sabino or arrest him, steps that would be expected from someone in his position. He later claimed that he had no legal right to intervene, although he had not hesitated to arrest and kill the Africans in the Malê revolt. Rebouças argued that in failing to stop Sabino, Gonçalves Martins was guilty of prolonging the Sabinada revolt.

The rest of the story is well known. Despite the disputes between Gonçalves Martins and Rebouças and despite the delay of the newly appointed president of the province, Barreto Pedroso, in cutting off supplies to Bahia, the government maintained a siege for five months that eventually left the city in famine. In March 1838, the Imperial troops took Salvador, where they arrested, wounded, and killed thousands of people.[40] During this time, while ships sat in the Bay of All Saints, preventing food from entering the city and awaiting arms and ammunition from Rio de Janeiro and the province of Pernambuco, Rebouças had taken his family to the Mataripe plantation, and from there to the town of Cachoeira. He spent the entire period of the rebellion living "in the same prestigious house full of happy memories of the cause of Independence in 1822," the house where the future engineer and abolitionist André Pinto Rebouças was born on January 13, 1838.[41] Rebouças returned to his home in the provincial capital once the rebellion was over, leaving again only in 1843 for Rio de Janeiro to assume his place once more in the National Assembly.[42]

Beyond his role in the conflict itself, undoubtedly motivated by his political beliefs, it is interesting to note the importance Rebouças attributed to the rebellion for strengthening his image as a defender of order. This was particularly important in the struggle for power among the moderate liberals after the beginning of the centralizing policy of the Regresso. The moderate wing of the liberals emphasized the need for basic reforms, such as judicial reform, which the conservatives also supported. After all, the judicial system was under the control of the local aristocracy and administered according to their political interests. Its reorganization meant greater efficiency and the rationalization of justice, which undoubtedly interested many liberals like Rebouças.[43]

Because of his position on order and legality, which was reinforced during the events in Bahia, Rebouças continued to be well received among the high authorities of the Brazilian Empire, even after the fall of Feijó. Pedro de Araújo Lima, for example, the future Marquis of Olinda and then one of the most influential men of the Empire, wrote to Rebouças shortly after assuming leadership of the ministerial cabinet, stating his confidence in Rebouças's actions in the repression of Sabinada: "You must have suffered with the disorder that arose there. I am sure that you were not indifferent to these public affairs, and I am thankful for all men who took part in this way. Where will we go without a common center, my dear Friend? At least your judgment is clear, and I count on your cooperation for the restoration of order."[44]

Letters such as this give the impression that Rebouças was secure in his political position, and that he had achieved enough prestige to guarantee his importance in both Bahian and national politics. But the local dispute with Gonçalves Martins reveals just the opposite. Despite his political involvement and his credibility on the national scale, Antonio Pereira Rebouças was still continually challenged to prove his commitment to the monarchical-constitutional order. Whenever he was involved in a political discussion, his opponents invariably invoked Rebouças's role in Sergipe as a way to suggest to the Bahian political elite to be aware of his alarming ideas. It was no different with Francisco Gonçalves Martins.

At a meeting of the Provincial Assembly in 1843, Gonçalves Martins accused Rebouças of propagating ideas that were dangerous for Brazil's future during the legendary Laranjeiras dinner, in Sergipe in 1824. Further, he challenged Rebouças's image as a defender of order because he was a mulatto, and it was mulattoes who had been primarily responsible for the recent riots in Bahia. Although many of his peers seemed to follow this reasoning, Rebouças argued that he could be the "guarantor of Brazilians" precisely because he was mulatto. As he explained a few years later to the General Assembly:

[Francisco Gonçalves Martins] misunderstood what I said in the
Provincial Assembly of Bahia, that I considered myself a guarantor
for the Brazilians. In fact I did say this, and I still say it . . . If I am a

guarantor of the union [of the Brazilians], it came in these
calamitous circumstances of 1837. . . . I effectively proved in that
difficult situation that my quality as a mulatto was worth a lot as a
great element of order and mutual trust among all Brazilians; it was
very reassuring to find myself, my brothers, my relatives, my friends,
and many honorable men of our quality on the side of order,
undoing with our example and our constitutional devotion the
intrigues of this man of fury. This is how I was, I am, and I will be
a guarantor for the general union of the Brazilian family.[45]

In fact, specifically in the case of the Sabinada, it was critical to Rebouças
to demonstrate that his position as a mulatto did not necessarily signify
agreement with the ideals of the rebels, in particular because he and Sabino had a lot in common. In addition to being a mulatto—with blue eyes,
as all descriptions emphasize[46]—Sabino was also recognized for having
achieved notoriety in his career as a surgeon and as a professor at Bahia's
medical school (where he was a colleague of Manoel Maurício Rebouças),
for his work in journalism, and for the size of his personal library, which
included works by Voltaire and Montesquieu, as were also found in the collection of Antonio Pereira Rebouças.[47]

Moreover, unlike upheavals that primarily involved Africans and enslaved persons, such as the Malê, the Sabinada involved all categories of
people of African origin, especially those born free in Brazil. It is always
difficult to assess information about color, but it is important to note that
many contemporaries considered the revolt to be fundamentally composed
of blacks and mulattoes. After all, despite the exclusion of Africans from
official participation in the rebel troops, many Brazilian-born slaves had
abandoned their masters in the hope that enlistment would guarantee their
freedom.[48] Other sources reference whites escaping from the city, as noted
by the British consul, who said Salvador had "become totally black, with
the exception of foreigners."[49] Barreto Pedroso estimated in a letter that
two-thirds of the rebel force was black. And according to the captain's note,
of the ten prisoners who died during the trip to the prison of Fernando de
Noronha after the rebellion, six were Brazilian-born slaves, three were
mulattoes, and one was a *cabra*.[50]

Even the spokesmen for the revolt tacitly recognized its racial dimensions. In an editorial published in the *Novo Diário da Bahia* in December 1837, the sabinos explained why the Bahian masters had so deeply hated
their ideas: "In the end, they started a war against us because they are white,

and [they think] in Bahia blacks and mulattoes should not exist, and especially not rise in the ranks, except for those who are very rich, and change liberal opinions, defend titles, honors."[51] The article continues by attacking one whose example they felt should not be followed: the mulatto Antonio Pereira Rebouças, who remained on the side of the government, after having abandoned his "liberal opinions": "whoever is not a rich mulatto, as Rebouças, and not, like him, a self-important turkey, can not be anything."[52]

The resentment of the rebels toward Rebouças is understandable. If one of the motivations of the Sabinada was precisely the frustration over those mulattoes who saw independence as a possible means of political and social ascension, mainly through a military career,[53] the figure of Rebouças meant just the opposite: he had managed to build a political and professional career, but he did not raise his voice to defend his peers—at least not in the way they believed he should. The sabinos tried to win over Rebouças and to convince him that he was fighting on the wrong side. In the same newspaper, they appealed to him directly:

> Do not suppose, Rebouças, and other men like you, . . . that on the side of the revolution there are not men who are educated; you are misled, and God willing, you will soon know that. Unite with us, if you want to save Bahia, and yourselves: the rights of equality and freedom will be defended by the brave of November 7 until death. The soil of Bahia will no longer be polluted by fake nobles; they will be equal in skills, and virtues . . . ; listen to our advice, and a salutary warning, which does not come from fear, because we fear nothing, but it is because we truly want the good of all.[54]

Rebouças paid no heed. Instead, he once again positioned himself as the "guarantor of the general union of the Brazilian family" and emphasized the importance of showing that there were mulattoes involved in the resistance against the Sabinada revolt. In this way, he definitively placed himself against Sabino and those who sought to turn race into a political argument through actions that, in his view, were extreme. Rebouças believed it was important to do just the opposite, dissociating the meaning of the revolt from any racial connotation, to show that race had no relation to political affiliation. Even if he agreed with the rebels on the state of affairs in the province, he would not protest through revolt and separatism, nor would he offer solidarity in an argument that was based on race.

With that, he refused Sabino's offer to save himself by joining the Sabinada. From the point of view of his own political project, the Sabinada and the Malê revolt were both tragedies. Rebouças had long been committed to fighting against the differentiation of citizens based on skin color, and both movements drew attention to the fact that blacks and mulattoes in Bahia had specific political demands. Thus his almost desperate emphasis on showing that race did not necessarily mean adherence to certain political principles was, in essence, an attempt to reinforce his principles of equal treatment for all citizens, whether white, black, or mulatto.

More than a personal political dispute, therefore, his issues with Gonçalves Martins lay in the fact that as chief of police, Gonçalvez Martins had done nothing to prevent the revolts from happening. Since they had occurred, Rebouças had no choice but to stay on the side of order, but this stance did not help him or strengthen his political position in any way. To the contrary, it revealed his vulnerability. The many revolts of the 1830s exposed the deep popular discontent with national politics, in particular for people of African origin, whether enslaved, freed, or free. For Rebouças, nothing could be worse. The recognition of the racial aspect of both the Malê revolt and the Sabinada led the members of the Legislative Assembly and the political cadres of the imperial government to view Rebouças's primary concern—the issue of civil rights—with extreme distrust. Although Rebouças survived politically for some time after the revolts that shook Bahia in the 1830s, his ideas were hopelessly condemned.

In the end, the national policy put into place by the conservatives, in power from 1837, considerably diminished the political spaces that the liberals could occupy, fueling competition between candidates for positions in politics and public administration. The events of the Sabinada exacerbated this situation in Bahia, as members of the troops sought their own political dividends after suppressing the revolt in Salvador in March 1838. After all, the victory was of great national importance—Bahia, with its strategic position and political significance, was fundamental for the Brazilian Empire to remain united.[55]

Chief of Police Francisco Gonçalves Martins gained great notoriety after the Sabinada. As a deputy in the General Assembly of 1838, he never tired of naming the revolt as an example of the government's victory over "barbarous customs, against the decline of civilization," against those who sought not only a change in government, but the complete destruction of the Brazilian Empire.[56] Given the political future that awaited him, it's clear that the Sabinada revolt was a great boost to his career.

It was this same impulse that began the slow decline of the political career of Antonio Pereira Rebouças. Having lost the battle against Gonçalves

Martins, Rebouças limited himself to complaining from time to time that Martins could not be considered a judge, since he had no legal training in Coimbra. It was a useless argument. Unlike Rebouças, who, having no formal education, never held a position in the judiciary, Gonçalves Martins did become a judge of law and chief of police, and from there continued to receive increasingly important positions. From then on, Rebouças had to face the political rise of his adversaries precisely at a time when Brazilian society was perceived as dangerously divided along racial lines.[57]

We see, then, that the racial tensions of the 1830s had considerable influence on the professional path of Antonio Pereira Rebouças. Although he consistently asserted himself as a defender of order, seeking to show that race had nothing to do with adherence to monarchical-constitutional principles, and continued to reinforce his total commitment to legality, Rebouças would always be thought of, precisely because of his visibility, as a defender of dangerous ideas.

In this sense, the politics of the Regresso affected Rebouças much more than any other liberal politician, despite the confidence and admiration he received from conservatives Bernardo Pereira de Vasconcelos and Pedro de Araújo Lima. His role in repressing the Malê revolt and the Sabinada had not yielded him any significant political dividend. Indeed, the racial imprint of the rebellions had actually compromised his ideas. Further, precisely because of the revolts, the fact that Rebouças was a mulatto became more important than the content of his ideas, which were considered dangerous for the very reason of the color of his skin. Rebouças was not the only liberal politician who suffered with the advance of the Regresso, but as one of the few to defend the notion of a liberal slave society and the extension of citizenship to a larger group, he became an extremely contradictory figure and difficult to understand in the eyes of his peers.

Thus, even already accustomed to the constant connection drawn between his skin color and his political ideas, it became ever more difficult for Rebouças to defend himself against the vulgarities thrown at him. In the middle of a provincial assembly, for example, Gonçalves Martins called him a "street urchin"; his countryman João Mauricio Wanderley, in a parliamentary debate of 1846, said of Rebouças that "impure and muddy water, no matter how filtered and purified, always shows its origin."[58] As we will see, these rude and dismissive references to Rebouças in the Assembly reflected that his political career was indeed coming to an end.

5   Terribly Anarchic Words

· ·

> Public interest, the trafficking of Africans, and elections
> are the ruin of Brazil.
> —Antonio Pereira Rebouças

In the legislative session of 1843, a significant number of the deputies were lawyers, and according to José Thomaz Nabuco de Araújo—himself a young deputy and lawyer—one who stood out was Antonio Pereira Rebouças. Although he had not crossed the ocean to study in Portugal, Rebouças was still considered part of the generation that had studied law in Coimbra and come to power between 1820 and 1840, not so much because of his age, but because he had entered public life so early.[1] In years, Rebouças was closer to people such as Bernardo de Souza Franco, who, like Rebouças, entered politics early and returned later to his studies. In 1821, with the proclamation of the Portuguese Constitution after the Liberal Revolution, Souza Franco, who was nineteen at the time, joined the national civic guard organized in the name of Brazilian independence. He was arrested and sent to prison at the Fortress of São Julião in Lisbon. It was not until a decade later, in 1831, that he took up his studies at the Olinda Law School,[2] together with other future (and younger) preeminent lawyers, such as Augusto Teixeira de Freitas, Urbano Sabino Pessoa de Mello, and José Thomaz Nabuco de Araújo.[3] By the time these colleagues entered formally into national public life as representatives from the provinces, Rebouças's reputation had already reached an almost folkloric dimension. As Joaquim Nabuco later wrote:

> The most original figure of this first Chamber that Nabuco [de
> Araújo] joined was old Rebouças. He was practically the only
> representative of the old historical liberalism before the closing in
> of the reactionary phalanx. Everything in him recalled another time,
> past and forgotten: spirit, manners, style of debate. . . . Although [he
> was] not formally trained, his knowledge of the procedures and his
> study of the interpretation of the law gave him one of the first places

in our forum. In the Chamber, where there was lively tradition, his conversation, his attitude, his language caught the attention of new members.[4]

By "old historical liberalism," Nabuco was most likely referring to the ideas embraced by those who supported independence and defended civil liberties, political rights, and the Constitution. But Nabuco depicted Rebouças as more than a rare representative of the "old historical liberalism"; he saw Rebouças as unique because of his particular situation as a mulatto. Rebouças was special, Nabuco wrote, because of his "singular nature, which brought together the aristocratic refinement and the spirit of equality proper to those who hold the same sense of pride and equity. Rebouças always spoke in the name of the 'mulatto population.' A man of two races, belonging to the white race, the purest Caucasian by intelligence, by moral conscience, by juridical intuition, and being proud of that origin, he felt himself the natural protector of the inferior race whose blood also flowed in the veins."[5] Setting aside his comment about the supposed inferiority of the "mulatto population," it is interesting to note that the very same characteristics that led Police Chief Francisco Gonçalves Martins to call Rebouças a "street urchin" are the ones that evoked praise from the abolitionist Joaquim Nabuco when he was writing in the 1890s. Of course, knowing Nabuco's path and the views he came to hold dear—as an abolitionist and also as a good friend of Rebouças's son André—it is not surprising that he held Rebouças in high regard for maintaining a critical political stance while holding onto his uncompromising commitment to order and legality.[6] Nabuco also noted that Rebouças felt himself to be "the natural protector" of mulattoes and blacks. Although Rebouças most likely did not use this very expression, he had specifically called himself "the guarantor of the general unity of the Brazilian family."[7]

It is perhaps because of these singularities—as a pardo occupying that particular social space—that Nabuco described Rebouças as "practically the only representative of the old historical liberalism before the end of the reactionary phalanx," which was a great compliment at the time. After all, this was in 1843, shortly after the revolts of 1842, when liberals from the provinces of Minas Gerais and São Paulo, dissatisfied with the government's centralizing reforms and frustrated by the failure of plans to overthrow the conservative cabinet, led armed protests.[8] But overall, the liberal leaders were too indecisive about their strategies, and the uprisings were poorly coordinated, and Rio quickly suppressed the provincial revolts. As a result, the liberals, having been increasingly excluded from local and provincial politics since 1837, were even further pushed out of the national realm—only Rebouças and a handful of other liberal deputies were part of the Legislative Assembly of 1843. "Our country is getting worse and worse, and where it will stop no one can say for sure," Montezuma wrote to Rebouças in those days, expressing a sentiment that most of his colleagues surely shared.[9] And he was proved right. Seven years later, in 1850, Souza Franco was the only liberal representative in the Chamber, and there were no liberals in the Senate.[10]

The election of 1842 is generally viewed as the turning point that marked the political decline of the generation of independence and the rise of newcomers who had studied law in Brazil, such as José Thomaz Nabuco de Araújo. In a letter to Rebouças prior to the elections, conservative Paulino José Soares de Souza, the future Viscount of Uruguay, wrote that while he was pleased that Rebouças's victory was practically guaranteed, he was also surprised that others are "at risk of not being elected, while men who were entirely new to public life will have this amazing number of votes."[11]

Leading up to that election, the main stance of the liberals had been opposition to the Regresso, the conservative group seeking to end the period of political and administrative decentralization under the Regency. In addition to the Lei de Interpretação (Law of Interpretation) of the Additional Act of 1840, which limited the power of the provinces, and the reform of the criminal code in 1841, a law was passed on November 23, 1841, that reestablished the Council of State and gave increased power to the Minister of Justice. With this legislation, the Minister could dismiss or appoint civil servants in both the Justice Department and the Police Department at his will—and indeed, these posts were immediately assigned to Regresso supporters.

This new political reality created several problems for the liberals. At the provincial level, representatives who were accustomed to controlling the offices of the police and the judiciary lost certain privileges when their conservative rivals were appointed to these positions. In this sense, the liberal revolts of 1842 were driven by landowners who sought to defend their local interests and felt ignored by the Empire's center of decision making. At a broader level, the revolts reflected a fundamental difference of interpretation about the hierarchy of political powers provided for in the Constitution. The main concern for liberal deputies was that the Legislative Assembly control the actions of the Executive Power to ensure that the Brazilian state maintain its autonomy and remain free from the interests of the oligarchies.

In other words, the liberals believed that civil liberties defended in the Assembly were the only guarantee of both national sovereignty, which had been previously threatened by the Portuguese presence, and provincial autonomy, put in danger with the strengthening of the Executive. They were particularly alarmed with the formation of the Council of State, which had been extinct since 1834, and viewed its reconstitution as leading to "the slavery of the people [understood figuratively] and the annihilation of constitutional guarantees." The liberals believed that the new Council would only strengthen "the oligarchy that today dominates the country, [attacking] the Crown, . . . which reduced the Monarch to listen only to the members of that faction."[12] The liberals were furious when the conservative Council advised the recently appointed Emperor to dissolve the National Assembly, as a means to protect the cabinet that was carrying out the reforms. These events ultimately caused the liberals to revolt.

The liberal rebels did not want their dissatisfactions to lead to social chaos, as they realized they were not strong enough to contain the revolts within the provinces, which they feared as much as the conservatives. They felt, however, that they had no choice, as they could not count on the Emperor to free himself from what they described as "coercion [of the State] by the dominant oligarchy." In the end, the revolt was defeated and the conservative cabinet remained in power, maintaining its centralizing policy. Indeed, when, two years later, the liberals returned to government, they supported the same policy themselves, in the name of maintaining social order and territorial integrity.

As historian Ilmar de Mattos argues, although the liberals returned to power, filling positions in the central government, the Senate, and even the Council of State, they failed to propose a direction for the Empire. They insisted on the limitation of the power of the Emperor, but still advocated for the principles of order, sovereignty, and monarchy to be valued more than national representation and will.[13] In the meantime, the Conservative Party was focused on the constitution of an "imperial master class," which relied on an ethos of "aristocratic sentiment" and on the maintenance of the hierarchical principles that constituted Brazilian society.[14]

The general impression is that after the liberal revolts, the liberals who remained in power basically adhered to the centralizing policy of the conservatives, with the exception of the liberals from the province of Pernambuco, where the last great provincial revolt of the Brazilian Empire took place in 1848, the so-called Praieira.[15] While this was in fact the case with a good number of the liberals, it was not true of everyone, and some continued to resist the new government. Urbano Sabino Pessoa de Mello, for example, a future praieiro leader, fought against the patronage system that led ministers to continually assign their own supporters and benefactors to political positions.[16] Bernardo de Souza Franco, who in the early 1850s became part of the Ministry of the Conciliação[17] and directed the Treasury with the Marquis of Olinda, defended arguments in favor of banking freedom, in particular for the circulation of multiple currencies rather than a single currency, which was considered fundamental for the government to centralize financial decisions.[18]

Rebouças sided with de Mello in denouncing paternalism and with Souza Franco on the banking question,[19] and shared other political views with Souza Franco as well, particularly on the end of the Atlantic slave trade for Brazil, the main political debate of their time. Since 1840, Souza Franco had been calling for a settlement policy in Brazil that could attract immigrant rural workers to replace slave labor.[20] Rebouças agreed. In his view, Brazil should honor the commitments made with England since at least the late 1820s to end the Atlantic slave trade. Furthermore, before 1845—when, with the Aberdeen Act, the British gave themselves the right to stop and search any Brazilian ship suspected of transporting enslaved persons—Brazil could claim the rights of indemnification for any ships illegally seized by England. Rebouças believed that as important as the end of the slave trade was the need for the country to establish stable contractual relations and honor its commitments, so as to profit from them. It was in this context that, in 1837, when a bill in the Senate proposed prohibiting the internal traffic of slaves and, curiously, of free blacks, Rebouças defended the repeal of the law of November 7, 1831, which called for the end of the slave trade to Brazil. Rebouças saw the law as depriving the country of taxes that could be collected on the importation of slaves and of important commerce with Africa. Given that illegal trafficking continued to take place, he argued, it was the state itself that was losing, as it was unable to enforce effective mechanisms of punishment and therefore unable to collect fees and taxes. Making his case to his liberal colleagues, who were in the majority at the time, Rebouças proposed a significant increase in import taxes so that the traffickers themselves would be economically motivated to discontinue the practice.[21]

Debating the legal aspects of these issues in the Chamber a few days after Rebouças defended his proposal, Minister Bernardo Pereira de Vasconcelos remarked: "Seeing that we are not in a position to suspend all trade with the coast of Africa, and that doing so would destroy our industry, I refuse to discuss the rights of Africans. I will be very frank, so as to express my position clearly: I will not take into account some of the opinions that have been expressed. I shall consider the question primarily from the perspective of the law."[22] While both Rebouças and Vasconcelos agreed that the issue should be considered in a legal context, they interpreted the law differently. Vasconcelos argued that as long as trafficking was legal in Brazil, it should continue, while Rebouças argued for the revision of the law itself. Thus in 1846, Rebouças put forward a proposal that Brazil stop importing Africans as slaves, and instead encourage them to come as free persons:

> Brazil lacks the hands that will serve agriculture and all the other occupations suitable for the Africans: but it does not, and should not, want Africans to come to us as slaves by means of forbidden trafficking. . . . It is always the same question: what is the recurring desire to violate the law prohibiting illicit trafficking? Certainly for some this is a question of profit, and for others, the conviction that it is impossible to live and thrive without the continuous service of the black Africans. Well, this will be achieved lawfully by importing them as settlers without breaking any law. Some will gain something through trade, and others by employing them.[23]

Rebouças believed his proposal promised great benefits for the country. In addition to encouraging the arrival of better workers—"having Africans come as settlers, whoever contracts with them in Africa will start by choosing the best"[24]—the plan would create a new market for Brazilian tobacco and *cachaça* (Brazilian rum), an argument that was popular among North American abolitionists. Some suggested that the African settlers would end up illegally enslaved in Brazil, and in response, Rebouças proposed that Africans be given manumission letters immediately upon their embarkation, an idea that came from the laws of September 19, 1761, and of January 16, 1773, which sought to limit the arrival of enslaved Africans to Portugal.[25]

Rebouças's position against trafficking and, at the same time, in favor of importing Africans as settlers seems to depict a startling logic. It was not the working conditions of Africans that concerned Rebouças, but their formal status, and in his view the work performed by the Africans would remain the same. Rebouças even proposed maintaining the role of the slave dealers, who would select those individuals most likely to be hired by Brazilian farmers. At no time did he consider the possibility that the Africans, as settlers, would not want to come to Brazil. In his scenario, Africans continue to be devoid of freedom and are seen as having no will of their own, as there is no concept of an interested party entering a contract that would be signed, in principle, between equals.

With this proposal, Rebouças was basically defending a position he had held for a long time, at least since 1830. He expressed a similar view during debates about the establishment of the death penalty in the criminal code of the Empire. Among the various arguments he made to convince others that the death penalty was unjust and unenforceable was the fact that it would not serve to prevent crimes and therefore would not function as a control tactic over the slaves:

In this case, the free, to whom the constitution belongs, should not be burdened because of the slaves, those pitiful beings. The death penalty is never terrible except for those who wish to enjoy social goods. . . . Slaves cannot care for life, because they do not enjoy it; if for anyone, death is less repressive, it is for them, who without hope rebel and die brutally; the most frequent suicides are theirs, who believe in transmigration, who believe that in dying they will pass from this land to their land. Make a separate law for the slaves; we should not do the wrong thing to the citizens, the free men, because of them. No one who neither gives nor restores life can take the life of a man; to take it is against the Divine Power, it is outside the realm of human power; no legislator can enact the death penalty.[26]

Referring to slaves as Africans "who believe that in dying they will pass from this land to their land," Rebouças argues that enslaved persons, as they do not enjoy life, would be indifferent to death. Understanding "social goods"—which the slaves did not have—as freedom, he claims that the only way to enjoy life is through the ownership of certain goods. Rebouças was borrowing from the English philosopher Jeremy Bentham when he argued that "the possession of material goods was so fundamental to the attainment of other non-material satisfactions that it could even be taken as the measure of all of them: 'each portion of wealth is connected with a corresponding portion of happiness.'"[27] In Rebouças's view, the enslaved African was not in a position to fully enjoy life, and was thus not fully a human. When Rebouças argues that separate legislation should be written for the slaves so as not to tarnish the laws of free men and that no one "can take the life of a man," he is claiming that a slave can be punished by death without taking away human life.

There was nothing particularly unique about Rebouças's position toward Africans in the 1830s and 1840s. He shared the general attitude of other politicians, and like them, he always referred to Africans as "barbarians," while at the same time recognizing and encouraging steps taken by the Brazilian government to restrict trafficking. In this sense, many of his proposals were prejudiced by the fear that dominated the political elites since 1835, the year of the Malê rebellion in Bahia. On the one hand, Rebouças shared the sentiment that Africans could not be trusted. On the other hand, however, his suggestion that Africans be brought over as settlers reflects a fundamental difference in his approach to the issue: he thought it reasonable to think of Africans as barbarians, but believed that their nature changed when they obtained freedom. Contrary to how all of the deputies of the time viewed this issue, Rebouças believed there were positive reasons to bring Africans into Brazil, and so he welcomed them. He did not support projects of immigration and colonization by European immigrants, as Souza Franco proposed. Since he saw no difference between the European and the African immigrant in terms of work done, he thought it better to maintain contact with Africa, as this would result in important trade inflow for Brazil.

Rebouças advocated his plan by highlighting the potential for ensuring the presence of Africans for labor while solving the trouble with the English over the repression of the slave trade. It was to no avail, however. The conservatives were not convinced. Perhaps the influence of the slave dealers prevented other deputies from understanding Rebouças's vision—it had been well known since the early 1840s that the slave dealers were closely connected to members of the Conservative Party. As Martim Francisco de Andrada e Silva ironically wrote to Rebouças about the composition of the ministry in April 1841, following his own resignation, "The party of the Portuguese and the *Africanist* have won.[28] Oh that God wants this for the happiness of Brazil!"[29] As the liberal movements of 1842 were being repressed, the conservatives were increasingly granting privileges to slave dealers and stimulating sectors of the economy directly linked to slave labor, such as coffee production, rather than encouraging an economy focused on the domestic market.[30]

As in the debates on provincial autonomy and administrative decentralization, the liberals also lost the discussion on the slave trade, particularly Rebouças, who was actively promoting his vision. The liberal agenda in the 1830s and 1840s thus came to represent the interests of rural landowners more than of the urban professionals, who identified with calls for civil liberties, political participation, and social reform. José Murilo de Carvalho argues that these demands only came to the forefront in the 1860s, when urban development and increased levels of higher education led to "better conditions to develop classical liberalism of individual rights."[31]

If this was indeed the case, it may be another explanation for the political isolation that Rebouças suffered starting in 1837, with the rise of the Regresso and the conservative shift in national politics. Any time he addressed issues relating to the defense of civil rights, Rebouças faced disapproval—even though his colleagues shared many of the same political concerns. This was the case, for example, when he responded to the decree suspending civil guarantees in Rio Grande do Sul, during the Farroupilha revolt (1835–1845), and denounced the provincial president's call to deport and exile the rebels. Citing Article 179, paragraph 6 of the Constitution, Rebouças claimed that deportation without trial disrespected a "man's natural right to preserve oneself, a citizen in the place of his birth and his home!!"[32] At the following session, deputy Paulino José Soares de Souza attacked the "noble deputy of Bahia," claiming that he was wrong to censor the decree when none of his colleagues had taken this stance.[33]

As a defender of civil rights for those who were and those who could become citizens, Rebouças occupied an increasingly uncomfortable position among the deputies in the 1843 Assembly. He viewed a horizon where the end of slavery was beginning to be visible, even though he believed that this future was still far off—indeed, further than the forty-five years that actually separated him at that moment from the abolition of slavery. Yet as a supporter of the end of the slave trade, he knew that slavery would eventually come to an end, and he believed that liberals should prepare for such a future, for the day when all Brazilians were born citizens.

This view, however, was at complete odds with the Regresso agenda, which promoted a hierarchy based on slavery, with limited opportunities for social mobility. The conservatives believed that Brazilian imperial society should continue to follow the traditional hierarchical principles of the former Portuguese Empire, in which only a small group had access to the rights and privileges granted by the state. It was in this sense that the conservatives read the Constitution of 1824 as granting political rights. The maintenance of the slave labor regime and the limitation of access to civil rights were understood as part of the continuities of the social structure of the former Portuguese regime—a regime of patronage where the King's authority was superior to the executive, legislative, and judicial powers through the exercise of Moderating Power—that should remain as such.[34]

It is thus not surprising that Rebouças's ideas did not resonate with his peers. Although his discourse was similar to that of several groups defending the end of the slave trade, such as the Société des Amis des Noirs, which advocated equal rights for blacks and free mulattoes in the French colonies without preaching the abolition of slavery, defending the universality of civil rights for free nationals was like throwing words to the wind.[35] This was a moment, after all, when several countries, invoking popular racial theories that claimed to prove the natural inferiority of certain peoples, had taken legal measures to restrict the access of freedpersons and blacks born free to the rights of citizenship. Just when persons of African origin were attempting to extend the rights of citizenship—established as universal by the newly founded American states—claims based on racial theories were being made to block the legitimacy of extending these rights.[36] It was no coincidence that racial theories became hegemonic precisely when civil and political rights were being systematically denied to populations of African origin.

In the United States, perhaps the place where racial theories were most often used as a justification for the denial of civil rights for blacks and free mulattoes, the slave labor regime had entered the nineteenth century with new fortification. The great plantation owners of the South emerged from the struggles for independence politically more powerful than they were in colonial times, especially after the period of instability and political turbulence in the 1790s. The U.S. slave states thus maintained respect for the large plantations, while securing a system of privilege—not rights—based precisely on the new racial theories that had gained prominence as the century advanced.[37]

In the Brazilian case, exclusion based on racial theories began in the 1820s, and continued through the entire 1830s and part of the following decade. Although racial lines were not totally impermeable, measures such as limiting access to the National Guard showed that race remained a crucial issue, and would for a long time. The victory of the conservative agenda reinforced this conception of society where social lines were based on the exclusion of the existing rights of citizenship. The defense of these rights made Rebouças unique in ways that Nabuco had not even imagined when he described the deputy in *Um estadista do Império*—and it was precisely this uniqueness that would soon ruin Rebouças's political career in Parliament.

The beginning of Rebouças's fall might be considered April 1843, when he made a forceful speech to the Assembly against the institution and privileges of the Council of State. He directly attacked the conservatives for turning the judiciary, the police, and the Chamber of Deputies into "instruments of an oligarchy," and argued that it was impossible to govern well without including different groups in power. Rebouças was referring both to the alienation of the liberals since 1837, and especially after the revolt of 1842, and to the exclusion of the "mulatto population" from the new political order:

> Another part of the Nation that lacks any representation in the Councils of State . . . is the mulatto population. Integrated into all other parts of the Nation in all branches of public service, it is very important that this identification have its complement in the Councils of State. Is it not so convenient, gentlemen, that the opinion of all Brazilians is known . . . and that national unity is represented everywhere? We all took part together in the sacred cause of Brazil's independence, united forever, and together we shared the dangers of the country, cooperating for its salvation and with the same loyalty and patriotic interest at all times, without exception.
> Consequently, . . . it can not but be fair that in the composition of the State Council some individuals of this essential part of the Nation enter into consideration due to their merits of patriotism, civilization, integrity, instruction, and possessions.[38]

Rebouças's speech provoked immediate controversy in the Assembly. When he began to chronicle the racial offenses since 1824, the president immediately interrupted him, saying that his statements were "out of order." Rebouças ignored the rebuke and continued, arguing that "the poison of these offenses" had contributed to the Emperor's resignation in 1831—now, Rebouças insisted, all Brazilians needed to be effectively represented before the throne. The president spoke again, saying that these matters had no place in the issue at hand—and again Rebouças carried on, proclaiming: "I personally believe that the Government of Brazil today represents only a third of the entire Nation."[39]

At this point, chaos broke out. The Minister of the Navy tried to interject, and then another deputy; the president no longer dared to interrupt. Rebouças continued his impassioned speech, making his case in his preferred style of argumentation: he corroborated his personal views with examples from other countries, all of which he considered to be more civilized than Brazil. Someone proposed that he request a closed session to discuss the matter, but Rebouças refused, claiming that he was tired of being "falsely portrayed [which would undoubtedly happen in a closed session] of things such as wanting the treaty with England simply because he loved the idea of manumitting all natives in the country."[40] Rebouças was furious when rumors circulated that he favored freedom for all slaves, including the Brazilian-born ones. This was not a position he embraced. Indeed, it ran counter to his long-term, adamant commitment to the respect of property rights above all else. What set Rebouças apart from others was his belief that enslaved persons had the right to become free, and therefore to become citizens—at the moment when they had proved themselves capable of accumulating property. He found himself constantly having to defend a social project that maintained slavery but was, at the same time, deeply liberal, in which the nation—the collective formed by the citizens of the country— was equally represented by all the groups and races that composed it.

Irritated by the interruptions—which, he claimed, caused him "to lose the consistent and methodical style he sought for presenting" his ideas— Rebouças abruptly ended his address. "So you're leaving?" his perplexed colleagues asked him. But he was not taking his leave just yet. He waited for a reply from the Minister of the Navy, to whom his speech was addressed, and in the next meeting, he returned to the attack: "I proclaimed that it was fitting that all national opinions be included in the Councils of State. . . . I said with all candor and loyalty that the Monarch, having in his Council all the opinions, all the sentiments of the Nation, would be certain of the love and loyalty of all its subjects, and free of the betrayal of some by the exclusion of others, and damage of the country: said in short, that the Council of the Monarch should be in accordance with the Constitution, a summary, an emblem of Brazilian nationality."[41] Rebouças was expecting an apology from the Minister of the Navy, on behalf of the government, for inadvertently failing to include all types of citizens in the Council of State, but this was not the response he received. As he later described in his memoirs, the minister, Rodrigues Torres, lashed back with "a horrible description of the liberals, known to be the contrarian party, and portrayed as the most harmful and dangerous individuals! . . . And he proclaimed that I was a torch of the most horrible anarchy, a most abominable inciting!"[42]

There was once again confusion and digression in the session, and it seems that the speech led to a succession of verbal attacks on Rebouças. Someone accused him of making this fuss because he wanted the position of Counselor of State for himself, another that his words sounded "terribly anarchic." Rebouças tried to defend himself, emphasizing that these were the opinions of a citizen who intended "seriously and prudently" to call his compatriots' attention to questions concerning the general good of the Brazilian nation.

It seems that what most upset Rebouças was the minister's accusation that he had raised ideas "that no one else has!" By portraying Rebouças as a lone voice for national integration without racial distinctions, Rodrigues Torres was positioning him outside all the political groups in the Empire: identified neither with the conservatives, who sought to form a "good society" with an "aristocratic sentiment" based on social divisions along hierarchical racial lines, nor with the radical liberals, or exaltados, because of his own commitment to maintain the slave order. Rebouças had also distanced himself from the moderate liberals because of his stance on the association between freedom and equality—a connection that they did not want to make. While Rebouças certainly shared the fundamental concerns of many moderate liberals about the scope and power of state intervention and the defense of constitutionalism as a way of reinforcing the boundaries between the public sphere and private life—as expressed in Benjamin Constant's maxim "How much am I ruled?" and in the conception of negative liberty later coined by Isaiah Berlin[43]—he did not share their fear about extending equality to a broader group of citizens. Rebouças rejected the notion that legal equality among citizens led to social disorder, and further, he believed that when social disorder did arise, the reasonable response was to repress it. The fear of social disorder, however, was no reason, he argued, to sacrifice the civil rights of Brazilians.

It is not surprising that Rebouças was totally defeated in this session of April 21, 1843. No one heeded his arguments about the participation of all citizens in the Council of State, and not a single colleague came to his defense in the verbal attack of the deputies. It is difficult to know whether his views on the inclusion of the "mulatto population" were exclusively related to his beliefs about the exercise of citizenship and political rights by all citizens, or whether he also raised the issue of racial exclusion as a metaphor for the exclusion of liberals from power after 1842, as historian Thomas Flory argues.[44] The important point here is that the mere mention of civil rights for descendants of Africans led other deputies to recall immediately old arguments that Rebouças harbored dangerous ideas and had played a role in inciting revolt. Indeed, in the eyes of most of his colleagues at the time, Rebouças's ideas were dangerous, precisely because he insisted on adopting unique and fixed criteria for the definition of citizenship.

In his final years in the Assembly, Rebouças continued to make his claims about the importance of maintaining a fixed definition of citizenship. This issue was often debated in these years, but Rebouças found himself in the middle of it again in 1846 when the reform of the National Guard was revisited. Rebouças repeated his arguments of 1832, saying that it was "unconstitutional, inadmissible, unjust, and absurd" that freedmen were forbidden from joining. He again pointed out that, even while not officially allowed, many freedmen were already members of the Guard, showing how little importance had been given to the condition of a citizen at the time of his birth, whether enslaved or free. Rebouças believed that income should be the only criterion to qualify as a citizen, which was not what the law stated at that point: in order to be an officer in the National Guard, one had to be an elector, and to be an elector, one had to be born free. In this case, what Rebouças proposed was not a change in the qualification standards for electors, but a disconnection between those and the criteria for choosing National Guard officers: following what the Constitution stated, he believed that individuals should be classified only according to their "skills and virtues."

Advocating that anyone be able to join the National Guard as long as he had the specified minimum income, Rebouças proposed increasing it from 200 to 400 réis. This reflected the minimum amount necessary to afford rent, clothes, shoes, and food, as well as to keep two slaves, because, as he claimed, "it is impossible for someone to be considered suitable for a National Guard officer . . . unless he has in his service at least two slaves, one at home, and one for things in the street."[45] As in 1832, Rebouças saw no contradiction in defending the rights of freedmen to become officers in the National Guard while advocating an increase in the minimum income criteria. In his view, this meant that the sole criterion for choosing National Guard officers would be property, a position that clearly had nothing to do with concerns about the representation of black citizens. It is curious that when it came to the National Guard, Rebouças did not pay attention to the race of those who possessed sufficient property, but with regard to the Council of State, race was precisely the way he described those who were excluded. Thinking about the two discourses together suggests that his reference to the "mulatto population" did not include the free black population in its totality, but only particular members of that group who had a prominent social position.

Even if Rebouças was referring to a specific privileged group of free blacks, as in the 1830s, his conservative opponents did not forgive him for using the term "mulatto population." They once again took advantage of Rebouças's reputation as the "natural protector of the inferior race" and of the fears that this association provoked. These were charged times when social conditions mingled with racial matrices in a very particular way, producing a situation in which "the different races not only were never confused but, further, in which each race and each class never ceased to know and maintain his place, more or less," as Francisco de Paula Resende had argued.[46] Thus, when Antonio Pereira Rebouças called himself out as representing the "mulatto population," he made himself even more vulnerable as a target of attack. He never stopped trying to dissociate himself from these so-called dangerous ideas, and emphasized, perhaps with a bit of exaggeration, his important roles in the Abdication and in the repression of the Malê revolt and the Sabinada revolt. But the use of any racial argument, even as a metaphor, allowed Rebouças's opponents to use the politics of racial tensions against him. He continued to be characterized as the defender of the "mulatto population," even though he always sought to deracialize his political arguments, insisting that people should be valued by their civil status, their skills and virtues, and the property they had acquired, and never by their race.

Rebouças did not believe that race should ever be a distinguishing criterion, whether negatively or positively, and this led to a disregard for his views on both sides of the political spectrum. His argument against using race to justify the exclusion of freedmen from full citizenship attracted the antipathy of the conservatives. At the same time, his position that racial identification was not a basis for constructing political solidarity attracted the antipathy of the sabinos. This is the irony: on all fronts, Rebouças tried to deracialize the structure of society, including the political discourse on race and the criteria of access to citizenship based on it. But it was impossible for him to do this without discussing the social exclusion of "mulattoes" or recalling the events in Haiti. Ultimately, this position backfired. Rebouças became the symbol of the very situation he wanted to combat, and as such he became politically vulnerable, because his views provoked fear in those who preferred a world of well-defined social and racial hierarchies. Yet the logic of Rebouças's propositions was based on the insistence that social distinctions depend only on wealth and property. In his view, it was possible to have a liberal slave society that was not racist, as long as any citizen, freed from slavery, would have equal social, political, and economic opportunities.

For the contemporaries of Rebouças, the problem with his view was that there were no qualitative distinctions among citizens. He proclaimed an effectively liberal society, where the most important element was the commitment to individual civil rights, which included security for citizens and respect for property. Within this logic, it made sense to modernize the

Ordenações Filipinas (1603) (book 4, title 11, paragraph 4), as in 1830, so that those slaves who were already free in real life had access to freedom and citizenship. Rebouças maintained that one was either free and thus a citizen, or one was enslaved. He did not believe there should be an intermediary condition, such as that which arose with the question of the National Guard, which would in practice make for a second-class citizenship.

Ultimately, the liberalism that Rebouças advocated, which prioritized civil rights, was not the prevailing view among liberal politicians of the 1830s and 1840s. By not allowing for exceptions to the Constitution, and by privileging individual rights over any logic of state, whether at the national, provincial, or municipal levels, Rebouças was seen as a radical. He distanced himself more and more from his colleagues, who believed that the main liberal critique of the Regresso government consisted of defending provincial autonomy and censoring the excessive power of the Emperor.

In that speech of April 1843, when Rebouças pointed out the lack of "mulatto" representatives, he surely did not anticipate that the tension over racial issues would so thoroughly affect conventional party politics, and particularly his own political career. His position as a deputy, vulnerable since losing the battle to Gonçalves Martins, was irrevocably weakened at this point, and he was further isolated from his peers. He was held in contempt on all sides. His insistence on taking the route of legal discourse to address the subject of civil rights, and insisting on the legislative forum as the legitimate site for expressing his ideas, caused other mulattoes to criticize Rebouças, especially those who had chosen the streets to express their political sentiments, as was the case with Sabino. And yet it was the radicalism of his legal views that led to such conflict with his fellow deputies, since he refused to go along with the social project advocated by most of the liberals of his generation.

After that fateful speech, Rebouças was never again elected to be a representative of his native province in the Brazilian Parliament. In 1845, he succeeded only in being elected to represent Alagoas, where there were fewer candidates. Three years later, when he ran again in Bahia, he obtained only 900 votes, which was not enough to win him one of the fourteen seats of that province. That year, 1848, marked the end of Rebouças's parliamentary life and his turn away from politics.

The project of the conservatives, consolidated in the 1850s, led to the defeat not only of the local liberal aims of political decentralization, but also of the liberal conception of overcoming the slave society as represented by Rebouças's discourse—a vision that embraced the slow move away from slavery by ending trafficking, allowing enslaved persons to buy their manumission, and advocating equal civil rights among citizens of all races. In the end, the failure of social movements such as the Balaiada and the Sabinada, which occurred in the 1830s, served to strengthen the political centralization headed by the conservative leadership. After those failed movements, any liberal leaders who had sought equal rights for citizens of all races were disregarded. Antonio Pereira Rebouças had gone even further than those peers, as, in his view, race had no place in discussions about citizenship.

Part III Civil Rights and Civil Law

. . . .

6 In the Empire of Property

Antonio Pereira Rebouças left public life in 1848. A year earlier, perhaps suspecting that he would soon need a different venue to defend his ideas, he had petitioned for the right to practice in the Court of Appeals in Rio de Janeiro. He already had authorization to practice in Bahia,[1] and in Rio, it was permitted to practice law occasionally—giving legal counsel, for example—without a diploma or license. Rebouças had actually long been practicing, as he specified in his request, explaining that "he continued to practice law [in the court], without the title of lawyer, as he had practiced in the capital of Bahia for more than 20 years."[2] In order to devote himself exclusively to his own law practice, however, he needed official permission. It is possible that he sought this authorization from the Court of Appeals because he did not want to return to Salvador, and was looking for an alternative way to guarantee his livelihood and support his family in the capital. Regardless of his motivations, he was certainly aware that if the legal profession became regulated, those without a degree risked losing their right to practice—and once Rebouças was no longer a deputy, he would need to rely on employment as a lawyer.[3]

At this point, although Rebouças had a comfortable situation, he was not yet firmly established in Rio. After returning from Bahia, probably in 1844, until at least 1848, he lived with his wife and eight children in a house on Matacavalos Street, which he rented from Eusébio de Queiróz Matoso.[4] Later, the family moved to Riachuelo Street, and sometime after that to the house where he lived the rest of his life, at 356 Aqueduto Street. This last residence was in Santa Teresa, a neighborhood known as a good location between the city center and the elite neighborhoods of Glória, Flamengo, and Botafogo, and as a popular destination for foreigners and people with delicate health because, high on a hill, the air was particularly clean.

We do not know for certain when the Rebouças family left Riachuelo Street to go up the hill to Santa Teresa. Most likely the move came after 1852, when his father-in-law, André Pinto da Silveira, died, leaving a sizeable inheritance, which included a house and a two-story mansion in the center of Salvador, large enough to be rented both as office space and as the residence of the chief of police. With some family money and his wages as a lawyer, Rebouças was able to provide a comfortable life for his family, as can be seen from his wife Carolina's many jewels, including a string of pearls with a gold cross, gold necklaces, and rings of emerald and sapphire. The interior of their home also reflected a certain level of wealth, as it contained a number of luxurious items such as jacaranda furniture, marble tables, chandeliers, and bronze candlesticks, and careful touches such as crocheted silk cushions carefully placed on six chairs upholstered in green silk. Silver was abundant in the Rebouças home, coffee was served in French porcelain, and beverages, whether water, wine, or champagne, were always poured into real glassware; even the daily towels were of linen, and the cutlery was of high-quality Christophle metal. Seven enslaved persons—a butler, a bricklayer, a potter, a tailor's apprentice, a washerwoman, and two children—took turns at domestic services, so that the Rebouças household always fulfilled the expectations of those in their social position.[5]

Even with the generous inheritance, however, Rebouças would never have been able to maintain this standard of living if not for his activities as a lawyer at the Court of Appeals, which was one of the more lucrative positions for lawyers. This is certainly why Rebouças persisted with his petition. A first request had been rejected on the grounds that there were plenty of trained graduates, and he submitted a second request in 1847. This time around, Rebouças emphasized his long-term engagement in juridical and political activities for the Brazilian Empire, arguing that they could not deny someone the right to practice law when he had already demonstrated "the most determined dedication to the field" and served on committees to review legislation in the Legislative Assembly. He cited examples of "true early jurists," none of whom were formally trained in the law, such as Minos, Licurgos, Pericles, Demosthenes, Catoens, Cicero, Caius Papirus—"the compiler of the first body of laws"—Hermes of Ephesus, and Salvius Julianus. For a more recent example, he continued, there was Montesquieu—"author of *The Spirit of Laws*, who, with no legal degree, formulated, compiled, and codified the principles and rules of judgment by which respective peoples governed themselves, and which even now, for the most part, continue to legislate and judge the most cultured and civilized nations of the old and the new world."[6]

With this second petition, Rebouças seems to have made a convincing enough case, and he received formal authorization from the Assembly to pursue his practice of law. In his request, Rebouças had sought to show that even without a degree, he had enough experience in court and in dealing with the law to allow him to practice. He was challenging what he saw as an erudite bias by showing that a diploma was not what reflected competence in a legal career.[7] And indeed, those who knew Rebouças personally seemed always impressed by the depths of his knowledge. He had an enviable library of over 2,000 volumes, some in his home, and others filling the polished wooden shelves of his office.[8] In addition to his legal library, which included general books on jurisprudence, legal journals, and various civil codes, Rebouças had a large collection of works in geography, mythology, and literature. He read Shakespeare and the Greeks in French, and had all the classics of English political economy and the French Enlightenment— Adam Smith, Voltaire, Montesquieu, Rousseau, and Robespierre—as well as the *Encyclopedia*, biographies, and histories of countries that served as examples in his speeches and opinions, such as Portugal, France, England, Italy, the United States, and Haiti.

With all that knowledge, it might be expected that Rebouças was one of Rio's most successful lawyers. And indeed, he was. Although not much is known about the cases he took part in aside from the freedom lawsuits, we do know that starting in 1859 he represented the Brazilian government in the Brazilian and British Joint Commission in charge of evaluating claims that had been pending since independence, and, as of 1866, he was the attorney of the Council of State, where he earned a good part of his income.[9] He also published some of his opinions from important cases, usually concerning claims of compensation against the state for expenses incurred during the battles for independence.

One of those cases involved the Teixeira Barboza family, which had been required to give over 570,000 cruzados in gold and silver coins along with other goods to the Brazilian troops in Bahia. The family asked for the restitution of the money and the property in 1823, but only the property was returned. A legal battle ensued, lasting thirty-five years; finally, in 1858, the court decided in favor of the family. Because it was such a substantial sum, however, the legislature continually postponed the payment. In his role both as lawyer and deputy, Rebouças published an extensive article about the case, establishing the return of goods confiscated during war as one of the first obligations of the "sacred cause of the Independence and the Empire of Brazil."[10]

In another case, also involving the Legislative Assembly, Rebouças defended the Viscount of the Torre de Garcia d'Ávila, who sought compensation for the office of the Secretary of the State of Brazil, a position that his grandfather had acquired at the end of the eighteenth century for 80,000 cruzados. Many offices that had once been purchased were dissolved with independence, and Rebouças argued that the owner should be compensated for the purchase value of the position and assigned to an equivalent public position by the government.[11] A law of September 15, 1827, ultimately established that the occupants of those positions should continue receiving wages and be given preference for new openings.

In both cases, the fundamental issue was the inviolability of the right to property. Although we do not know the outcomes of either case, Rebouças seems to have taken pride in his role, and not solely because he was defending important people. In practicing law, he had found a way to defend his most fundamental principle: that the right to property mattered above all else, including even the "skills and virtues" defended in the Constitution. His position was particularly pronounced in the case of the Viscount. In his explanatory statement, Rebouças claimed that an individual should be given a public office *independent* of his skills and virtues, even though this was in many ways contrary to the principles he had defended throughout his public life, both for others and for himself.

Perhaps the most important point here is that Rebouças was regularly hired and his opinions were often published, confirming that he was indeed considered an expert in matters of civil law and property. Colleagues frequently asked Rebouças, along with other well-known law graduates such as Bernardo de Souza Franco, José Thomaz Nabuco de Araújo, and Augusto Teixeira de Freitas, to provide opinions on judgments and to advise clients who had already received an unfavorable ruling either on the legal impossibility of winning a case or on how best to pursue the dispute.[12] In the handbook *Consultas jurídicas* (Legal Consultations), a compilation by João José Rodrigues of opinions on a wide variety cases, Rebouças appears right alongside other important Brazilian jurists, such as Ramalho, Sayão Lobato, Perdigão Malheiro, and Carlos Arthur Busch Varella.[13]

Rebouças also came to be seen as an expert on freedom lawsuits, and between 1847 and 1867 he was involved with nine such cases at the Court of Appeals in Rio de Janeiro. Although this might seem like a low number, the outcomes of these cases give a good indication of how he actually acted—as opposed to how he portrayed his views in speeches at the Assembly—when confronted with an enslaved person's request for freedom. In five cases, Rebouças defended an enslaved person, and in four he defended a master. In the nine cases overall, he won four and lost four, and one was undetermined—he only lost once when defending a master, and he only won once when defending an enslaved person.[14] Apparently he was more skilled at convincing the judges when defending a master, and less so when he was arguing on behalf of the enslaved.

In some of these trials, Rebouças's participation was primarily technical. For example, in his first freedom lawsuit—in which he was appointed to defend an enslaved person—Rebouças's only action was a half-hearted request to release the person while the lawsuit was taking place; in another case, he tried to slow the pace of the proceedings through legal recourses. In other instances his participation was more central. In a case where he was defending a master, he challenged the primary document presented by the attorney of the enslaved—a baptismal record, which included the word "free" next to the name of the said enslaved person. Rebouças argued that ecclesiastic documents, such as baptismal records, could not serve to prove the civil condition of an individual, as they were only relevant to Church issues, and that only a civil registry, which at that time did not exist,[15] could serve as evidence in these legal matters. Shrewdly claiming that it was impossible to present proof, as the law required, Rebouças was victorious in the case.[16]

Rebouças used a similar argument in another case, this time defending an enslaved person from Curitiba, who claimed that he had been granted freedom before his master died. Although there was no letter of manumission, Rebouças argued that, as the name of the alleged slave was not mentioned in the master's will, he certainly must have been freed. Contrary to what he had earlier argued on behalf of a master, Rebouças tried to use the baptismal record as legal evidence in this case. Rebouças lost this case, and the plaintiff remained enslaved. It seems that his earlier argument on behalf of a master about the necessity of civil registration and the invalidity of the ecclesiastical document had set the precedent.[17]

In another case, the descendants of slave owners hired Rebouças to contest the freedom granted to one of the enslaved persons, Casimiro, on the basis of a conditional letter of manumission from the wife. Rebouças used all possible means to stop the case: first, he said that the plaintiff, as a slave, should seek a license from the judge to initiate the lawsuit; he then sought reimbursement from the person assigned to keep Casimiro for the days of lost labor;[18] lastly, he tried to argue that a married woman could not divest such a significant portion of property without her husband's consent. Upon learning that the woman in question was in the process of divorce, he claimed that, especially during this time, her assets would be unavailable. The case went on for over two years, often resulting in lengthy discussions about conditional freedom; ultimately, Rebouças's arguments did not convince the judge, and Casimiro was officially granted freedom.[19]

Rebouças's interventions in these freedom suits revolved primarily around three issues: the legitimacy of ecclesiastical documents as evidence, the possibilities of bequeathing goods, and the conditions for the possession of freedom. In grounding an argument in any of these three core issues, Rebouças always came back to the concept of property. He invoked the baptismal record to prove—or to deny—someone's ownership over an alleged slave. He approached disputes over the transfer of property—whether it was in the will, whether it was by the wife or the husband—in terms of the legality of the bequest in view of existing laws. And in cases of conditional freedom, he raised the core question of when the enslaved person was in possession of his or her freedom—at the time of the agreement, or only once the terms of condition were filled. Thus, in debating civil status, he brought up the complicated issue of quasi-possession.

The relationship between the possession of civil status and property was extremely complicated from a legal point of view, starting with the very definition of "possession," as jurist Coelho da Rocha explains in his book on Portuguese civil law: "The article on possession is one of the most encumbered in the body of jurisprudence: its rules are as difficult to put into theory as to apply in practice, because of the different meanings given to the word and the various relationships presented in the court."[20] The variety of meanings of the term can be traced all the way back to Portuguese medieval law. Until at least the middle of the thirteenth century, the words "possession" and "property" were designated by a single expression, *iur* (from the Latin *ius*), which is why the concept was considered "tentative, uncertain, and confusing."[21] Over time, the concepts of possession and property became increasingly disassociated, and it required a greater number of years for a possessor of something to be considered its proprietor. Even so, when the right of ownership was contested, the maintenance of possession remained guaranteed to the possessor until proven otherwise, as emphasized by the Portuguese jurist José Homem Correia Telles in his book *Digesto português* (Portuguese Digest): "Title XIII: The Rights and Obligations Resulting from Possession: The possessor is presumed to be master of the thing until someone proves otherwise. Nonetheless, if another does not prove that the thing is his, the possessor is discharged from showing the title of his possession. All other rights being equal, [the possessor] is the one who has the better conditions. Every owner or possessor must be protected by Justice against any intended violence."[22] In lawsuits where freedom was demanded, the question thus arose: Who is the "master of the thing"—the master of the slave, the "thing" being the slave, or the slave, the "thing" being freedom? The text allows for both interpretations, and since "the possessor is discharged from showing the title," in the end the master cannot be obliged to prove his ownership, and nor can the slave be obliged to show the manumission letter, as, according to Ordenações Filipinas book 4, title 11, paragraph 4, the cause of freedom should always prevail.

This discussion was at the core of Rebouças's most thorny case, which was about the issue of conditional freedom, or, in legal terms, quasi-possession. The core issue at debate was when a person enters into freedom—immediately upon receiving conditional manumission, or only after rendering the required services. Rebouças, in this case, was representing Dona Anna, who sought to keep the African Joaquim Rebollo as her slave until he had finished paying what he owed her, so that he would be in possession of his freedom only after satisfying the necessary conditions. Rebollo's lawyer argued that his client should be freed even if he had not yet paid the full sum, because anyone should be presumed free, and in addition, he already possessed his freedom.[23]

The process began in 1861, and thus Rebouças was writing after both the 1831 ban and the 1850 ban on the Atlantic slave trade to Brazil. Yet Rebouças sought to refute the possibility that the case concerned a free African—even though many were clearly free, as they had been illegally brought to the country after the prohibition of the slave trade.[24] That is, as much as there may have been consensus that those who were Brazilian-born, regardless of race, could be free, he argued that any African-born person was presumably a slave, simply because he, or his ancestors, had arrived in Brazil as slaves.

Later in the brief, Rebouças went on to argue that services should first be fulfilled, so that freedom could be granted and the freedperson could take possession of freedom; until then, this could not be considered a freedperson: "D. Anna Garcia Duarte . . . inherited the ownership and possession of the Slave Joaquim Rebollo, on the death of her father Miguel Garcia Duarte and her Mother D. Bernarda Jesuina da Silva. . . . Thus, in favor of the freedom of the slave Joaquim Rebollo, what could be done for him in court would be to give and pay her the price at which he was valued . . . so that, after finishing the payment, he could enter into the possession of his freedom."[25]

Rebouças's argument is understandable from a legal point of view; Portuguese law, and by extension Brazilian law, had maintained the Roman rules that ownership was acquired only when the buyer took possession of the property. The person who acquired something cannot be considered the owner prior to possessing it, even if stated in a contract. According to this reasoning, in the case of Joaquim Rebollo, there would be no point in having a contract with the master that guaranteed the transaction of freedom; until Rebollo paid the debt, he would not be in full possession of his freedom. Yet, Rebollo's attorney, Domingos de Andrade Figueira, challenged the argument. Figueira suggested that, in fact, what Rebouças was calling the possession of freedom was actually the "obligation of all persons to provide certain services."[26] He proposed differentiating between possession, which the soon to be freedperson would have at the very moment of his release, and the obligation to provide services, guaranteed by a contract, signed between equal parties in law.

Figueira's argument was interesting, but as the judges pointed out, it did not apply to Brazilian law. Figueira was actually relying on a concept of property transfer established by French law after the 1789 Revolution—in France's civil code, it was determined that the transfer of possession should be done through the contract. Thus, as long as there was an agreement, property would not depend on possession.[27] In invoking this particular legal concept, Figueira was certainly not being simpleminded; he was well versed in Brazil's legislation. The fact that each of these lawyers relied on different definitions of possession and property demonstrates how the concepts were being contested at the time, and not just in relation to slavery. Jurists such as José Antonio Pimenta Bueno, the most important commentator on the Brazilian Imperial Constitution, defined property rights as "the broad and exclusive faculty that every man has to use, enjoy, and dispose of freely what he lawfully acquired, that which is his own, with no limits other than those of the ethical or rights of others."[28] Yet, although property rights were fully guaranteed, it was also written in the Constitution that "if the public good legally verified the need and use of a citizen's property, he will be hitherto compensated for its value."[29] In other words, property was absolute, but not totally absolute.

There was thus no consensus at the time about property as an inviolable good, a situation that was not specific to Brazil or to the legal tradition it had inherited from Portugal. In France, although the Declaration of the Rights of Man and of the Citizen of 1789 established that property was natural, indefeasible, sacred, and inviolable, there was dispute over the concept of property, and even the Napoleonic civil code of 1804 continued to adopt legal elements both from the revolutionary traditions and from the Ancien

Régime. The code's new definition of property was as vague as the previous one, namely, "the right of enjoying and disposing of things in the most absolute manner, provided that they are not used in a way prohibited by the laws or statutes."[30] The absence of a clear definition of property, which lasted throughout the nineteenth century, meant that many questions concerning private, familial, collective, communal, and public property in France were difficult to resolve, not least because certain rights with their origins in the Ancien Régime had not been repealed. As Thomas Kaiser has pointed out, late eighteenth-century French jurists had a difficult time solving issues related to allodial law and to property from the old fiefs, even after the famous night of August 4, 1789, when the French Constituent Assembly decreed the destruction of feudalism.[31]

The French civil code's definition of property as an absolute right had its origin in John Locke's conception, later adopted by Pothier and Portalis, that property was a natural right that existed prior to the state. In the state of nature, man had the right to make use of those goods he took for himself, but once men agreed to form a society and create the state, property would also be under certain laws derived from this contract.[32] The point is that this concept continued to be controversial: ownership was simultaneously a natural law, and therefore absolute, and its regulation, or the guarantee that the state would protect it, was a positive right, as based in social relations.

It is important to consider the circumstances under which the French Declaration of the Rights of Man and of the Citizen and then the civil code were promulgated. At that moment, after the abolition of feudal property during the Revolution, the priority was to protect the property of those who had purchased lands formerly belonging to the nobility and to ensure that there would be no counterrevolution that would remove the new owners and restore the land to the previous owners. Even so, the possibility of restricting property—perhaps because there was no consensus about the definition of the term—continued to disturb several judges. The Cours et Tribunaux de France tried to legislate the interpretation of this concept in the Declaration of the Rights of Man and of the Citizen, stating that "no one may be constrained to give up his property if it is not for a public cause, receiving a fair and prior indemnity,"[33] but doubts nonetheless continued to persist.

In other countries, such as Canada, medieval conceptions of property continued to exist, often in conjunction with modern notions adopted more recently from the French civil code. In legal terms, feudalism continued to exist in Canada until 1856. In common law countries, the acquisition and transfer of assets, even with the enactment in England of Real Property Laws in 1922 and 1925, remained permeated by medieval terminology.[34] In Portugal, despite the attempt since the mid-eighteenth century to establish a definition of property as complete and absolute, based exclusively on natural law, the ambiguities of the term permeated the legal realm of daily life, not only in Portugal, but also in countries that had inherited its legal tradition, such as Brazil.[35] The competing uses of the term reflect the fact that the understanding of the concept of property had changed dramatically over the course of the nineteenth century. Works such as the Declaration of the Rights of Man and of the Citizen and the civil code in France and the Constitutions in Portugal and Brazil were essential—not only for changing how property was acquired, but also for changing how it was talked about. The discourse on the legitimacy of property came to revolve around natural rights, and no longer around the privileges of certain groups. Even recognizing this change in the concept of property, and keeping in mind that it is more difficult to change these relations in everyday life than to enunciate them in documents, the legal dogma of the nineteenth century nonetheless remained dominated by the paradigm of the inviolable right of property, even if it never became a reality.[36] It was of course a fallacy that property always trumped all other rights, but a fallacy so widespread that possibly men like Pimenta Bueno and Rebouças came to believe in it.

This broad transformation of the concept of property in modern times led to a variety of views on the conceptions and customs about goods acquired legitimately and illegitimately. Thus, starting in the mid-nineteenth century, many of the cases involving property issues had no legal precedent. The issue of quasi-possession, for example, had not been revised since the seventeenth-century Ordenações Filipinas, and the arguments made by lawyers and judges were always a matter of juridical interpretation. As one would expect, opinions diverged radically depending on individual juridical-political views. Most Portuguese-Brazilian jurists chose to maintain the primacy of Roman law.

In the case of Joaquim Rebollo's freedom lawsuit, the Court of Appeals agreed with Rebouças's defense of Dona Anna, that the burden was on the enslaved to prove his possession of freedom. Rebollo's attorney did not give up, however. Likely realizing that it would be difficult to win the case based on who had to prove possession, Domingos Figueira shifted his focus when the case was appealed to the Supreme Court. He turned to a strategy that was more typical in these cases, claiming that freedom was a different type of property from any others. The attorney thus argued that the case should be judged as an exception to the rule, as recommended in the Ordenações Filipinas (book 4, title 11, paragraph 4). Put simply, Domingos Figueira argued that freedom, as quasi-possession, could never be revoked, even if it was not being exercised at the time the former enslaved would be rendering services.[37] Of course, the argument ran counter to prevailing law, according to which "the possession of rights that do not depend on the possession of the thing is acquired only by the exercise of the same rights."[38] Thus, quasi-possession would only be achieved if the enslaved person were exercising the freedom, which, in this view, could not be the case until the conditions were satisfied. This was the unanimous opinion of all jurists, even those like Francisco de Paula Batista, who had just published a work of jurisprudence that considered the concept of quasi-possession itself strange and outdated, precisely because the transmission of ownership took place only after taking full possession.[39]

In the end, jurists writing on the subject never referred explicitly to the concept of quasi-possession in relation to the enslavement and freedom of individuals. In fact, in legal terms, quasi-possession in relation to slavery was never established. It remained only an abstract definition, as the law was vague and did not address slavery specifically, and was thus not a sufficient basis on which to argue the case in court. And this is indeed what happened: the judges in question ruled that Joaquim Rebollo remain enslaved while he was rendering services, and that he would only enter into his freedom when he had finished paying his debt. Rebouças, on behalf of Dona Anna, was therefore victorious in the case.[40]

In defending their cases, both attorneys invoked various legal traditions. Figueira made use of two distinct concepts of property in his arguments, appealing to two conflicting legal traditions: one that gave precedence to Roman law over other more modern sources of law in the argument of quasi-possession, and one that honored new forms of property transfer established by the French civil code. Rebouças, defending the opposite argument, also made use of both the Roman and Portuguese legal traditions. Even in arguments that were legally opposed—and in this case also politically opposed—the abstract character of the law enabled a blending of legal traditions.

Although Figueira was defeated, his position—at least as of the mid-1850s—was far from marginal. This very issue of conditional freedom was discussed a few years later at the Institute of Brazilian Lawyers, in a heated debate between Caetano Alberto Soares[41] and Teixeira de Freitas.[42] Caetano

Alberto Soares, known for his legal work on behalf of the emancipation of enslaved persons, noted the frequency of conditional manumission and worried about the range of interpretations on the subject. He posed the following question to his colleagues:

> As it is very common for a person to free a slave in his will with the condition of serving a person for as long as that person is alive or for a certain period of time; and as it is no less frequent to leave the slaves temporarily to serve someone, and to give a letter of manumission at the end of that period, the question arises: 1) In the first scenario, if the slave is a woman and has children during the time that she is forced to provide services, are the children legally free, or slaves? If they are free, will they also be obliged to provide services? If slaves, who will they belong to? 2) In the second scenario, if the same circumstances occur, will the decisions be the same or different?[43]

He then summarized the opinions of his colleagues about whether these two scenarios would be identical with regard to the legal status of the slave while fulfilling the stipulated work requirements.

The group concluded, after much discussion, that "the two scenarios were [not only] different, but also at the core of the question; because in the first case the slave was free and in the possession of his freedom at the moment of the bequeather's death, only with the burden of providing services for a certain time, and in the second, the slave had the right to his freedom, but the enjoyment of this right was dependent on the determined time set, if he was still alive at this time."[44] The members of the Institute of Brazilian Lawyers thus established a difference based on when the letter of manumission was granted, that is, whether the services were performed before or after the granting of manumission. In the case of a verbal agreement, they decided that freedom had already been granted and that the individual maintained full possession of his rights, regardless of how things transpired. Children would also be free from any possible transfer of their mother's services to them.

This understanding was thus contrary to what the Court of Appeals had decided in the case of Joaquim Rebollo a few years earlier. Teixeira de Freitas had taken this same position, arguing that according to a literal interpretation from Roman law—which, in his view, was the only legitimate interpretation—the children of slaves freed conditionally should remain slaves, at least for as long as the conditions stated.[45] When his position was rejected, he left the Institute and severed his relations with several of his preeminent colleagues.

Analyzing the issue some years later, jurist Perdigão Malheiro showed that there were many potential legal solutions to the problem of conditional freedom even more favorable to the idea of freedom than the one adopted by Domingos Figueira.[46] Revisiting the Roman concept of *statuliber*, meaning a slave with conditional freedom, Malheiro argued that, initially, the slave remained in this condition until the service was complete, but that the legislation was modified over time in order to consider him or her a freedperson, or, in Figueira's words, already in quasi-possession of freedom. Arguing that the *statuliber* should be considered totally free from the moment of the granting of freedom, Perdigão Malheiro based his belief on the assumption that legislation continued to evolve and, moreover, that manumission should not legally be considered a gift like any other, because it was merely the restitution to the slave of "his natural state of freedom, in which all men are born."[47] This is a good example of how certain meanings can be expanded at particular moments in time—in making these observations, Malheiro was trying to give legal credence to an argument that already had social legitimacy in certain sectors of society.

This is precisely the view that Rebouças did not take. Even when he was legally defending slaves, he considered the question of ownership of human beings the same as ownership of any goods. Thus, in a lawsuit in which a master alleged that he owned a person who was living as if she were free, already in possession of her freedom, Rebouças did not argue that the individual, once freed, could no longer be enslaved. On the contrary, he argued that in such cases gifts could not be revoked, referring always to the status of the donor, not of the beneficiary. He maintained that when a letter of manumission was granted, the slave owners remained in the full possession of their property, as the other alleged possessors had given up their custody, and the husband, who had granted freedom against his wife's will, had every right to do so, since the gift did not constitute more than a third of their total worth, as stipulated by law. Rebouças approaches the situation like any situation involving goods—there would be no issue as long as the gift did not exceed the amount stipulated by law.[48]

Rebouças addressed two different categories of gifted goods: those made by spouses who shared their possessions and those bequeathed in a will. According to legislation that had been adapted from Roman law and adopted in Portugal, and was then in force in nineteenth-century Brazil, any gift was the "irrevocable concession of the domain of something to someone."[49] If the gift was made by one spouse of a couple, there were some limitations: it could never exceed one-third of the couple's total worth, and it must be confirmed if it were to exceed 360,000 réis, in case of the husband making the gift, and 180,000 réis if it were the wife.[50] In the case of gifts left in a will, the rules were similar, except that the donor's acceptance was not necessary for it to be made. The law stipulated that the will of the deceased be obeyed such that his heirs, in particular his widow, should not be left in poverty. The only restrictions on gifts were in situations when the right of possession of other owners was at stake.

The point here is that while there were a number of different ways to argue on behalf of an enslaved person in the case of gifting, since there were so many exceptions when the issue was manumission, Rebouças always chose to discuss the legitimacy of the gift itself. Whether on behalf of the masters or the enslaved, Rebouças consistently followed the logic of the law of property, and never the primacy of freedom. He formulated the issue in the same basic way no matter what side he was defending, invariably beginning his argument with the assertion that manumission is a form of gift that does not depend on the beneficiary's acceptance. In other words, he emphasized his view that manumission was a contract that dealt with the transference of property, like many other contracts. In this case, specifically relevant is that the beneficiary could not refuse the gift: at the heart of the case is the action of the donor, not the object of the gift.

It is interesting to see how this played out in the case of Joaquim Rebollo, in which Rebouças and Domingos Figueira engaged in a broad discussion about conditional freedom. Rebouças's first line of argument referenced only the law of the Ordenações Filipinas, which dealt directly with the granting of freedom: "Ord book 4, title 11, which is entitled: 'Let no one be constrained to sell his inheritance and things which he has against his will,' says in [paragraph] 4 that 'in favor of freedom many things are granted against the general rules of law,' consists of the benefit that the Slave may be released after having given and paid to the master the price at which he is appraised." As Joaquim Rebollo had not paid his debt, it was evident to Rebouças that he should continue to be enslaved. Domingos Figueira, on the other hand, dismissed Rebouças's interpretation of the ordinance, especially because he failed to cite the maxim that "the reasons for freedom are greater."[51]

Reading these exchanges, it is impossible not to think back to 1830 and the bill Rebouças submitted for consideration by the Legislative Assembly.

He was advocating, at that time, the use of that very ordinance to provide for the granting of manumission through self-purchase, with the assumption of the possession of freedom only once the debts were paid. Rebouças had wanted to eliminate the phrase "the reasons for freedom are greater," precisely to prevent interpretations such as the one put forward by Domingos Figueira. This concurrence of ideas between Rebouças's argument in the Assembly and his position during his defense of Dona Anna thirty years later leaves little doubt that in the courtroom he was putting into practice principles he had deeply believed in for many decades.

Rebouças also faced these issues in his personal life. He possessed several enslaved persons, most of whom he had inherited from his father-in-law, André Pinto da Silveira, on behalf of one of his children. Those who obtained manumission did it through the purchase of their own freedom, such as the African Leocádia, who, having been given to Anna Rita Rebouças, bought her freedom and that of her daughter Laulina for 900,000 réis; the cook, Mileto, also purchased manumission after putting together the vast sum of 2.5 million réis. When Carolina, Rebouças's wife, died in 1865, her will specified that the slave Damiana was to take possession of her freedom "after her daughter Guilhermina is 21 years old and her son Izidro 14, and if her daughter and son are missing before those listed ages, Damiana herself will be released after giving ten years of service to any of her daughters to whom she would belong for a period of ten years." Damiana, according to this document, was worth 1.5 million réis. It seems she was already working the years of service, because the will included a clause about the arrangement: "Her services for the four years she has to work until she enters the possession of her freedom are valued at 600,000."[52] Rebouças and Carolina thus made use of conditional freedom as a way of guaranteeing a few more years of slave labor, and they expressly maintained that, in order for Damiana *to enter into possession of her freedom*, she had either to provide services for four more years or pay the stated amount. The action that Rebouças took in his personal life thus coincided with the position he defended both in the Legislative Assembly and in the courtroom.

Rebouças also established the centrality of the concept of property in his speeches, making a strong case to suggest that his legal and political opinions were consistent over time and across venues. It seems fair to conclude that when acting in a freedom lawsuit, Rebouças was protecting neither the master nor the enslaved—but rather, the property, regardless of the possessor. As Rebouças's primary concern was regulating civil relations, in the case of someone owning someone else's freedom, he believed that the relationship between the owner and the deprived person must first and foremost be regulated by law, like any other contract.

Clearly, the position Rebouças took in defending enslaved persons had nothing to do with advocating the end of slavery. Consistent with the liberal principles he demonstrated both in the field of civil law and through his political role as a deputy, he reinforced the necessity of maintaining contractual relations. If we want to take his argument to the extreme, we could extract from Rebouças's argument that the master may own the freedom of another, but not the power of life and death. These same liberal principles, however, did not lead Rebouças to criticize how the property of an enslaved person was acquired or its legality. He defended the inviolability of the right to property as a natural law without questioning the social origins of this right, and without giving importance to the fact that this right, to use the language of the jurists of revolutionary France, constituted a usurpation of the rights of others.[53] If he had thought differently, he would have chosen to free his slaves without claiming compensation, payment, or labor.

· · · · · ·

The legal ambiguity of Brazilian law in the 1850s and 1860s was such that both Rebouças and Figueira made arguments that could be considered both legally and logically valid. For example, when Domingos Figueira changed the strategy of his argument away from the logic of property law to the issue of the exceptionality of the laws on slavery, he relied on old laws that actually had nothing to do with the freedom of slaves descended from Africans: the law of April 1, 1680, and of June 6, 1755.

Abundantly cited throughout the nineteenth century, both of these laws addressed the prohibition of enslavement of natives in Brazil. The law of 1680 was about the unjust enslavement of Indians by the inhabitants of the state of Maranhão, and the law of 1755, based on the earlier law, claimed that the illegal enslavement of Indians in that state and in the state of Grão-Pará, rather than ceasing, had been growing in frequency. The text of both laws reinforced the intention of the King of Portugal to instruct the Indians in the Catholic faith, a mission that "can never be achieved if it is not for the proper and effective purpose of civilizing these Indians," which was of course impossible if they were reduced to slavery.[54] The laws clearly were of no direct relevance to the freedom lawsuits involving individuals of African origin, even though they were also illegally enslaved. Even so, lawyers referred to them, along with the charters of July 30, 1609, and March 31, 1680, in their effort to justify any argument that might be favorable to freedom.

Invoking this legislation was of course incorrect from a legal point of view. Lawyers referred to these older laws because their use made sense in the context of the nineteenth century, especially since there were no recent laws that could be used in the argument. In fact, in referencing a law that had no express relation to the case, in addition to drawing attention to the lack of specific legislation, lawyers such as Figueira were trying to broaden the possibilities of interpretation in freedom lawsuits, precisely at a time when the so-called new humanitarian winds were blowing through the Empire of Brazil.

As the historiography of slavery in the nineteenth century has shown, the prohibition of the Atlantic slave trade and the increase in interprovincial trade created a context in which enslaved persons began to exert various forms of pressure to gain their freedom, including in the legal arena.[55] Although slavery was still legal from a juridical point of view, it was increasingly viewed as illegitimate by some sectors of Brazilian society. Although an individual's right to possess another human being as property was still guaranteed by law, the right to freedom—even though not based in a legal definition—was becoming equally valued. It was a true dilemma, as Machado de Assis portrayed: "That I like freedom, for sure; but the principle of ownership is no less legitimate. Which one would you choose? It existed thus, like a shuttlecock, between the two opinions."[56]

Lawyers who were defending enslaved persons and advocating for their freedom made use of existing legislation according to how it would work in a particular argument. The more abstract the legislation, the more necessary it was to introduce other criteria beyond legal ones—in other words, as the laws were often unclear, the decision of each case depended primarily on a particular judge's political opinions. The legal ambiguity resulted in unpredictable outcomes to freedom lawsuits, which posed challenges for both sides. Precisely for this reason, the Institute of Brazilian Lawyers organized their discussion about conditional freedom, hoping to guide decisions in these types of cases and in that way, as it were, *create new law*. On this point Rebouças was decidedly conservative: for him, a lawsuit was a lawsuit, and its results should be based only on judgments based on the rule of law. The place for politics, he believed, was in the Assembly, and until a new law was proclaimed by members of the legislative body, judges should continue to decide cases according to the current legislation. Adamantly against the Institute's strategy, Rebouças believed that due process required putting bills forward in the Assembly, as he himself had already done.

While the pressure to change the rule of law was very high throughout the 1850s and 1860s—whether on the side of broadening the meaning of the law or restricting it—the question would still take many years to resolve. Meanwhile, the Brazilian legal field was a territory that seemed open to interpretation, with lawyers and judges deciding to free or enslave individuals at their will.

7   Lawyers in Action

· ·

In an excerpt from the novel *O Coruja* (The Owl), by Bernardo Guimarães, the attorney Teobaldo asks: "Indeed, what is the mission of the lawyer, if not to use ways and means to persuade the jurors to judge in favor of his client?" When he hears someone respond that "the lawyer serves many other things; he serves to prevent an innocent person from suffering a punishment he does not deserve; he serves to . . . ," Teobaldo interrupts, snapping back: "Come on! . . . A lawyer hardly ever believes in his client's innocence. He defends him because his life is to defend the accused, and he is willing to use all the traps and snares of rhetoric to obtain his goal!"[1]

Teobaldo clearly does not hold the legal profession in high regard. He imagines the lawyer as a pathetic old guy, "loaded with books, stomping his foot . . . , pedantic, clean-shaven, glasses sitting atop his head." The type of guy, Teobaldo suggests, who blithely resorts to sophistry if it helps to win a case: "In law, sophisms are everywhere; everything can be reversed; everything is subject to a thousand and one licenses and two thousand and many reforms!"[2] Teobaldo condemns the tendency to apply the law loosely. For those who study the relationship between the practice of law and slavery in nineteenth-century Brazil, however, this tendency had a positive place in the legal culture. After all, if a lawyer could interpret the laws as he pleased, then he was free to interpret them for noble reasons, such as freeing enslaved persons.

Historians Sidney Chalhoub and Hebe Mattos, both pioneers in the study of freedom lawsuits in Rio de Janeiro during this period, emphasize the critical role of lawyers when enslaved persons turned to the legal system as a strategy to obtain freedom. Ultimately, each argues that lawyers contributed to undermining the politics of slavery by questioning the legal boundaries between slavery and freedom and the legal framework that legitimated slavery.[3] Chalhoub examines the increased pressure for freedom that enslaved persons exerted in the second half of the nineteenth century, while Mattos analyzes the conditions that made freedom lawsuits possible—such as access to the legal system—and how relationships among enslaved, freed, and free persons influenced the outcomes. Chalhoub and Mattos focus on different aspects of the issue, but each convincingly maintains that the field of law was a "decisive arena" in the struggle against slavery.[4] Both also highlight how lawyers and judges who took a political position in favor of freedom made use of the multiplicity of laws that existed at the time.

Chalhoub specifically examines legal battles in the context of freedom lawsuits to consider the conflict between the right of property and the principles of freedom. He argues that given the myriad possibilities of interpreting legal texts, lawyers and judges were able to apply legal norms according to their own political positions, moving in an "open field of interpretive possibilities." Furthermore, he claims, in the freedom lawsuits, the "conflicting interpretations of general rules of law had important political meanings."[5] He concludes that lawyers and judges who were sympathetic to the cause of freedom used their legal arguments—whether defending the prerogative of private property (including one's own freedom) or using "openly militant" claims about the right of freedom—to make political statements.[6]

Chalhoub raises the question of whether we can know the political motivations of a lawyer or judge based on his professional conduct. To a large extent, this depends on how much interpretive autonomy these legal agents really had—an issue that, even in the nineteenth century, had already long been debated. For centuries, dating back to the period of Roman-canon law, jurists throughout Europe were occupied with this question, in particular once common law began to be replaced by statutory law that was specific to each nation. Roman law had provided lawyers and judges with a wide variety of laws and resources for use in legal rhetoric and decision making, but it made it impossible to arrive at a unified conception of justice. Jurists thus sought to reduce the sources of law and regulate juridical activity—an effort that, in Portugal, can be traced back to the fifteenth century, at the time of the promulgation of the Ordenações Afonsinas. This marked the first attempt of the Portuguese state to unify the body of laws and the systems of justice and administration, thus imposing a national system and dispensing with the more regional sources of medieval laws and customs.

The compilation of the Ordenações Afonsinas in 1448 sought to systematize the national sources, establishing general rules for the application of Roman-canon law and custom. It was a particularly important moment because, up to that point, the King was arbiter with the full authority to create law, based on the customs and traditions of either canonical or Roman law.[7] The Ordenações Afonsinas were replaced in 1512 by the Ordenações Manuelinas and, at the beginning of the seventeenth century, by the

Ordenações Filipinas. The updated ordinances changed little from the original compilation, simply incorporating new laws.[8] The fifteenth-century foundation, therefore, was still the basic reference for jurists and judges of succeeding centuries in adopting the sources of law and establishing subsidiary law: as set out in the ordinances, the first recourse was local law; second, Roman and canonical laws; then the "common interpretations of the judges"; and, finally, the King, who would decide based on custom. In practice, however, the first resource was most often Roman law, and eventually national law served as a subsidiary.[9]

By the second half of the eighteenth century, this legal tradition was at odds with the political aspirations of the Portuguese state, and more generally, with legal discussions throughout Europe. In post-revolutionary France, for example, Robespierre advocated the abolition of the French word "jurisprudence," since "in a state which has a constitution, a law, the jurisprudence of the courts is nothing other than the law."[10] It was in this spirit that France created the Tribunal of Cassation in 1790, which was given the power to annul any judicial decision that had misinterpreted, or failed to honor, the law.

A similar process occurred in Portugal. The architects of the Pombaline reforms—issued by Prime Minister Sebastião José Carvalho e Melo, Marquis of Pombal (1699–1782)—sought to delimit the body of laws that served as the basis for legal decisions, and to clearly establish what constituted the work of interpretation. Pombal's goal, after all, as the head of state during the reign of King José, was to strengthen the nation-state through absolute power and administrative centralization. To this end, and with a concern for secular education, the Portuguese expelled the Jesuits—who were at the time the greatest threat to the Crown—from the territories of the Empire.[11] The dispute with the Jesuits encompassed several fronts, including the establishment of official censorship, the supervision of national and foreign publications, and educational and legal reforms.[12] Pombal thus saw a pressing need to reform not only the education system, but the whole legal structure. In an attempt to eliminate doctrine and limit interpretation, he sought to decrease the sources available for judges and to condition the validity of Roman law to its conformity with *good will*. Because of that, the use of the Roman Index came to be viewed as an attack on the aims of the Portuguese state.

This effort to eliminate interpretation in Portuguese legal doctrine dates more exactly to 1768, when, after a series of decrees, it was specified, through the law of November 3, that only national law would be considered the real law of Portugal. The process was completed by the promulgation of the Lei da Boa Razão (Good Will) of August 18, 1769, which, abolishing title 64 of book 3 of the Ordenações Filipinas, established that Roman law would be considered subsidiary, canon law applied only in ecclesiastical courts, and the Casa de Suplicação, then the highest court of Portugal, the only body empowered to unify legal interpretation.[13] At the core of this ruling was a doubt about whether the interpretation of the law would always be made according to the ideals that the law was intended to uphold. The jurists were seeking to guarantee, into the future, the preservation of the juridical presuppositions put into place with Pombalism—and thus, as they saw it, the fewer people involved in the interpretation of the law, the better. These Portuguese guidelines continued to be followed in Brazil, even after the creation of law schools in São Paulo and Olinda in 1828. The continuity was built into the organization of the judiciary after independence: the Constitution of 1824 and the regulation of the high courts of 1833 specified that the Court of Appeals and the Supreme Court of Justice were the only bodies that could interpret the law, granting or denying revisions.[14] The aim was to reduce the number of laws used in courts, so judges and lawyers would have no space to create their own interpretations.

We see, then, that at the very moment when lawyers were making the most of their legal creativity to argue in freedom lawsuits—as Rebouças and Figueira did in the case of Joaquim Rebollo—laws and regulations were being put into place to limit their possibilities of interpretation. It is actually difficult to ascertain how much liberty lawyers and judges really had to reference a breadth of arguments, but we can get a sense by analyzing the citation pattern of legislation during this period. Even with the Lei da Boa Razão in effect—which should have resulted in fewer of the older laws being cited—for some decades, there continued to be an abundance of citations to the Ordenações Filipinas as well as to the older laws and charters.

As the data in graph 1 indicate, the legislation referenced in legal arguments—and thus the possibilities for juridical interpretation—changed over the course of the nineteenth century. With the passing of time, older legislation that was less applicable to concrete cases, such as charters and the Ordenações Filipinas, gradually lost its relevance, especially as new laws, decrees, and regulations were promulgated. In the mid-nineteenth century, the Ordinances accounted for 65 percent of the legislation cited in freedom suits, but that number dropped to only 32 percent as more recent laws, codes, and regulations were cited. This decrease throughout the century effectively reflects how the freedom of interpretation became

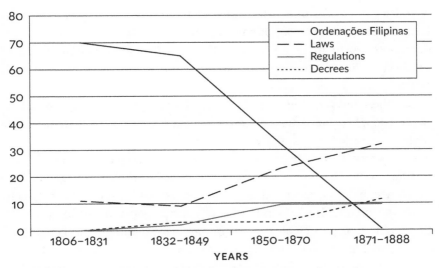

GRAPH 1 Pattern of legal quotes in freedom lawsuits, Court of Appeals,
Rio de Janeiro, 1808–1888

limited over time. In the last decades of the nineteenth century, the Ordenações Filipinas practically disappeared as a valid legal reference in freedom lawsuits.

With this, we are back to the starting point of this digression: while
Chalhoub was certainly correct in observing that lawyers and judges enjoyed
a great deal of interpretive autonomy, it seems that it was less broad than
once thought. Attorneys did not cite laws and doctrine at their whim.
Although they did manipulate the relative interpretive autonomy at their
disposal, legal rules also demarcated clear limits to the maneuvering.[15]
Even the most politicized advocates—whether on the side of freedom or of
maintaining slavery—ultimately had to conform to standard arguments
if they wanted a chance to win the case. We are left asking, then, to what
extent lawyers, as far as possible, interpreted laws and cases with political
motivations in mind.

Interest in the political behavior of lawyers during nineteenth-century
Brazil is not new. The classic debate about the character of the state—
whether patrimonial or bureaucratic—led to a number of historical works
that analyzed the actions of state agents, including politicians, military officers, judges, and also lawyers.[16] Carvalho was the first scholar to use em-
pirical data to look at law graduates in the politics of the Brazilian Empire,
suggesting that, along with priests and soldiers, lawyers too formed a

cohesive group.[17] He argues that although these young men were originally from different social backgrounds, their training in law school (whether at Coimbra in Portugal, or at Olinda or São Paulo in Brazil) brought them together as a political group that shared a common core of knowledge and skills.[18]

It is these lawyers, the elite of the Brazilian Empire who participated in the freedom lawsuits, whose actions I analyze here. In order to understand their interpretations and the political motivations of their arguments, we need to know better who these lawyers were and how they argued in the freedom suits. The cases I accessed—those filed at the Rio de Janeiro National Archives in a specific drawer labeled "Slaves"[19]—occurred between 1806 and 1888 and, while in the lower courts, involved 620 lawyers. Of those, only four participated in five or more cases, and 513, or 83 percent, participated in only one case. Apparently, there were no lawyers dedicated specifically to freedom lawsuits, as the vast majority (96 percent) participated in one or two cases. As the lawsuits took place in many cities and over several decades, it is not surprising that many different lawyers acted in them. Effectively, the few lawyers who worked on more than four freedom suits in the lower courts all lived in Rio.

We cannot, therefore, really talk about "freedom activists" among the attorneys who tried the freedom suits in the lower courts in the first decades of nineteenth century. The work of abolitionist lawyers, such as Luiz Gama, seems to have started in the late 1860s, and grown in the following decade, when abolitionists initiated collective processes in rural areas of the provinces of Rio of Janeiro and São Paulo.[20] This certainly does not eliminate the possibility that before that time, here and there, lawyers existed whose actions could be characterized as favorable to the emancipation of the slaves. For example, this seems to be true of Joaquim José Affonso Alves of Pelotas, who tried four cases between 1858 and 1867 in the Court of Appeals of Rio de Janeiro. In each of the cases, the lower court had decided in favor of freedom for the enslaved, and the master appealed.[21] Each took place on the border between Rio Grande do Sul and Uruguay, and Alvez used a skillful argument: based on the law of November 7, 1831—the first law to prohibit the slave trade to Brazil, which became known as a "law for the English to see"—he argued that slaves who crossed into Uruguay, even if by chance, accompanied by their masters, or having fetched cattle, would have the right to freedom, since, having entered free territory, they were then free. According to the Penal Code of 1830, a return to Brazil as an enslaved person could be legally characterized as illegal trafficking or enslavement.[22]

With regard to the freedom lawsuits that reached the Court of Appeals in Rio de Janeiro, of 279 attorneys involved, 167 were involved in only one case, while 26 took part in five or more cases. At first glance, the participation of lawyers in the higher court seems similar to that in the lower courts, since most lawyers (almost 60 percent) participated in only one case. A closer look, however—as detailed in table 1—reveals a different pattern in the Court of Appeals: while 26 lawyers (or 9 percent) participated in five or more suits, together those lawyers were involved in 154 cases. Recalling that there were 402 cases, it can be inferred that this small group was asked to participate in more than one-third of the freedom suits sent to the higher court, which demonstrates a much greater concentration than we might at first assume. This was probably due to the smaller number of lawyers—those formally trained in law or given special permission to practice, such as Rebouças—who were qualified to work at the Court of Appeals.

The first interesting observation is that all of these lawyers represented both masters and enslaved. This applies even to well-known attorneys such as Nabuco de Araújo and Perdigão Malheiro, whom Edmundo Campos Coelho called the "bigwigs of the Empire," concluding that they were not "professionals available for any sum," and "in a freedom suit would certainly be at the service of the masters."[23] In fact, Nabuco de Araújo participated in eight cases, representing masters in five and enslaved persons in three; and Perdigão Malheiro participated in seven, representing enslaved persons in two. Nabuco, after serving as Minister of Justice in 1853 and as senator as of 1858, lost a case in 1860—defending Theodosia, who had been taken from her mother, then sold and resold several times—for not being able to prove that the girl was really who he said she was.[24]

The lawyers were clearly not exclusively defending one group or the other. With the exception of Severo Amorim do Valle, who defended twenty masters in twenty-three cases, no one can be characterized at first sight as either an activist for the enslaved or for the masters. Most likely, these lawyers were requested the most frequently in any kind of law case, not only in freedom lawsuits, because they were professionals of great renown, recognized for their skills and competence. We also know that the enslaved person did not choose the lawyer for the appeal. In cases where the judgment in the lower court had gone against freedom, there was an ex officio appeal, and the judge appointed an attorney once the case reached the Court of Appeals in Rio. Indigent people, as well as widows and orphans, had the right to obtain an attorney free of charge.[25] One can imagine that a lawyer would not always willingly accept defending a slave. This was the case, for

TABLE 1 Performance of lawyers acting in more than five freedom lawsuits in the Court of Appeals

Lawyer	Period of activity	Party represented	Outcome	Number of cases
Agostinho Marques Perdigão Malheiro	1852–1872	5 masters 2 slaves	6 victories 1 defeat	7
André Pereira Lima	1849–1874	5 masters 2 slaves	3 victories 3 defeats 1 undetermined	7
Antonio Correia Picanço	1834–1847	6 slaves 4 masters	5 victories 5 defeats	10
Antonio Ferreira Lima	1823–1844	3 masters 9 slaves	5 victories 7 defeats	12
Antonio Pereira Rebouças	1847–1864	4 masters 4 slaves	3 victories 4 defeats 1 undetermined	8
Augusto Teixeira de Freitas	1844–1871	9 masters 5 slaves	8 victories 5 defeats 1 undetermined	14
Bernardo de Teixeira Moraes Leite Velho	1838–1860	3 masters 6 slaves	7 victories 2 defeats	9
Bernardo de Souza Franco	1843–1855	3 masters 2 slaves	2 victories 3 defeats	5
Caetano Alberto Soares	1835–1864	9 slaves 5 masters	8 victories 5 defeats 1 undetermined	14
Carlos Arthur Bus e Varella	1854–1878	3 masters 3 slaves	3 victories 3 defeats	6
Domingos Miz. de Faria	1858–1862	5 masters 8 slaves	4 victories 7 defeats 1 no outcome 1 undetermined	13
Galdino de Freitas Travassos	1865–1870	1 masters 5 slaves	3 victories 3 defeats	6
Honório Augusto Ribeiro	1862–1872	1 masters 9 slaves	10 victories	10
Joaquim Gaspar de Almeida	1813–1846	10 masters 10 slaves	8 victories 10 defeats 2 undetermined	20

(*continued*)

Lawyer	Period of activity	Party represented	Outcome	Number of cases
Joaquim Theodoro de Souza Soares	1834–1852	4 masters 1 slave	2 victories 3 defeats	5
José Figueiredo de Andrade	1864–1872	1 master 5 slaves	3 victories 3 defeats	6
José Pedro Carlos da Fonseca	1836–1860	3 masters 3 slaves	3 victories 3 defeats	6
José Thomaz Nabuco de Araújo	1860–1871	5 masters 3 slaves	3 victories 3 defeats 2 undetermined	8
José Xavier da Silva Capanema	1860–1872	3 masters 4 slaves	3 victories 3 defeats 1 undetermined	7
Luís Antonio da Silva Nunes	1862–1872	4 masters 1 slave	1 victory 3 defeats 1 undetermined	5
Manoel Francisco Rodrigues Pereira Galvão	1819–1844	10 masters 2 slaves	3 victories 9 defeats	12
Miguel Borges de Castro Azevedo e Mello	1815–1860	13 masters 14 slaves	9 victories 16 defeats 2 undetermined	27
Paulino José Soares de Souza	1862–1865	2 masters 3 slaves	1 victory 2 defeats 2 undetermined	5
Sebastião Navarro de Andrade	1836–1850	5 masters 4 slaves	5 victories 3 defeats 1 undetermined	9
Severo Amorim do Valle	1860–1875	20 masters 3 slaves	8 victories 12 defeats 3 undetermined	23
Urbano Sabino Pessoa e Mello	1840–1858	2 masters 7 slaves	4 victories 5 defeats	9

Source: Tribunal da Relação—Arquivo Nacional-Rio de Janeiro

example, of Augusto de Carvalho, representative of the enslaved Ricarda, who, in introducing his argument, lamented his own situation more than Ricarda's: "Now I have to perform the arduous task of defending this indigent plaintiff, who imposes my duty on me by oath."[26] It seems, then, that these men were not defenders par excellence of either masters or slaves, but rather, attorneys who took on freedom lawsuits as they would any others.

The twenty-six lawyers we are considering followed a variety of trajectories. Half of them enjoyed at least some prestige in the public life of the Empire—whether by obtaining honorary titles, publishing books, participating in political debates about legal reform, holding positions in the executive or legislative powers, or even working as provincial presidents or ministers of state. Nine of the thirteen simultaneously served as officials in higher levels of politics and practiced as lawyers. Others, such as Domingos de Faria, built their careers singularly in the field of law, defending clients. Faria was a white man of "ordinary stature with a long, pocked face." Born in Portugal in 1799, he studied at Coimbra and was later appointed Knight of the Order of Christ and served as a judge in Paranaguá, on the southern shore of the country.[27] Between 1858 and 1865, living in a rented room on Ourives Street, Faria was one of the lawyers who most frequently participated in the freedom suits that reached the Court of Appeals. In the higher courts, those who dedicated themselves exclusively to practicing law, with the exception of Teixeira de Freitas, were precisely the ones who took on the majority of freedom suits. Having gained a certain level of prestige through their work in the courts, they clearly were assigned regularly to cases.

In some cases, an exclusive dedication to service in the law has obscured interesting life histories, such as that of Miguel Borges de Castro Azevedo e Mello, who tried cases at the Court of Appeals of Rio de Janeiro for decades. He was the lawyer involved in the greatest number of freedom suits, representing thirteen masters and fourteen enslaved. Azevedo e Mello was born in Portugal, in the region of Viseu, the son of the judge of the Court of Appeals of Porto, Miguel Borges Tavares de Azevedo Gouveia e Castro. After participating in the war against France in 1808, he returned from battles to face a series of misfortunes—his house had been destroyed, his furniture looted, and his possessions stolen, and on top of that he fell ill. Finding himself destitute, Azevedo e Mello had no choice but to seek help from the state, eventually immigrating to Rio de Janeiro to directly petition the King for assistance.[28]

In Rio, Azevedo e Mello was perhaps the first to claim compensation for being a volunteer soldier in the war against France, demanding the "extraordinary remuneration" of 500,000 réis.[29] Although impoverished from his travails, he did not receive financial retribution, but only the honor of Knight of the Order of Christ and permission to practice in the Court of Appeals in Rio de Janeiro. He worked in this position for the rest of his life, participating in well-known cases such as the defense of the liberal journalist Cipriano Barata in 1830.[30]

The greatest difference among this elite group of lawyers was most likely their social positions. Some were notoriously wealthy, like Teixeira de Freitas, who was a dealer in "land, houses, farms, and slaves," or Honório Augusto Ribeiro, who owned buildings on the prestigious street of Arcos. Others were very poor, such as Domingos Martins de Faria and Manoel Francisco Rodrigues Pereira Galvão. Both of these lawyers died alone and without heirs, Martins de Faria in the Santa Casa de Misericórdia Hospital and Galvão in his rented room in a boardinghouse. The property of the two of them together barely reached 100,000 réis, consisting of little more than broken furniture and old clothing.[31] Although he was a lawyer for more than twenty years in the Court of Appeals "with irreproachable conduct," Galvão's greatest asset was certainly his profession, and indeed his diploma was found in a tightly closed tin in a locked drawer.

These individuals were thus far from composing a socially homogeneous group. And yet, as José Murilo de Carvalho has argued about the Brazilian political elite, the homogeneity of their education compensated for their social differences: each of these lawyers, with the exception of Antonio Pereira Rebouças, was trained in law in Coimbra, Olinda, or São Paulo.[32] The study of law was not so much evidence of belonging to the elite as it was a passport of access to it: a law degree guaranteed the fortunate ones a reliable career in the judiciary. Not counting individuals dedicated exclusively to practicing law, such as José Xavier da Silva Capanema and Miguel Borges de Castro Azevedo e Mello, lawyers who studied law in the first generation of post-independence Brazil all pursued a career in the judiciary. The exception, again, is Antonio Pereira Rebouças, who did not occupy any of these positions. In formal discussions about the judicial system, however, Rebouças made clear his indignation that only formally trained lawyers were eligible to be appointed as judges, surely reflecting his personal wish to be appointed a judge himself.[33]

Over the course of the century, as the legal field grew increasingly important, a law degree was extremely valuable and highly sought after, especially by those who, like Rebouças, had no assets other than their "virtues and skills." When the first students graduated from the law schools of São Paulo and Olinda in 1832, the professionalization of the field began to occur on a large scale. Lawyers trained in these institutions, many of whom were ambitious, often served as judges in small towns right after finishing their studies, and later moved to Rio—because it was the political center, but also because there were more opportunities for work and for social and professional development. By the middle of the century, the next generation of graduates included such high numbers that, for the first time, it was difficult to obtain a government position. This is when many lawyers began to dedicate themselves primarily to the practice of law, setting up their own offices. But it is the earlier generation who interest us here. When younger lawyers such as Carlos Arthur Busch e Varella and Perdigão Malheiro began to make their names in Rio, those of Rebouças's generation—some of whom studied in Coimbra, and many in Olinda—began to lose the status they had enjoyed during the political consolidation of the Brazilian Empire. Using the political prestige accumulated since independence, they too sought to set up private law practices.

Indeed, despite Edmundo Campos Coelho's assertion that "as a rule, these notable lawyers used the law firm as an initial station from which they embarked on the adventure of politics,"[34] it seems that the opposite occurred. As Joaquim Nabuco wrote about his father, "When he had ceased to be a minister in 1857, [José Thomaz] Nabuco [de Araújo] established himself as a lawyer in Rio de Janeiro. He soon joined the profession as one of the first in a forum that included experts such as Teixeira de Freitas, Rebouças, Caetano Alberto Soares, Urbano Pessoa, Perdigão Malheiro, Zacarias, Silveira da Mota, Octaviano, Taylor, and others."[35]

We already know that this was the story of Antonio Pereira Rebouças. It was also true of Urbano Sabino Pessoa de Mello, who was a municipal judge of Goyana, then a judge in Recife and Assu, and provincial deputy of Pernambuco in the General Assembly. Only in 1849, when he definitively left the judiciary, did Pessoa de Mello begin to practice law himself. Many of his colleagues followed a similar path; among them were Bernardo de Souza Franco, deputy and president of the province of Pará, who, despite having participated in some cases while his political career was developing, only started to practice law after retiring as a judge in 1854; Antonio Ferreira Lima, who was *juiz de fora*[36] and had other bureaucratic positions in the towns Santo Antonio de Sá and Magé before participating in freedom suits; and Joaquim Thomaz Nabuco de Araújo, who was active in freedom suits only after having been public prosecutor, judge, deputy in the National Legislative Assembly, president of the province of São Paulo, senator of the Empire, and Minister of Justice.[37]

By the time these deputies started practicing law, they were already experienced politicians, and many, such as Nabuco de Araújo and Bernardo de Souza Franco, would continue to occupy prominent positions in Brazilian public life. They certainly had their ideas about the state of legislation in Brazil, about the situation in the courts, and, of course, about the subject that had shaken the Assembly since the mid-1840s: measures that should or should not be taken to stop slave trafficking and, in the future, slavery. All the lawyers who stood out in Brazilian public life in the first half of the nineteenth century were either members of or identified with the Liberal Party, except for José Thomaz Nabuco de Araújo, who turned to liberalism only in the late 1860s. This confirms José Murilo de Carvalho's claims that liberal professionals made a coalition with landowners who were interested in greater regional powers to form the Liberal Party. He argues that the judges and lawyers in the party represented the doctrinal positions of classical liberalism, which would only gain greater expression from the 1860s onwards, with the increase in the number of liberal professionals willing to participate in politics.[38] Following this reasoning, it is understandable why we only find liberal deputies among the lawyers who participated in the freedom lawsuits; virtually no Conservative Party members were liberal professionals.

The trajectory of the lawyer and priest Caetano Alberto Soares is a good example. Leaving Madeira Island to be a liberal deputy at the Lisbon court in 1828, Soares emigrated from Portugal to Brazil when liberals were being persecuted by supporters of the Portuguese King Miguel. Although he never again engaged in political-parliamentary activities in Portugal—he became a Brazilian citizen in 1833—Soares was distinguished for his participation in various committees that reviewed legislative works and for his work with the Institute of Brazilian Lawyers, of which he was president from 1852 to 1857.[39] He also participated in fourteen freedom suits, defending nine slaves and five masters; nevertheless, he came to be known as an abolitionist, according to the obituary published in the *Revista do Instituto Histórico e Geográfico Brasileiro*: "In matters of manumission, he was the champion of the freedman, fighting for freedom, a constant leader in this generous endeavor; the most delightful music to his ears was the jingle of the handcuffs, smashed by his liberating hands, that fell from the arms of slaves."[40]

Like Rebouças, other well-known lawyers also identified themselves with the ideas and movements that together came to define "liberalism," even if they included diverse practices and ideas and were applied to different conjunctures of Brazilian politics. Urbino Sabino Pessoa de Mello, for example, was one of the leaders of the Praieira rebellion (1848), and often the representative of Pernambuco in the Legislative Assembly, where, between the 1840s and the 1860s, he became a strong voice of the Liberal Party.[41] For a good part of his political-parliamentary trajectory, Pessoa de Mello's main rival was José Thomaz Nabuco de Araújo, the conservative who adopted the liberal platform in the mid-1860s.

All these lawyers were considered liberal by their contemporaries, and judging by their legal opinions, they seem to have been favorable to the end of trafficking and the later abolition of slavery. Joaquim Nabuco referred to them, especially those who served as president of the Institute of Brazilian Lawyers, as the precursors of abolitionism in Brazil: "It will always be the honor of the Institute of Lawyers to be able to say that its first Presidents (and those who followed them, Nabuco and Saldanha Marinho), Montezuma, Carvalho Moreira, Caetano Alberto Soares, Urbano Pessoa, Perdigão Malheiro, even before emancipation was discussed seriously in politics, were all abolitionists. At a time when the principle of slavery was accepted by all as a sacred mystery, those names represent the solitary protest of the law."[42]

Nabuco emphasized the "noble attitude" of Caetano Alberto Soares, who gave a speech in 1845 about improving the situation of slaves,[43] and the judgments of Urbano Sabino, who, in a letter of 1869, claimed that "Brazil will never be considered a civilized nation in the world as long as we have slaves."[44] However, as historian Eduardo Spiller Pena pointed out using the same passages cited by Joaquim Nabuco, it is important to look with caution at the apologies Nabuco makes about the trajectory of these lawyers, as he was specifically interested in highlighting the jurists as pioneers in the condemnation of slavery.[45] It is not surprising that they were identified with the Liberal Party in the 1830s and 1840s, but had not made use of their offices to act politically in favor of the freedom of the slaves. At the risk of drawing the obvious conclusion, it is worth noting that while there were perhaps certain lawyers who used the legal arena to fight for the manumission of slaves before the mid-1860s, they were not *necessarily* activists for freedom. And indeed, most of them definitely were not.

Participation in lawsuits of enslaved persons seeking freedom did not imply a political view on the social status of freedpersons or the formalization of access to manumission. On the contrary: judging by their legal work in the freedom lawsuits, these attorneys took a stance toward the question of slavery similar to that of Rebouças. If they were concerned with the extension of civil rights to freedpersons, they viewed this on an individual basis, defending those who, having the right skills and virtues, showed that they deserved to enter the world of the free. In this sense, they were acting in a distinctly liberal fashion, defending individuals and their property, without, however, ceasing to support the institution of slavery—views that ultimately enabled slavery and liberalism to coexist in nineteenth-century Brazil.

The problem for these liberal lawyers took shape after the prohibition of the Atlantic slave trade in 1850, when it became increasingly difficult to look at attempts to gain manumission through legal measures as an individual issue. While freedom suits had been primarily individual until that time, from this decade onwards there was an increase in the number of slaves collectively demanding freedom, as Hebe Mattos has shown. It thus became much more complicated to politically legitimize a suit favorable to the freedom of an individual and to deny the same rights to all enslaved persons.[46] With the end of the Atlantic trade and the pressure for the abolition of slavery, the political landscape in the Brazilian Empire changed radically, which led to a politicization of these freedom suits. If the movement to regulate civil law had been seen as problematic since the founding of the Empire, it had now become a pressing issue. The increase in the number of freedom suits only showed how disputes over property—and most of them were considered as such—could no longer be resolved without addressing the problem of civil rights.

Not by chance, in 1855, five years after the enactment of the promulgation of the law that finally prohibited the Atlantic slave trade and the promulgation of the commercial code, Augusto Teixeira de Freitas was hired by the Brazilian government to write the *Consolidação das leis civis*, a preparatory work for the drafting of the civil code. In this new landscape, while some young people were beginning to discuss ways to reinterpret the existing laws, using them as tactics to pressure and criticize the monarchy itself, old jurists such as Antonio Pereira Rebouças clung increasingly to the law as the only means for introducing legitimate change into society.

8   At the Edge of the Civil Code

In 1859, Antonio Pereira Rebouças and Augusto Teixeira de Freitas engaged in a polemical dispute in the pages of Rio's newspapers. Teixeira de Freitas had just published his book, *Consolidação das leis civis* (Consolidation of Civil Laws), a compilation of all Brazilian civil laws that were then in force, intended as a precursor to preparing a national civil code. Rebouças felt obliged to comment on the work in a published letter to Teixeira de Freitas, hoping, he claimed, to contribute to the improvement of "the best and most comprehensive repertoire of our current civil legislation."[1] Rebouças was perhaps revealing his disappointment that he was not chosen to be part of the commission to review the work, which included José Thomaz Nabuco de Araújo, Caetano Alberto Soares, and Paulino Soares de Souza, the Viscount of Uruguay. And so he shared his opinions in an open letter to Teixeira de Freitas in the newspaper *Correio Mercantil*, pointing out that while the review commission had recognized that there were a number of omissions in the work, they had not specified what they were.

Rebouças was writing the letter, he stated, because he feared that the status of laws would be chaotic and "wild given the uncertainty and the diversity of opinions," and that the commission's review would further aggravate this situation. He was, however, supportive of the project itself. Worried that existing laws might be put to use in ways that contradicted their original meaning, Rebouças welcomed a work that sought to clarify and organize the meanings of civil laws. Even with the occasional mistake, he argued, such a volume would be useful not only in the country's courts, but for teaching law as well.[2]

After praising the overall importance of Teixeira de Freitas's work, Rebouças itemized one criticism after another—eventually leading him to publish an entire volume in response to *Consolidação das leis civis*. In reply, Teixeira de Freitas issued two more editions of his compilation: one with Rebouças's comments, and a second with his own replies to the concerns. Teixeira de Freitas was not bothered at all by the debate with Rebouças, or by the extra work that ensued—on the contrary, he was honored by the words of the former deputy. In one of his responses, he wrote: "Fortunately there are still noble hearts who feel the pulsations of love for all that is great and glorious for the nation. The illustrious jurist Mr. Antonio Pereira Rebouças, who had already expressed his appreciation of my work, published in *Correio Mercantil* a series of remarks about some of the legal articles in *Consolidação das leis civis*. . . . We cordially thank our distinguished colleague for this commendable effort. All your praiseworthy remarks will be carefully taken into account. Brazil would be a much happier place . . . if it contained more virtuous and patriotic men as this honorable jurist."[3]

Rebouças was also pleased. Although many thought Teixeira de Freitas might react unfavorably, he had thwarted any "malicious expectations" by praising Rebouças's initiative. In fact, Rebouças appreciated the comments about himself printed in the press, and replied, "In the situation in which I live—on the margins if not completely in obscurity—perhaps Mr. Freitas's expressions of generosity toward me seem hyperbolic. I myself would have viewed the praise as excessive, if . . . I had not already heard similarly honorable expressions from men notorious for their great talent, knowledge, prudence, and seriousness of character."[4] The passage continues with Rebouças's usual praises of himself, emphasizing his contributions to the "history of our homeland" and the recognition he had received from the greatest authorities of the Empire. Apparently he had little concern that he might be accused of lacking modesty.[5]

It may seem strange that Rebouças describes himself as living on the margins, almost in obscurity. After all, he was one of Rio's most successful lawyers, called upon for advice in a variety of civil law disputes and assigned to be the attorney for important cases. And yet, by all indications, it was not appreciation of his legal skills that he sought. Accustomed to participating in legislative reform committees in the Assembly, Rebouças clearly had not recovered from the political ostracism he suffered at the end of his parliamentary career ten years earlier. It seems he yearned for recognition not only of his legal knowledge, but also of his contributions to the nation. Such acknowledgment, however, was not on the horizon.

At the same time, Teixeira de Freitas was experiencing his own frustrations. The publication of the *Consolidação* had not caused the stir he had expected, and he was resentful that there was so little discussion on the legal content of the work. Likely Teixeira de Freitas was still smarting from a defeat suffered two years earlier in a controversy at the Institute of Brazilian Lawyers. President of the Institute at the time, he had argued that children of conditionally freed enslaved mothers should retain the same status as the mother, *at least* while she remained enslaved. Many of his colleagues, including highly regarded lawyers and jurists such as Caetano Alberto Soares, Perdigão Malheiro, and Urbano Sabino Pessoa de Mello, rejected his position. An indignant Teixeira de Freitas accused them of ignoring Roman law, and an animated disagreement ensued—including purposeful provocations, such as Freitas's offer to purchase a copy of the basic work of civil Roman law, *Corpus Juris Civilis*, which, he argued, was lacking in the library of the Institute. The strife ended with Freitas resigning as president of the Institute.[6]

The most heated part of the conflict was between Teixeira de Freitas and Caetano Alberto Soares. Teixeira de Freitas recognized his colleague's "many praiseworthy tendencies toward freedom," but reproached him for always allowing his "beloved idea" to "overshadow the process of debating a legal question, which should be calm and reflective."[7] It was no coincidence, then, that two years later the committee in charge of reviewing *Consolidação*— of which Caetano Alberto Soares was a member—remarked: "It is sensible to omit . . . any provisions regarding slavery; for reasons of political and public order, these must constitute a special law, and it is first necessary to know the state of the legislation in this respect."[8]

The fact that Antonio Pereira Rebouças and Augusto Teixeira de Freitas had both felt marginalized by other prestigious lawyers may explain the mutual accolades that marked their legal exchange. It is possible that both men had legitimate reasons to complain about the lack of professionalism among their colleagues; it could be, however, that Rebouças and Freitas were isolated precisely because of the position each took on the legal debate about slavery.

The first discussions about preparing to write a civil code dated back to 1854, when Minister of Justice Nabuco de Araújo had a number of conversations with Teixeira de Freitas about how to proceed with this critical undertaking. Teixeira de Freitas suggested that he begin by compiling "a systematic classification of all branches of legislation, which in the future will serve as a basis for further improvements and reforms."[9] The proposal was approved, and the imperial government commissioned Teixeira de Freitas for a five-year period "to classify and consolidate . . . all of the country's legislation, including that of Portugal, prior to the Independence of the Empire."[10] This contract between Teixeira de Freitas and the government was an important step in recognizing that Brazil needed to organize its civil laws—as jurists, politicians, and lawyers had long been saying. In a famous statement, Francisco Ignacio de Carvalho Moreira, then president of the Institute of Brazilian Lawyers, claimed that the lack of a civil code would continue to "delay our civilization, delay the aggrandizement of our industry, and consequently of our wealth and national opulence."[11] Carvalho Moreira charted the history of attempting to codify civil laws in Brazil, arguing that the multiplicity of legislation had created "social anachronism," as, even after independence, the country continued to be regulated by laws that had already been repealed even in Portugal. He warned that the use of old laws related to customs and practices no longer current in Brazil would result in dire consequences for the "stability of justice, and the security of civil rights, for the peace and happiness of families, the effectiveness of contracts, and the maintenance of property."[12] Implementing a civil code, he argued, was thus of the greatest urgency. Carvalho Moreira's powerful reflections convinced many that codification was a historical necessity and that, indeed, Brazilian society could not progress until the code was accomplished. He also conveyed in his article the shared belief that this task would not be easy.

Although Teixeira de Freitas may not have been familiar with the encumbrances inherent in writing any codification, he certainly must have realized the challenges before starting to work on the code—a task he was hired for by the Brazilian government in 1859, two years after the publication of the *Consolidação*.[13] The committee charged with reviewing the *Consolidação* had already pointed out a number of the issues specific to Brazil in their report, requesting that Teixeira de Freitas revise certain parts of the work. In particular, the committee emphasized one major point: the question of slavery. In addition to questioning Teixeira de Freitas's omission of anything related to the slave labor regime, the report highlighted his definition of persons, from which enslaved were excluded:

> In the first section—Persons—the author considers the acts of birth and death; and distinguishes people only as to age, family, property, and absence. For the reasons that the author mentions on p. 11, the state of slavery is excluded from this category. Considering rights only as civil or political, of the man or the citizen; political rights being those that refer to participation in public power and functions, and consequently only and exclusively of the Brazilians, and civil rights being the same for Brazilians and foreigners, the author does not indicate that there are different categories of national and foreigner.[14]

Teixeira de Freitas probably anticipated reaction on this first category, and not only because of his previous conflict with Caetano Alberto Soares.

In his introduction to *Consolidação*, he explained that he had expressly chosen not to include slaves in this project, so as not to "tarnish himself with the evil that still afflicts Brazilian society":

> It should be noted that slaves are not considered in any part. It is true that we have slavery among us; but if this evil is an exception, which we regret, and one destined to extinguish itself in a time that is more or less remote; let us also make an exception, a separate chapter, in the reform of our Civil Laws; let us not sully them with shameful dispositions, which cannot serve posterity: let the state of freedom be without its odious correlative. The laws concerning slavery (which are not many) will therefore be classified separately and will form our Black Code.[15]

Rebouças, in summarizing what he viewed as the errors in Teixeira de Freitas's *Consolidação*, also highlighted the issue of slavery; however, it was not the absence of the topic that bothered him as much as the author's attempt to address the omission by inserting footnotes. In Rebouças's view, including exceptions all the time would prevent the code from being useful at all, while for Teixeira de Freitas this was meant to be a temporary solution. In the second edition, however, Teixeira de Freitas addressed the possible elaboration of a "Black Code," adding a comment that he was "indicating how little civil legislation we have concerning slaves." He had thus included the available Roman law, he explained, in order to "provide a service to the courts, because the issues that arise with this subject are frequent and delicate."[16] Was Teixeira de Freitas alluding to discussions with Caetano Alberto Soares when he portrayed the issues surrounding slavery as "delicate"? It is quite possible, and if so, it is interesting to note that after some time he too had come to consider these issues in the same light.

Rebouças's main contention with the work was Teixeira de Freitas's interpretation of contractual relations and gifts under slavery. In particular, he questioned Article 63, in which Teixeira de Freitas claimed that the "only exception to the completeness of property rights . . . will take place when the public good requires the use of a citizen's property because of necessity or utility."[17] For Rebouças, a main exception was when a slave paid for his or her own manumission, which, he argued, could be considered either a matter of necessity or of the utility of the public good. He was referring to the law of 1823 promulgated in the period of independence, which stated that the government should promote the fair treatment of slaves and their gradual emancipation. Rebouças could thus claim that the possibility of buying one's own manumission was indeed a public good, and therefore an exception to property rights.[18]

Teixeira de Freitas disagreed with Rebouças, arguing that there had been no cases of a master being obligated to manumit a slave in Rio de Janeiro. He maintained that compulsory manumission was a very limited custom and did not imply the obligation to allow any enslaved person wanting freedom to purchase his or her manumission. In fact, he considered this practice an abuse, agreeing with the recently issued Notice 388 of December 21, 1855, that established rules for the purchase of manumission and the gifting of freedom by heirs.[19]

Teixeira de Freitas's claim that there had been no cases of compulsory manumission was not true. He knew very well that such a case existed,[20] as he had successfully defended a slave in one of them in 1844, in a lawsuit whose opposing lawyer was none other than Caetano Alberto Soares.[21] Either Freitas had forgotten that he had succeeded in freeing a slave precisely through forced manumission, or, despite having acted as a lawyer in the case, he held such an opposing political position that he purposefully forgot the episode. It is more likely that he disagreed with the legitimacy of compulsory manumission, which confirms Eduardo Pena's argument that Freitas's commitment to the emancipation of enslaved persons was indeed quite narrow.[22]

It is important here to highlight Rebouças's position—that there existed instances of compulsory manumission, but also that they should be considered legal because they were legitimate, that is, because they were widely practiced and already recognized by some courts. In this instance, Rebouças was less concerned with formalism than with the juridical changes necessary to the situation engendered by the end of the Atlantic slave trade. At the same time, however, he thought it was wrong to introduce legislative changes when the object was the civil code, which, he argued, should be discussed and approved only by the Legislative Assembly. He was against the introduction of new conceptions of law within the judiciary, but very much in favor when in the hands of the legislative branch.

Rebouças's remarks on Teixeira de Freitas's *Consolidações* reveal his views on the ideal conditions for moving from slavery to freedom and for acquiring civil rights. At the same time, they demonstrate the difficulties in trying to legislate definitively—since the final objective would be the composition of a civil code—on issues that kept changing all the time, such as customs related to slavery. For example, in two articles referring to free manumission, legally considered a gift, Rebouças disagreed with Teixeira de Freitas's interpretation. The first article set a limit for men and women to make gifts without having to submit a written record of proof.[23] In the note, Teixeira de Freitas drew attention to the fact that this included the gift of free manumission, legally understood as an individual act that transpires after the gift is delivered. The emphasis is in the last words: "after it is delivered." A letter of manumission found at the time of death, according to Freitas, should only be valid from the date of death. Conclusion? "The children, therefore, of a slave freed in these circumstances born before the letter of manumission produced its effects, before it was known, . . . are slaves."[24]

It seems unbelievable that, after all the discussion at the Institute of Brazilian Lawyers, Teixeira de Freitas returned again to the subject in an article that did not require this observation. He took the opportunity to insist once more on the legitimacy of the rules of Roman law, once interpreted by the legislators of the Ordenações Filipinas and applied to the Brazilian law of the mid-nineteenth century. In his disagreement, Rebouças referred to precisely the same arguments as Teixeira de Freitas, noting that, according to the Ordenações Filipinas, book 4, title 63, paragraph 7, manumission was not dependent on the beneficiary's acceptance. That is to say, it is considered a reasonable assumption that no slave would refuse the freedom—especially if there was no fee—offered by a master. When a slave was bequeathed to an heir, Rebouças argued, even if the heir did not take possession of the property at the time the letter of bequest was written, the slave would nonetheless immediately become the heir's property at the time of death. The same should happen with freedom:

Thus, whenever a letter of manumission appeared or was presented after the death of a master, it must be assumed that the freedperson has been [free] as of its date; and, if of the feminine sex, all the fruits of her womb that were born after the date the letter was signed, must be recognized as freed and as if they were born free; in fact, it would be absurd if all gifts between the living were valid and effective and on the contrary only freedom was a *causa mortis* [only taking place after death], just because the freedmen do not have in their possession their respective letters or written titles. . . . How would the freedman not have gained manumission granted by the master even if he didn't know and hadn't yet benefitted from it? How can children of freedwomen not be free, if born after the date of the title of the concession of their manumission?[25]

Teixeira de Freitas was not convinced by these arguments. In the third edition of *Consolidação*, in response to Rebouças, he argued that it was not inconceivable that a slave might refuse freedom offered by a master; moreover, he maintained, without citing any specific cases, that there were actual examples of Brazilian slaves who had refused.[26] As we already know that Teixeira de Freitas was not particularly committed to accuracy in his arguments, we can only analyze their legal aspects. He disagreed that manumission declared in a will could be considered a gift between two living persons; quite the contrary, actually, as it was to be given only once the donor had died, like the gifting of animals. Thus he argued: "Strictly, in such situations, it is logically possible that there was no gift."[27]

Teixeira de Freitas had actually made his argument more complicated than it already was: if "strictly" manumission could not be considered a gift, why would there be a note about the specifics of the gift of freedom in an article about gifting? Once again, Teixeira de Freitas concluded that the legal decision on an issue like this was mainly political, and he accused the members of the Institute of Brazilian Lawyers of acting on political grounds. He said of Rebouças's comments that "questions continue to arise when principles do not exist,"[28] a view he confirmed at the time of the debate in the Institute. Freitas clearly believed that the only argument that was free from "opinions" and in accordance with correct legal principles was his own. But Rebouças had also formulated an interpretation of the law: to support his argument, he chose to regard the gift of free manumission as an endowment contract in which the gift of manumission was a *bilateral act*. He maintained that the slave entered into possession of freedom at the moment the master signed the letter of manumission, and not at the disclosure of the will—exactly the opposite, therefore, of his argument in the freedom lawsuit with Domingos Figueira in the early 1860s.

In keeping with his earlier arguments, Rebouças continued to insist that transactions involving manumission were the same as any contractual operation involving the transmission of goods. As in any commercial transaction, he argued, if conditions were not fully met, the contract was annulled. This led to surprising conclusions, such as his response to Article 421 of *Consolidação*, which dealt with the possibility of revoking manumission. Teixeira de Freitas maintained that it was impossible to revoke the freedom of a freedperson born in Brazil, because he had already acquired citizenship rights.[29] Knowing Rebouças's history of defending the civil rights of freedpersons, one might expect him to agree. He did not, however. Instead, he argued that if a freedperson was ungrateful, regardless of birthplace, he or she must be returned to slavery.[30] It turns out that he was not referring to ingratitude in general, but rather to a specific case: "It has often been seen that enslaved men invest themselves in being citizens and soldiers pretending to be free-born or freed, and after being returned to the dominion and possession of their masters, when this has been fairly demanded, can no longer be citizens and soldiers."[31] That is, according to Rebouças, those freedpersons who had paid for their freedom, or who had acquired it through another legitimate form, being Brazilians, should become full citizens, without restriction clauses, such as those suggested during the discussion about the National Guard. But those who sought to gain freedom by illegitimate and deceptive means should lose their citizenship rights, as they had been illegally obtained, and be returned to slavery.

Teixeira de Freitas found it difficult to accept Rebouças's arguments because this would be "one more instance of a loss of citizen rights beyond the three that were expressly designated by Article 7 of the Constitution of the Empire." Ultimately, however, he acknowledged that his own argument could also be refuted. Like Rebouças, Teixeira de Freitas too believed that the Constitution—which declared that freedpersons are Brazilian citizens—did not mean to include those who had obtained freedom through fraudulent manumission. His conviction was such that he even returned, one more time, to discuss the status of children of freedwomen: "Admitting this possible case of revocation of manumission, if the freedwoman had children after manumission? It is the same solution as in the case of revocation for ingratitude. . . . Children conceived after revocation are slaves, but not those conceived before."[32] He thus assumed that the Ordenações Filipinas, book 4, title 63, paragraph 7, concerning the possibilities of revocation of manumission, had not been fully annulled, although he considered this practice no longer acceptable in Brazil.

This was after all the prevailing view in the legal realm from the late 1850s until the middle of the 1860s. Lourenço Trigo de Loureiro, in his work *Instituições de direito civil brasileiro* (Institutions of Brazilian Civil Law), first published in 1851 and adopted in the course on national civil law at the Faculty of Law of Recife, established that only the "partially freedmen," those who were still fulfilling conditions, could have their manumissions revoked for ingratitude, since, as they were not yet in full enjoyment of their civil rights, they could not be considered citizens. But if the person had already been "completely manumitted," he could no longer be reduced to slavery by reason of ingratitude, because he was already a citizen and could not lose citizenship rights for any reason other than the three cited by the

Constitution.[33] It is clear that Trigo de Loureiro was the resource for Teixeira de Freitas on this issue, as he considered manumission a restitution of natural freedom, and although the form was sometimes illegal or unjust, as he put it, it could not be revoked if the individual was a native of Brazil.

Several jurists supported the positions of Trigo de Loureiro and Teixeira de Freitas in condemning the legal possibility of annulling manumission due to ingratitude of the freedperson. Antonio Joaquim Ribas and Agostinho Marques Perdigão Malheiro, in their important works of civil law in the 1860s, practically repeated the opinions of their predecessors. As Ribas wrote: "One of the questions that has been the most debated among us is whether this Ordenação book 4 title 7 is revoked or not [he cites text from *Consolidação* and the work of Lourenço Trigo de Loureiro]. We hope that this opinion, which we cannot discuss here, prevails in the courts, tending, as it does, to limit slavery."[34]

Perdigão Malheiro, who was dealing specifically with laws relating to slavery, showed how, even in Roman law, freedmen were often exempt from their obligations. It did not make sense, he argued, that ingratitude, for whatever reason, was still considered a valid reason to annul a person's manumission.[35] All these authors, although they had differing opinions on other subjects related to slavery, agreed that manumission was the restitution of the natural freedom due to any enslaved person and that revoking it was in fact reducing a free person to slavery, which was a crime under the laws of the Brazilian Empire.[36]

It is important to note, however, that they omitted an important element of Trigo de Loureiro's argument. He believed that only cases of manumission that had no conditions, and that were not illegal or unjust, could be considered "complete." Thus in the case described by Rebouças, Trigo de Loureiro would probably have agreed that manumission should be revoked. Although Rebouças's stance on annulling manumission for those who, according to him, had obtained freedom illegally was in decline, there were nevertheless still those who agreed with him. And yet, there is no reference in books written in the 1860s to exceptions made when manumission was acquired in a supposedly illegal manner. This was most likely because of the increasingly widespread belief that manumission was a restitution of natural freedom to the one from whom it had been improperly usurped. Of course this view did not mean that Perdigão Malheiro, Antonio Ribas, or even Caetano Alberto Soares defended the immediate abolition of slavery; but it certainly distinguished them substantially from people like Antonio Pereira Rebouças, who believed that freedom and, by extension, citizenship rights, were solely for those who deserved them.

Rebouças continued to treat manumission as a prize won through merit rather than a restitution of natural freedom, showing that he never came to conceive of slavery itself as illegitimate. On the occasion of his seventieth birthday, he celebrated by granting freedom to one of his slaves, who had already been freed in his will, as his son recalled in his diary: "[On turning seventy], my father celebrated the dawn of this welcome day by granting freedom to our slave Guilhermina, Damiana's daughter, released in the will by my mourned mother."[37]

The truth is that Antonio Pereira Rebouças, even in the 1860s, continued to consider freedom and civil rights as he had in the Assembly in the 1830s and 1840s, when the defense of property and the individual rights of freedpersons did not appear contradictory, and slavery was still viewed as legitimate by the great majority of political representatives. But Brazil had changed signficantly in those thirty years. The increasing number of freedom lawsuits—especially those in which several slaves from a rural region tried to gain their freedom at the same time—reflected the growing pressure to consider manumission and the rights attached to it as a collective issue, which would ultimately encompass all slaves.[38] Likewise, there were more lawyers, such as Joaquim José Affonso Alves in Rio Grande do Sul and Luiz Gama in São Paulo, who were willing to use legal provisions with the express purpose of freeing as many slaves as possible.

Rebouças, by contrast, never stopped treating the freedom of slaves as an individual matter. His fundamental concern was always the defense of civil rights, even in a slave society. The editor of *O Novo Mundo*—a newspaper "illustrating the Progress of the Age," published in Portuguese in New York with the collaboration of André Rebouças—made this very observation about Rebouças. In 1875, the paper devoted a cover story to the history of the illustrious lawyer: "We are adorning the front page of this issue with a beautiful portrait of the famous Brazilian jurist, Mr. Antonio Pereira Rebouças, and we are sorry for not having more biographical information about him. . . . There are few—very few—men in Brazil whose political opinions would be the same now as they were forty-seven years ago. Mr. Rebouças is the only one about whom we can say that his political ideas, as far as we know, are the same today as when Bahia sent him to the National Assembly [as a representative] for the first time."[39]

This is perhaps the key for why Rebouças's criticisms of the *Consolidação* of Teixeira de Freitas were disregarded. The remarks that he had so carefully elaborated did not, after all, have the intended effect—even after the publication of the second edition of Freitas's work, which included parts of Rebouças's notes. His obvious attempt to influence the process of codifying civil law, albeit with no invitation, fell into the void. Besides Teixeira de Freitas's own replies, no mention was ever made of Rebouças's careful reading of the work—except of course in the speeches and tributes given at the time of his death, when all tend to bear witness with more benevolent eyes.[40]

In fact, it was not only Rebouças's intervention in the process of Brazilian civil codification that went unnoticed. His entire career as a politician and jurist was symptomatically forgotten, despite his own numerous efforts to preserve his legacy. A liberal among conservatives in the 1830s, he was regarded as a conservative among the new liberals of the mid-1860s. But perhaps there were other reasons for his descent into oblivion: throughout his life, Rebouças maintained a discourse in which he refused to include race as a valid criterion for obtaining and exercising citizenship. Thus, for both those who saw African descent as a negative trait and those who saw it as a positive one, Rebouças's ideas were off.

Antonio Pereira Rebouças strongly believed in the universality of civil rights, which, in turn, reinforced the individual effort for the daily exercise of citizenship. For him, the struggle for the possession and guarantee of civil rights had to be made through individual activism or at most by a group of individuals, but never by a community that defined itself on an ethnic basis and made a joint claim to rights. Race, for good or ill, should not differentiate anyone.

This is the context, then, for understanding Rebouças's bitterness about his exchange with Teixeira de Freitas in the 1860s, and also his effort to perpetuate the memory of his political achievements. It clearly crushed Rebouças that no one seemed to remember the important political role he felt he had played. After the death of his wife, Carolina, in 1865, the first signs developed of the blindness that would mark the last ten years of his life. Indeed, one of his final projects was dictating his memoires to his son André which he did from 1867 to 1870, culminating with the publication of two books: *Recordações da vida patriótica* (Memories of a Patriotic Life) and *Recordações da vida parlamentar* (Memories of Parliamentary Life).[41] It was also in 1870 that Rebouças last worked as an attorney.

In fact, in the 1870s Antonio Pereira Rebouças no longer participated in any of the important public discussions related to the slow process of ending slavery in the country. He made no public comment about the Law of the Free Womb, issued in 1871, that declared, among other things, that all individuals born from the womb of an enslaved woman were free and that slaves had the right to accumulate money in order to pay for their manumissions. We know these were topics dear to Rebouças's heart, and it's a sad irony that this law was promulgated at the end of his career, validating a position that he had initiated in the Assembly, even though, at the time, it was considered too subversive and dangerous. But it seems that after the death of his beloved Carolina and the completion of his memoirs, nothing really mattered to Rebouças. Blind and widowed, he spent the last years of his life remembering past achievements and attending occasional ceremonies celebrating Brazilian independence. Soon before he died, he was last seen at the celebratory mass of his eighty-second birthday held at the local church.

Conclusion

The Legal Stains of Slavery

. . . .

Finally, Law 3353 of May 13, 1888, abolished slavery from that very day
forward. This vital decision of the Brazilian Legislature . . . affirmed and
guaranteed the freedom of work. And for those codifying Brazilian civil law,
it marked an end to one of their nightmares.

—A. Velloso-Rabello, 1911

Antonio Pereira Rebouças died in 1880. It was a rather sad end for this "guarantor of the Brazilians." Rebouças had always believed that he—a self-
educated black man, moderate in politics, and adamant that change should
occur through legal means—was the best reassurance that universalizing
civil rights to all Brazilians without distinction would provide a positive
path beyond slavery. Rebouças did not live to witness the abolition of slavery in 1888 or the ending of the Empire in 1889, and certainly not the promulgation of Brazil's civil code in 1917—an event that he would have
celebrated. As we have seen, Rebouças had long insisted that only the civil
code would guarantee the civil rights of citizens, and ensure the practice of
these rights.

In the early 1880s, however, despite his own efforts and those of contemporaries such as Augusto Teixeira de Freitas and Nabuco de Araújo, a civil
code for Brazil was far off. Although the process of codifying civil legislation had formally begun in 1855 when Teixeira de Freitas began to work on
his compilation of existing laws, there was still a long road ahead. Indeed,
the drafting of a civil code was never carried out while the Brazilian Empire still existed. Even after writing and publishing the *Esboço* (Sketch) of
the civil code, Teixeira de Freitas abandoned the task in 1867, claiming that
his own views differed too much from those of the government.[1] In 1872,
José Thomaz Nabuco de Araújo set out to complete the task, but he died six
years later, leaving dozens of volumes of notes, but no book.[2] The jurist Felí-
cio dos Santos was the next to take up the cause, and in 1881 he wrote a
proposal to complete a draft of the code, an extensive work in itself, entitled
Apontamentos (Notes), and presented it to the Legislature. The commission

that evaluated dos Santos's proposal rejected it, and was then asked to draft a new code. The group, made up of jurists such as Lafayette Rodrigues Pereira and Felicio dos Santos himself, had so many conflicts between them that they barely managed to work together, and dissolved in 1883. The last attempt to publish a civil code during the Empire came too late: the final commission, formed in 1889, included Afonso Pena, Candido de Oliveira, and even the Emperor himself, but it was dissolved with the end of the regime, in November of that year. From then until 1899, when Clóvis Beviláqua was hired to write the code, only individual efforts to elaborate the civil code kept the issue active.

Various stories speak to the troubled history of codifying civil law in the Brazilian Empire. Some say that the failure to complete a civil code was the actual cause of death of Nabuco de Araújo.[3] It has also been suggested that the alleged incompatibility of Teixeira de Freitas's conception with the government's was in fact a first sign of his mental illness—an affliction, so the suggestion goes, that developed from his singular dedication, with no respite, to this project of creating a civil code. These two hypotheses, along with others, have often been explored in the historiography.[4] What matters here, and deserves further exploration, is that for the duration of slavery, there was no civil code in Brazil.

• • • • • •

The issues that Antonio Pereira Rebouças highlighted throughout his political career and in his response to the *Consolidação das leis civis*—regarding everyday relations between free and enslaved persons and the definition of the *status* of freedpersons—were not solved while Brazil was an empire. The Law of the Free Womb, however, promulgated in 1871 after intense legislative debate, did address these questions. There were endless discussions, for example, on the status of children born to enslaved women who had been granted conditional freedom, with an obligation to provide services for a certain time.[5] In fact, the Law of the Free Womb radically altered the status of enslaved persons in Brazil. Although no one dared to proclaim it publicly,[6] by establishing that thereafter all children born to enslaved women would be considered free, the law effectively guaranteed that the end of slavery in Brazil was approaching. And this was no small thing, as Nabuco de Araújo noted in his defense of the approval of the Law of the Free Womb in the Senate, however critical he may have been: "In this notion [of the Free Womb] there is a great principle, a principle that satisfies our patriotism; in effect, the legality of slavery ends, and only the fact of slavery, a transitory fact, subsists; it must be gradually abolished, because it cannot be extinguished immediately."[7] He completed his argument with a soon-to-be famous phrase: "[In Brazil] no one else will be born a slave."[8]

Nabuco de Araújo seemed to believe what he said. After all, in his notes for the civil code there was not a single mention of slavery. In his view, in legal terms, the issue was solved, and the former population of enslaved persons would have a civil status assured for the future, as free citizens like anyone else. While many argued that such legal terms do not necessarily secure those rights—which of course is true—we must nonetheless agree that, from the perspective of the making of civil legislation, the problem no longer existed. Thus, the law of 1871 established—in principle, if not in practice—the end of the theoretical dilemma between freedom and property.

· · · · · ·

It has long been maintained that the abiding presence of slavery and the monarchical regime were the main reasons for the absence of a civil code in Imperial Brazil. Surely it lies more in the first cause than the second, as many European monarchies had elaborate civil codes that never questioned the political system. At issue was the impossibility of reconciling a civil code in which citizenship rights should be granted to all persons with slavery, legally grounded in the distinction between persons who are free, and the enslaved, legally considered things. Indeed, as we have seen, this was the main argument of Teixeira de Freitas when he refused to tarnish the civil code with provisions on slavery.

Paulo Mercadante in the 1960s was probably the first to develop the idea that a civil code and slavery were irreconcilable. Mercadante argued that the fact that a commercial code was enacted in 1850 without a corresponding civil code or, as Teixeira de Freitas wanted, without subordination to a code that encompassed all the activities of private law, was due to the very existence of slavery in the country. As a civil code that sought to govern relations between masters and slaves would have been impossible, the commercial code was ultimately responsible for framing virtually all areas of civil law.[9]

When we look at the process of codifying civil law in other countries, it becomes clear that although slavery was a great impediment to the codification of Brazilian civil law, it was certainly not the only one. There were additional obstacles, including issues concerning family relations, inheritance, and the legal status of women, as Sueann Caulfield demonstrates.[10]

The relationship between the Brazilian state and the Catholic Church was another site of great contention. Because state and church were so closely connected, there was never a civil registry or civil marriage in Brazil during the nineteenth century; there were only Catholic cemeteries, and only Catholics could be elected to public office. This of course constituted a clear limitation of citizenship, since those who did not profess the Catholic faith could not exercise the full rights of citizenship even if they met all other requirements. Nabuco de Araújo weighed in on the debate, explaining why the fact that the Empire had an official religion was a problem for the Liberal Party: "The State owes all protection to the Church, the State must maintain the freedom and independence of the Church; but the Church must know that the State has laws for itself, as it has for all citizens, and laws that are inflexible. . . . Indeed, if as stated in the constitution all religions are allowed, how can you deprive citizens of political rights because [they have] a religion other than that of the state? . . . This is not possible . . . because it is not about the tolerance of faith, but civil or political tolerance."[11]

Even Nabuco, however, believed that some of these questions could only be resolved with a civil code, not with stopgap measures. In 1877, for example, he disagreed with the Clube da Reforma (Reform Club), a group that sought to institute a civil registry of births and deaths and a mandatory civil marriage contract.[12] Such individual reforms were not useful, he argued, if there was no civil code. When the Republic decreed the end of the Padroado in the early 1890s,[13] one of the first decrees of the new regime, some of these issues began to be resolved. However, only with the promulgation of the code in 1917 was civil life fully regulated.

The regime of slave labor and the civil code were not necessarily incompatible, just as slavery and liberalism had not been irreconcilable in the Brazilian Empire, as the long historiographic debate on the subject makes clear. In the U.S. state of Louisiana, which, because of French rule, had laws rooted in the Roman legal tradition rather than common law, a civil code was enacted during the period of slavery. Promulgated in 1825, the Louisiana Civil Code contained at least four articles pertaining to slaves: Article 174, on the inability of the enslaved to enter into any type of contract except those relating to their own emancipation; Article 177, which established that the enslaved could not be a party to any civil action, except when they claimed their freedom; Article 189, which ruled that it was impossible for manumission to be revoked for any reason; and Article 461, which specified that enslaved persons were considered property by law.[14]

In Brazil, by contrast, the only references to slavery in Teixeira de Frei-tas's draft civil code asserted that, even though enslaved persons should be regulated by a specific law, they should nevertheless be legally considered persons because they were capable of acquiring rights: "It is known that this bill leaves aside the slavery of blacks, reserved for a special bill of law; but it should not be thought that I will regard slaves as things. Even with the many restrictions, they still have the ability to acquire rights; and that suf-fices for them to be considered people."[15]

In Louisiana, since the beginning of the nineteenth century, high prices for sugar and cotton on the world market had encouraged the reopening of the Atlantic slave trade and an increased commitment to slave labor, while also creating a wider distance between African plantation slaves and their descendants who lived free in New Orleans. These factors led to the restric-tion of manumission in the state.[16] In Brazil, on the contrary, the abolition of the Atlantic slave trade and the slow delegitimization of slavery, espe-cially after 1850, actually meant that freedom was more available to en-slaved persons than ever before.

Thus, one of the reasons for the difficulty in codifying Brazilian civil law in the nineteenth century may have been the changes in the status of en-slaved persons, and not the very existence of slavery. After all, slavery it-self posed no problems of regulation. Yet, even though the regime of slave labor did not seem seriously threatened, manumission had become a pos-sibility in the lives of many enslaved persons. This in the end was more dif-ficult to reconcile with a civil code than a full-on commitment to the institution of slavery.

It was no coincidence that, as early as 1830, Antonio Pereira Rebouças was concerned with regulating, from a legal perspective, the movement from enslavement to freedom. His work in this regard reveals the insight—and, at the same time, the ambiguities—of his reading of nineteenth-century Brazilian society: Rebouças was not preoccupied with slavery itself, but rather with the regulation of moving from slavery to freedom and the sub-sequent conditions of having access to rights and exercising citizenship. Re-bouças cared about the acquisition and the loss of civil rights, but was not particularly concerned about the very existence of slavery.

In Rebouças's view, the emancipation of all enslaved persons was going to be a slow process, and he did not consider slavery a stain that impeded the development of the nation, as jurists of the early twentieth century later argued. He did not see any logical incompatibility between slavery and the civil code. What concerned him was the incapacity of the political leaders of the 1840s—that is, those responsible for the Regresso—to visualize a society in which the movement from slavery to freedom was effectively allowed and regulated, rather than always a random result of special circumstances.

At the heart of the difficulties of completing a civil code in nineteenth-century Brazil were the disputes around the definition of the concept of citizenship. These difficulties were common to all countries that sought to construct a liberal state, formed by a set of citizens. As we have seen, in all slave societies of the Americas that were discussing the end of slavery, a fundamental question arose: If Africans and their descendants cease to be enslaved and become free workers, will they also be citizens?[17]

The originality of the thought of Antonio Pereira Rebouças lies precisely in his realization that none of the great issues discussed during the construction of the Brazilian nation and state could be solved without regulating the access of formerly enslaved persons to citizenship rights. From his own experience, he understood that the existence of an intermediary group between citizens and enslaved persons was totally inconsistent with the principles set forth in the Constitution of 1824. This is why, in the 1830s, Rebouças—at the risk of being viewed as a radical—proposed to regulate terms for the purchase of manumission and repudiated the exclusion of freedmen from becoming National Guard officers. This is also the context for his stance against the conservative policy of the Regresso, which supported a society founded on hierarchical principles that had already ceased to exist in Portugal. And finally, for his steadfast committment to formalizing a coherent body of laws in a civil code—the sole safeguard, he believed, for anyone who transitioned from slavery to freedom.

Ironically, the originality and radicalism of Antonio Pereira Rebouças fell into oblivion. Despite being a hero of independence, Rebouças could not create his own place in posterity, but rather entered into history as the father of the abolitionist and engineer André. In the end, Rebouças was remembered in the way Joaquim Nabuco described him: a man divided between "two races," misunderstood on the one hand by those who viewed the slave past as a stain that should be eliminated from the collective memory of the nation, and on the other hand by those who wanted to construct a positive idea of race.

For scholars in the early twentieth century who sought to highlight the African origins of Brazilian politicians and abolitionists, it was surely difficult to understand how one could have been deeply liberal and also defend slavery. Rebouças's approach to the racial issue and his defense of a universal definition of citizenship went against assumptions about the role of black legislators and lawyers. And yet, Rebouças was consistent in his belief of what he thought was a true and liberatory concept of liberalism; throughout his career, he never ceased to insist—in both the General Assembly and in the courts—on the principles of equality, arguing that what was then called "race" did not, in the end, matter. Or, at least, *ought* not to matter.

Notes

Preface

1. Some of the recent works include Pinto and Chalhoub, *Pensadores negros*; Godoi, *Um editor no Império*; Castilho, *Slave Emancipation and Tranformations*; and Miki, *Frontiers of Citizenship*.

2. On Mattos's concept of racial silence, see her "Prefácio," in Cooper, Scott, and Holt, *Além da escravidão*. See also Mattos and Rios, *Memórias do cativeiro*; and Fischer, Grinberg, and Mattos, "Law, Silence and Racialized Inequalities."

3. Gilroy, *The Black Atlantic*; Mbembe, *Critique of Black Reason*.

4. I am following Hendrik Kraay's use of Brazilian (especially Bahian) eighteenth- and nineteenth-century racial terminology, as discussed in *Race, State, and Armed Forces*, 20–22. See also Andrews, *Afro-Latin America*.

5. The term could also include a free black person born in Africa, but for the most part, a *preto* was someone whose life was close to slavery.

Introduction

1. *O Bahiano*, May 23, 1829, 4. Rebouças bought a letterpress to run the newspaper *O Bahiano* after it was closed and forbidden to be in circulation; from 1828 at least into 1831, he directed and contributed writings to the paper. "Apontamentos Biographicos do Conselheiro Antonio Pereira Rebouças," n.d., Coleção Antonio Pereira Rebouças, Seção Manuscritos, Biblioteca Nacional.

2. Salvador, in Bahia, was the capital of Brazil until 1763, when it was relocated to Rio de Janeiro.

3. On André Rebouças, see Veríssimo, *André Rebouças através de sua autobiografia*; Maria Carvalho, *O quinto século*; and Alonso, *Flores, votos e balas*.

4. Tavares, *A independência do Brasil*; Nunes, *História de Sergipe*; Freire, *História de Sergipe*.

5. Reis, *Slave Rebellion in Brazil*; Reis, *Death Is a Festival*.

6. Nabuco, *Um estadista do Império*, vol. 1, pp. 74–75. Joaquim Nabuco, son of José Thomas Nabuco de Araújo, was an abolitionist from the same generation as André, and one of the most important politicians and diplomats of the Empire, as well as a highly regarded historian.

7. Mott, "A revolução dos negros do Haiti e o Brasi." See by the same author: "Brancos, pardos, pretos e Índios em Sergipe, 1825–1830"; "Violência e repressão em Sergipe"; "Pardos e pretos em Sergipe."

8. Spitzer, *Lives in Between*, 101–26.

9. See Grinberg, "Manumission, Gender and the Law."

10. Surely the archives of Bahia and Sergipe have relevant documentation, but I was not able to include them in this study. I begin to explore these sources in H. Mattos and Grinberg, "Lapidário de si."

11. On the expansion of slavery in nineteenth-century Brazil, see Marquese, Parron, and Berbel, *Slavery and Politics*; Tomich and Marquese, "O Vale do Paraíba."

12. Schwarz, "Misplaced Ideas." About that debate, see Bosi, *Brazil and the Dialectic of Colonization*, chap. 7, "Slavery between Two Liberalisms."

13. Pontes de Miranda, *Fontes e evolução*, 456.

14. Pontes de Miranda, 441–42.

15. Pontes de Miranda, *Sistema de ciência* and *Tratado de direito privado*.

16. The jurist Tobias Barreto (1839–1889) was also a lawyer, a deputy in the province of Pernambuco, and a professor at the Faculty of Law of Recife, where he was responsible for the introduction of positivist ideas.

17. The Pernambuco juridical tradition emerged from the School of Recife, which inaugurated a tradition of criticizing Catholicism, monarchy, and romanticism, based on positivism, evolutionism, and Darwinism, beginning in the 1870s; the racial question, based on racial determinism, in which the human race was believed to be at different levels of biological evolution, was one of the major concerns of the intellectuals associated with this movement. See Schwarcz, *O espetáculo das raças*; Venâncio Filho, *Das arcadas ao Bacharelismo*. On Pontes de Miranda, see J. Silva, *Pequeno opúsculo*; Correia, *Pontes de Miranda*; and S. Macedo, *Pontes de Miranda*.

18. Meira, *Clóvis Beviláqua*.

19. Beviláqua, "Instituições e costumes," 2–3.

20. See, for example, Graham, "Ciudadanía."

21. See, for example, H. Mattos, *Escravidão e cidadania*; Mendonça, *Entre a ação e os anéis*; Ribeiro, *A liberdade em construção*.

22. J. Carvalho, *Pontos e bordados*, 277.

23. J. Carvalho, 285–86.

24. J. Carvalho, "Cidadania: Tipos e percursos" and *Desenvolvimiento*, 51. See also, by the same author, "Dimensiones de la ciudadanía." Carvalho has reviewed important aspects of his work in more recent studies, many of which are the product of collective research projects. See, for example, J. Carvalho and Neves, *Repensando o Brasil*; J. Carvalho and Campos, *Perspectivas da cidadania*. See also T. H. Marshall, "Citizenship and Social Class," in his book *Citizenship and Social Class*. On Marshall's work, see Hirschman, *The Rhetoric of Reaction*; Turner, "Outline of a Theory of Citizenship"; Roche, "Citizenship, Social Theory, and Social Change"; Marx, "Contested Citizenship"; Bulmer and Rees, *Citizenship Today*.

25. The description of the process of secularization, organization, and bureaucratization of the modern state is one of the central themes of Max Weber's work. See especially Weber, *Economy and Society*.

26. J. Carvalho, *Desenvolvimiento*, 356.

27. This question grew out of reflections from Cooper, Holt, and Scott, *Beyond Slavery*.

28. For a reflection on the final period of slavery in the United States, see Berlin, Fields, Miller, Reidy, and Rowland, *Slaves No More*. On the Reconstruction in the United States, the classic work is Foner, *Reconstruction*. On a similar discussion about Jamaica, see Holt, *The Problem of Freedom*.

29. On Cuba, see Scott, "Fault Lines, Color Lines"; Ferrer, *Insurgent Cuba*; Helg, *Our Rightful Share*.

Chapter 1

1. Since the second half of the eighteenth century, Bahia had been divided into six administrative districts, or *comarcas*; the Recôncavo was the territory that surrounded the bay, located in the same *comarca* as Salvador, which had been Brazil's colonial capital until Rio de Janeiro supplanted it in 1763. See Mattoso, *Bahia século XIX*, 43.

2. According to Governor Fernando José de Portugal, in 1798 there were 138 *engenhos* (sugar mills) and 90 *alambiques* (stills) in Bahia, in addition to other plantations. Arquivo Público do Estado da Bahia, *Cartas ao governo 170*, pp. 10–13, May 24, 1798, in Schwartz, *Sugar Plantations in the Formation of Brazilian Society*, 425.

3. Luis dos Santos Vilhena (1744–1816) served in the military in Setúbal, Portugal. He became a professor of Greek in 1785, and in 1787 accepted a position in Salvador, Bahia, where he lived and worked until his death. Known for his descriptions and criticism of eighteenth-century Bahian society, he wrote several letters to the Portuguese minister Rodrigo de Souza Coutinho, in Lisbon. Vilhena, *Recopilação de notícias soteropolitanas e brasílicas contidas*, book 1. On the economy in late eighteenth-century Bahia, see Schwartz, *Sugar Plantations in the Formation of Brazilian Society*.

4. Vilhena, *Recopilação de noticias soteropolitanas e brasílicas contidas*, book 1, p. 48. For additional information on the population growth, see Alden, "The Population of Brazil in the Late Eighteenth Century"; Mattoso, *Bahia século XIX*, 82–87; Reis, *Slave Rebellion in Brazil*, chap. 1.

5. Spitzer, *Lives in Between*, 101–10.

6. "Apontamentos biograficos do Conselheiro Antonio Pereira Rebouças," n.d., Coleção Antonio Pereira Rebouças, Seção de Manuscritos, Biblioteca Nacional, I-3/24/60.

7. Spitzer, *Lives in Between*, 101–10.

8. The baptismal records of José and Antonio Pereira Rebouças are in the book of baptisms of the Parish of São Bartolomeu, in Maragogipe. *Livro de batismos 1788–1803*, Registros paroquiais, Arquivo diocesano de Salvador. "Brasil, Bahía, Registros da Igreja Católica, 1598–2007," images, Family Search (https://familysearch.org /ark:/61903/3:1:9392-8R9D-Y?cc=2177272&wc=M7ZY-1Z3%3A370085001%2C3700 85002%2C370085003: 22 May 2014). American historian Leo Spitzer cites the Marriage Registry in the Curia of Salvador and the Baptismal Registry of Maragogipe to confirm his claim that Rita dos Santos was freed. I believe he made this assumption based on the reference to the children as pardos. Spitzer, *Lives in Between*, 101.

9. On reenslavement and illegal enslavement, see J. Freitas, "Slavery and Social Life"; Chalhoub, "The Precariousness of Freedom"; Grinberg, "Re-enslavement, Rights and Justice."

10. On biographies and autobiographies of Antonio Pereira Rebouças, André Rebouças, and Antonio Pereira Rebouças Filho, see Apontamentos Biograficos do Conselheiro Antonio Pereira Rebouças, n.d., I-3/24/60; "Biografia," n.d., I-3/24/61, Coleção Antonio Pereira Rebouças, Seção de Manuscritos, Biblioteca Nacional; André Rebouças, *Apontamentos para a biografia do Engenheiro Antonio Pereira Rebouças Filho*; André Rebouças, *Diário e notas autobiográficas.* Very little is known about Escolástica, Luisa, Maria, Anna Rita, and Eugenia Rebouças; on José Pereira Rebouças, Mauricio Rebouças, and Manoel Pereira Rebouças, see chapter 2 and Spitzer, *Lives in Between,* 111–13.

11. Jancsó, *Na Bahia, contra o Império,* 157–212; Jancsó, "Adendo à discussão da abrangência social da Inconfidência Baiana de 1798"; Blaj, "Questões a respeito do movimento baiano de 1798."

12. Jancsó, *Na Bahia contra o Império,* 124.

13. Vilhena, *Recopilação de noticias soteropolitanas e brasílicas contidas,* book 1, pp. 13–14.

14. Geggus, "Slavery, War and Revolution in the Greater Caribbean, 1789–1815."

15. Genovese, *From Rebellion to Revolution*; Blackburn, *The Overthrow of Colonial Slavery.*

16. Thomas Paine, "How can Americans 'complain so loudly of attempts to enslave them' . . . 'while they hold so many hundreds of thousands in slavery?,'" quoted in Berlin, *Many Thousands Gone,* 220.

17. Drescher, *Capitalism and Antislavery*; Knight, "The American Revolution and the Caribbean"; Quarles, "The Revolutionary War as a Black Declaration of Independence."

18. On the rebellion led by Denmark Vesey, see Egerton, *He Shall Go Out Free*; Rasmussen, *American Uprising*; Robertson, *Denmark Vesey.*

19. Costa, *Crowns of Glory, Tears of Blood.*

20. Writing specifically about the Caribbean in the 1790s, Geggus refers to the revolts of Guadaloupe (1793) and Curaçao (1795 and 1800) that involved over 1,000 enslaved people; Grenada and Saint Vincent (1795/1796); Santa Lucia (1795/1797); and Guadaloupe again (1802). Geggus, "Slavery, War and Revolution in the Greater Caribbean, 1789–1815."

21. Maxwell, "The Generation of the 1790s and the Idea of Luso-Brazilian Empire."

22. Letter from Manuel José Novais de Almeida to Jacinto José da Silva, May 25, 1792, "Auto de exame que fizeram o desembargador ouvidor geral do crime Francisco Alvarez de Andrade e o Dr. Intendente General do Ouro, Caetano Pinto de Vasconcellos Montenegro, em todos os papéis do Dr. Jacinto José da Silva," Rio de Janeiro (January 8, 1795), in *Anais da Biblioteca Nacional do Rio de Janeiro* 61 (1939): 241–370.

23. Letter from Manuel José Novais de Almeida to Jacinto José da Silva, May 25, 1792.

24. On the Hausas, see Schwartz, "Cantos and Quilombos." The Hausas came from West Africa, and the majority were Muslims who were enslaved during holy wars in the late eighteenth and early nineteenth centuries.

25. On escravos "ao ganho," see Karasch, Slave Life in Rio de Janeiro, chap. 7; Nishida, Slavery and Identity, 35.

26. Conrad, Children of God's Fire, 404–6.

27. Vilhena, Recopilação de noticias soteropolitanas e brasílicas contidas, book 1, p. 136.

28. On manumission in Bahia, see Mattoso, "A propósito das cartas de alforria"; Schwartz, "The Manumission of Slaves in Colonial Brazil"; Nishida, "Manumission and Ethnicity in Urban Slavery." On manumission in other cities in Latin America, see Karasch, Slave Life in Rio de Janeiro; Hunefeldt, Paying the Price of Freedom; Sharp, "Manumission, Libres, and Black Resistance"; Dantas, Black Townsmen; Higgins, "Licentious Liberty" in a Brazilian Gold-Mining Region; Johnson, "Manumission in Colonial Buenos Aires, 1776–1810."

29. Although not comparative in perspective, there are many studies about the buying of freedom and manumission. To cite a few of these works, see Philips, Freedom's Port; Whitman, The Price of Freedom; White, Somewhat More Independent; Harris, In the Shadow of Slavery; Landers, Against the Odds; Brana-Shute and Sparks, Paths to Freedom; Schafer, Becoming Free, Remaining Free; Fede, Roadblocks to Freedom.

Chapter 2

1. "Apontamentos biograficos do Conselheiro Antonio Pereira Rebouças," n.d., Coleção Antonio Pereira Rebouças, Seção de Manuscritos, Biblioteca Nacional, I-3/24/60. (There are no dates or page numbers on the two handwritten manuscripts.) There were no law schools in Brazil until 1827, when the first ones were created in Olinda (Pernambuco) and São Paulo. Until that time, wealthy Brazilians could pursue a law degree in Coimbra, Portugal. As there was a lack of lawyers in the country, those who were self-educated in law could apply for special permission to practice.

2. In 1842, José Pereira Rebouças was a musician at the Imperial Camara. See Graças Honoríficas, "Pasta Antonio Pereira Rebouças," April 16, 1862, Arquivo Nacional, Rio de Janeiro. The same information can be found in codex 933, p. 2, also at the Arquivo Nacional. About José, see also André Rebouças, Diário e notas autobiográficas, 218. Antonio Pereira Rebouças's references to his brothers can be found in his book Recordações da vida patriótica do advogado Rebouças, 31–32 and 73. See also Spitzer, Lives in Between, 112–13.

3. The battalion, officially called Voluntários do Principe Dom Pedro (Volunteers of Prince Dom Pedro), was known by the name "periquitos" (parakeets) due to the green color of their uniform.

4. Manoel Maurício Rebouças, Tratado sobre educação doméstica, 6–7. Manoel Maurício also received the titles of Cavaleiro da Ordem Imperial do Cruzeiro and Conselheiro do Imperador.

5. Writing about the fight for independence in his memoirs, Antonio Pereira Rebouças specifically includes the participation of his brother, Manoel Maurício. He makes no mention of José Pereira, which suggests either that José Pereira was no longer in the army at this time or that the two brothers did not fight in these battles together.

6. In 1815, Brazil became part of the Kingdom of Portugal and Algarves, officially named the United Kingdom of Portugal, Brazil, and Algarves. On the Kingdom and on the 1820–1821 movement in Portugal, see Schulz, *Tropical Versailles*; Marquese, Parron, and Berbel, *Slavery and Politics*.

7. Antonio Rebouças, *Recordações da vida patriótica*, 30.

8. "Notas políticas de Antonio Pereira Rebouças," Rio de Janeiro, December 29, 1868, Coleção Antonio Pereira Rebouças, Seção Manuscritos, Biblioteca Nacional, I-3/24/59; and Antonio Rebouças, *Recordações da vida patriótica*, 30.

9. Antonio Pereira Rebouças, Junta Provisória da Cachoeira, June 26, 1822, Coleção Antonio Pereira Rebouças, Seção Manuscritos, Biblioteca Nacional, I-3/24/64.

10. "Biografia de Antonio Pereira Rebouças," n.d., Coleção Antonio Pereira Rebouças, Seção Manuscritos, Biblioteca Nacional, I-3/24/61. For other biographical works, see Antonio Rebouças, *Recordações da vida patriótica*; "Notas políticas de Antonio Pereira Rebouças"; "Apontamentos biográficos do Conselheiro Antonio Pereira Rebouças"; "Nota dos primeiros movimentos dos brasileiros na Bahia para a independência do Brasil redigida pelo advogado Antonio Pereira Rebouças, dirigida à Sociedade dos Veteranos, Salvador, November 12, 1865"; and Antonio Pereira Rebouças, "Discurso de sete de setembro pela Sociedade Ipiranga," located at the Coleção Antonio Pereira Rebouças, Seção Manuscritos, Biblioteca Nacional, I-31/30/5 and I-3/24/66. Portraits of heroes of independence can be found in Sobrinho, *Dicionário bio-bibliográfico brasileiro*; A. Souza, *Bahianos ilustres*; O. Souza, *História dos fundadores do Império do Brasil*; Taunay, *Grandes vultos da independência do Brasil*.

11. Francisco Gê Acaiaba de Montezuma's real name was Francisco Gomes Brandão (1794–1870). A mulatto lawyer from Bahia, son of the Portuguese merchant Manuel Gomes Brandão and the Brazilian parda Narcisa Teresa de Jesus Barreto, Montezuma got his law degree in Coimbra before joining the Brazilian independence movement. In 1822, after Brazil's victory, he changed his name to incorporate all elements of the Brazilian nation (Gê for the indigenous non-Tupi; the Acaiaba Tupi; and Montezuma in honor of the Aztec emperor). On his change of name, see Pena, *Pajens da casa imperial*, 23.

12. Antonio Rebouças. *Recordações da vida patriótica*, 83.

13. "Biografia de Antonio Pereira Rebouças," Coleção Antonio Pereira Rebouças.

14. Antonio Rebouças, *Requerimento dirigido*. Rebouças writes that he has great respect for Montezuma, even though the latter held an "illegally obtained" position, as he had managed to be elected deputy "by the most unusual means." See Pena, *Pajens da casa imperial*, 42–46; Venâncio Filho, *Francisco Gê Acaiaba de Montezuma*. A few years later, Rebouças reconciled with Montezuma: when he returned to Sal-

vador in 1823, he visited Montezuma in prison, where he had been sent for his stance against the dissolution of the Constituent Assembly. No grudges seem to have remained between the two, at least politically (see chapter 4). Carta do Visconde de Jequitinhonha a Antonio Pereira Rebouças, May 26, 1835, Coleção Antonio Pereira Rebouças, Seção de Manuscritos, Biblioteca Nacional, Rio de Janeiro.

15. At the session of September 27, the Constitutional Committee presented its opinion to the whole Assembly at Rebouças's request. In the presentation, the parliamentarians recognized that the determination of the votes in Cachoeira "had not been made with that gravity that the act required," but that they lacked information to draw any conclusions. The Committee indicated, however, that the government of Bahia required "an exact narration of all that had happened, and specifically with the citizen Antonio Pereira Rebouças," so that they could then issue a final verdict on the case. This most likely never happened, as the National Constituent Assembly was dissolved shortly thereafter. See *Anais do Parlamento Brasileiro 1823*.

16. Antonio Rebouças, *Recordações da vida patriótica*, 3. Leo Spitzer makes the suggestion that Rebouças, who had gone blind in his old age and had to dictate his memoirs, most likely dictated them to his son, André.

17. There are diverging beliefs about Montezuma's social origins. Katia Mattoso refers to him as coming from a "relatively simple" social environment, the son of a captain of a brig who worked in the slave trade; Eduardo Spiller Pena however, writes that "he actually was the son of a powerful slave trader from Bahia" who owned multiple ships. Mattoso, *Bahia século XIX*, 273–74; Pena, *Pajens da casa imperial*. See also note 16, p. 63.

18. "Biografia de Antonio Pereira Rebouças," Coleção Antonio Pereira Rebouças.

19. The Andradas brothers were José Bonifácio de Andrada e Silva (1763–1838), Martim Francisco Ribeiro de Andrada (1775–1844), and Antonio Carlos Ribeiro de Andrada Machado e Silva (1773–1845). The brothers were very influential during the years of Brazilian independence and the Emperor's Reign (First Reign, 1822–1831). José Bonifácio, in particular, was known as the Patriarch of Independence, as he was the Emperor's main political advisor and Minister of the Kingdom and Foreign Affairs (1822–1823). See Schultz, *Tropical Versailles*, chap. 6.

20. "Biografia de Antonio Pereira Rebouças," Coleção Antonio Pereira Rebouças.

21. São Cristóvão is a neighborhood in Rio de Janeiro, where the palace was located.

22. "Biografia de Antonio Pereira Rebouças," Coleção Antonio Pereira Rebouças.

23. "Biografia de Antonio Pereira Rebouças," Coleção Antonio Pereira Rebouças.

24. Rebouças recounted episodes like this one to André Rebouças many years later. On the dinner and the silence on racial discrimination, see Spitzer, *Lives in Between*, 121.

25. The president of the province was equivalent to a governor; the secretary was the second to the president of the province, or the vice-governor.

26. Freire, *História de Sergipe*, chap. 1. Nunes, *História de Sergipe*, chap. 4; Nunes, *Sergipe no processo de independência do Brasil*.

27. Manoel Fernandes da Silveira was born in Estancia in 1757. It is possible that he met Rebouças during the fight for independence in Bahia, when he became a leader of the Brazilian resistance against Portuguese troops in Salvador. Nunes, *História de Sergipe*, chap. 4.

28. Ofício de Manoel Fernandes da Silveira ao president da provincial da Bahia, April 21, 1824, cited in Nunes, *História de Sergipe*, chap. 4.

29. On the events in Pernambuco, see Quintas, "A agitação republicana no Nordeste."

30. Queen Njinga (c. 1582–1663) was the legendary and controversial Queen of the Kingdoms of Ndongo and Matamba, in Angola. See Heywood, *Njinga of Angola*. Rebouças was derogatorily referred to as the "grandson" of Queen Njinga in "Sergipe—Apontamentos para sua história," December 2, 1825, Seção de Manuscritos, Biblioteca Nacional, 19/4/13; also cited in Nunes, *História de Sergipe*.

31. Freire, *História de Sergipe*.

32. Proclamação do Presidente da Província de Sergipe, April 28, 1824, in IG1105—Ministério da Guerra—Sergipe—Correspondência do Presidente da Província, Arquivo Nacional, p. 215. In addition to works already cited, see also "Memorial Histórico da Província de Sergipe desde a época de sua independência, escrita com toda a imparcialidade oferecida ao Ilustríssimo e Excelentíssimo Senhor Presidente Dr. José Pereira da Silva Moraes por um sergipano," n.d., Seção de Manuscritos, Biblioteca Nacional, 22/2/33.

33. After the proclamation of the Brazilian Constitution of 1824, every authority had to swear loyalty to the Constitution in a public ceremony, normally at a local church. I. Souza, *Pátria coroada*.

34. In Portuguese, "morra tudo quando é maroto." This episode was recounted by the vicar himself, representing the commander of arms on July 10 of that year. IG1105—Ministério da Guerra—Sergipe—Correspondência do president da provincia, Arquivo Nacional, Rio de Janeiro, 131. See also "Biografia de Antonio Pereira Rebouças," Coleção Antonio Pereira Rebouças.

35. IG1105—Ministério da Guerra—Sergipe—Correspondência do president da provincia, 128.

36. A *zabumba* is a type of bass drum.

37. In the original, *marotos* (instead of Portuguese). IG1105—Ministério da Guerra—Sergipe—Correspondência do president da provincia, 123.

38. IG1105—Ministério da Guerra—Sergipe—Correspondência do president da provincia, 119. Also cited in Mott, "A revolução dos negros do Haiti e o Brasil."

39. IG1105—Ministério da Guerra—Sergipe—Correspondência do president da provincia, 161.

40. See Mott, "Violência e repressão em Sergipe."

41. "Ofício de Francisco Vicente Vianna de 20 de setembro de 1824, autorizando o transporte para a provincial de Sergipe, junto com Antonio Pereira Rebouças, sua família, e escravos Abrahão, Benedita do Gentio da Costa, e Antonio Cabra, e um crioulo de nome João," Seção de Manuscritos, Biblioteca Nacional, Rio de Janeiro, I-3/24/67. See also Arquivo Público do Estado da Bahia, Passaportes, G1-603, cited in Mott, "Violência e repressão em Sergipe," 10. Leo Spitzer's claim that, based

on the memories of Rebouças and his son, Rebouças would have acquired slaves only after his marriage to Carolina Pinto da Silveira does not seem accurate. Spitzer, *Lives in Between*, 123n52.

42. It states that Rebouças screamed "vivas ao Haiti." A copy of excerpts from the trial can be found in the document Carta ao Redator do Soldado da Tarimba, located in the folder titled Ofício de José Egídio Gordilho de Barbudo dirigido a Pedro de Araújo Lima sobre rebelião de negros, Bahia, 1828, Seção de Manuscritos, Biblioteca Nacional, Rio de Janeiro, I-31/13/13.

43. "The offenders have grown up in this way, and they are almost all men of color, because the Secretary of the Government Antonio Pereira Rebouças, a *pardo*, has indoctrinated and persuaded them that every *pardo* or *preto* can be a General." IG1 105—Ministério da Guerra—Sergipe—Correspondência do presidente da provincial, Arquivo Nacional, Rio de Janeiro, 128. My interpretation is corroborated by Felisbelo Freire, who argued that Rebouças was not a revolutionary, but a "free spirit," revolted by "the authoritarianism and arrogance that the aristocracy of Sergipe exercised over the people." Freire, *História de Sergipe*, 266–68.

44. Testemunho numero 5, Carta ao Redator do Soldado da Tarimba, Bahia, 1828, Seção de Manuscritos, Biblioteca Nacional, Rio de Janeiro, I-31/13/13.

45. IG1 105—Ministério da Guerra—Sergipe—Correspondência do presidente da provincial, 128.

46. Citizenship and voting rights are discussed in chapter 3.

47. Spitzer, *Lives in Between*, 122.

48. Hobsbawm, *The Age of Revolution*.

49. Ribeiro, *A liberdade em construção*, 307. See discussion in next chapter.

50. Antonio Pereira Rebouças, "Satisfação do dinheiro em moedas de ouro e prata dos Teixeira Barbosa, empregado de novembro de 1822 a julho de 1823 na manutenção vital do Exército pacificador empenhado na Guerra da Independência" (Rio de Janeiro: Typographia Nacional de J.M.N.G, 1860).

51. Proclamation of Pedro I on April 23, 1821, cited in Ribeiro, *A liberdade em construção*, 350–51.

52. Carta ao Redator do Soldado da Tarimba, Bahia, 1828, Seção de Manuscritos, Biblioteca Nacional, Rio de Janeiro, I-31/13/13.

53. *O Bahiano*, May 26, 1829; for a general overview of these events, see the editions from May 16 to 30, 1829. See also Silva, "Na trilha das garrafadas," available at http://www.scielo.mec.pt/scielo.php?script=sci_arttext&pid=S0003-25732012 000200002&lng=pt&nrm=iso. Accessed on June 26, 2018.

54. *O Constitucional*, no. 5 (April 20, 1822), 1.

Chapter 3

1. The National Guard was created in 1831 as an alternative "army" composed of the "good citizens" of the country, with the goal of "protecting the Constitution, and the integrity, freedom and independence of the Brazilian Empire," which basically meant "tranquility and public order." Kraay, *Race, State, and Armed Forces*.

2. *Anais do Parlamento Brazileiro*, session of August 25, 1832. Hebe Mattos analyzes the same speech in *Escravidão e cidadania no Brasil Monárquico*, 39–46. Miguel Calmon Du Pin e Almeida (Santo Amaro da Purificação, Bahia, 1796–Rio de Janeiro, 1865) was the main leader of Bahian resistance in Cachoeira against the Portuguese in the conflicts during the independence movement, presiding at the Conselho Interino (Temporary Council) in 1822 and 1823. Later, he received the title of Marquês de Abrantes and had a long career as a lawyer, politician, and diplomat.

3. *Anais do Parlamento Brasileiro*, session of August 25, 1832.

4. *Anais do Parlamento Brasileiro*, session of August 25, 1832.

5. The French decree of March 8, 1790, was ambiguous about the status of freed and free blacks as citizens and voters. Singham, "Jews, Blacks, Women, and the Declaration of the Rights of Man."

6. *Ingênuos* refers to Afro-descendants who were born free.

7. *Anais do Parlamento Brasileiro*, session of August 25, 1832.

8. *Anais do Parlamento Brasileiro*, session of July 28, 1830. José Paulino de Almeida Albuquerque (Pernambuco, unknown birth date) was president of the province of Rio Grande do Norte from 1826 to 1830. He died in 1830 while serving as deputy at the National Assembly in Rio de Janeiro.

9. P. Castro, "A experiência republicana, 1831–1840." Basile, "O laboratório da nação."

10. *Anais do Parlamento Brasileiro*, session of August 25, 1832.

11. On April 7, 1831, Pedro I resigned. He had been in power since his father, João VI, returned to Portugal in 1821, and Emperor of Brazil since independence in September. After years of political turbulence in Brazil and in a drawn-out battle with his brother Miguel over the Portuguese crown (Pedro I wanted his daughter Maria to be named successor), Pedro I decided to resign and return to Portugal. In his place, he left the young Pedro II, then a five-year-old child. About that period, see Ribeiro, *A liberdade em construção*.

12. From then on, conservatives loyal to Portugal were called the *restauradores*, signaling those who sought to restore political power to the Portuguese.

13. Rebouças referred to that episode in "O dia 30 de julho de 1832," *Correio Mercantil*, September 16, 1857; and in *Recordações da vida parlamentar*, vol. 1, pp. 239–50. See also O. Souza, *Diogo Antonio Feijó*, 176–78; Valladão, *Da aclamação à maioridade*; Ricci, *Assombrações de um padre regente*.

14. About this period, see P. Castro, "A experiência republicana, 1831–1840"; Barman, *Brazil*; Basile, "O laboratório da nação." Constitutional reform, discussed in October 1831, included a number of proposals, such as the constitution of a federal monarchy, the extinction of *poder moderador* (reserve power), a biennial election for the Chamber of Deputies, the change of the Senate to an elective and temporary—rather than lifelong—body, and the establishment of provincial legislative assemblies with two chambers.

15. According to the law of June 12, 1831, the "regência trina" was subordinate to the National Assembly in many ways. It could not, for instance, declare war, confer titles or honors, or dissolve the Assembly; the responsibilities of the Regency did include, however, naming ministers, senators, and civil servants.

16. Barman, *Brazil*, 168. On the conflicts between Portuguese and Brazilians, see Ribeiro, *A liberdade em construção*.

17. A reduction in spending for the military was attributed at the time to the large presence of Portuguese officers; however, most of the budget cuts had already been proposed and approved during the First Reign in an attempt to balance state finances. See Holanda, "Prefácio," xiv–xv.

18. P. Castro, "A experiência republicana, 1831–1840," 16–17.

19. Moreira de Azevedo, "O Brasil de 1831 a 1840," 23, cited in Valladão, *Da aclamação à maioridade*.

20. *Anais do Parlamento Brasileiro*, session of May 25, 1831, cited in J. Castro, *A milícia cidadã*, 23. Almost twenty years later, the conservative politician Justiniano José da Rocha ironically recalled that the liberals only decided to support the creation of a National Guard in Brazil when they became fearful of the "disorder" provoked by popular classes following the resignation of Pedro I. *Anais do Parlamento Brasileiro*, session of June 25, 1850, cited in J. Castro, *A milícia cidadã*, 18–19.

21. According to Jeanne Berrance de Castro, recruitment lists of the regular troops show that the majority of soldiers were poor and primarily black, freed only because they joined the military. Even though it was usual to grant freedom to enslaved persons who would voluntarily serve in the military, this tendency was highly criticized by many citizens. J. Castro, *A milícia cidadã*. On the recruitment of enslaved persons during the era of independence, see Kraay, "Arming Slaves in Brazil."

22. Bernardo Pereira de Vasconcelos was the Minister of Finance while Feijó was Minister of Justice. See O. Souza, *Bernardo Pereira de Vasconcelos*; J. Carvalho, *Bernardo Pereira de Vasconcelos*.

23. In the Cisplatine War (1825–1828), also known as the Argentine-Brazilian War, the Uruguayans living in Cisplatine Province declared independence from Brazil, founding the Republic of Uruguay.

24. On enslaved persons as soldiers and the struggles for independence in the Spanish American world, see Blanchard, *Under the Flags of Freedom*.

25. *Anais do Parlamento Brasileiro*, session of September 30, 1823. The speech is also cited in José Rodrigues, *A Assembleia Constituinte de 1823*.

26. Henriques de Rezende (1784–1866), born in Pernambuco, was a priest, canon at the Imperial Chapel, and vicar of Santo Antonio do Recife, and received the honorary titles of Commander of the Order of Christ and Officer of the Order of the Cross. Described as an "exalted Republican" in the national biographical dictionary, Rezende participated in the Pernambuco rebellions of 1817 and 1824 and was deputy multiple times starting in 1822. After a visit to the United States, he changed his political views and became a member of the Conservative Party. Blake, *Dicionário biobibliográfico brasileiro*.

27. José Rodrigues, *A Assembleia Constituinte de 1823*, 104–6.

28. After the dissolution of the Constituent Assembly of 1823, the Emperor appointed a group of ten persons to write the Constitution, which was then issued on March 25, 1824.

29. *Anais do Parlamento Brasileiro*, session of September 23, 1823.

30. On slavery and citizenship in classic antiquity, see Finley, *Ancient Slavery and Modern Ideology*.

31. *Anais do Parlamento Brasileiro 1823*, vol. 5, p. 167.

32. *Anais do Parlamento Brasileiro 1823*, vol. 5, p. 184.

33. José Rodrigues, *A Assembleia Constituinte de 1823*, 115.

34. *Anais do Parlamento Brasileiro 1823*, vol. 5, p. 205.

35. On the comparative "status" of different patterns of citizenship, see the debate initiated by Marshall, *Citizenship and Social Class*. In Brazil, this debate was developed by W. Santos, *Ordem burguesa e liberalismo politico*; J. Carvalho, *Cidadania no Brasil*; and others.

36. Fitzsimmons, "The National Assembly and the Invention of Citizenship"; Sewell, "Le citoyen/la citoyenne"; Kent, *The Election of 1827 in France*; Singham, "Jews, Blacks, Women, and the Declaration of the Rights of Man."

37. Berlin, *Slaves without Masters*; Greene, *All Men Are Created Equal*; Foner, *The Story of American Freedom*; Grinberg and Peabody, *Free Soil in the Atlantic World*.

38. Marshall, *Citizenship and Social Class*, 19.

39. Constant, *Cours de politique constitutionelle*.

40. *Anais do Parlamento Brasileiro 1823*, vol. 5, p, 168. This quote is from Henriques de Rezende.

41. J. Carvalho, "Cidadania: Tipos e percursos." The first analysis of electoral participation and political citizenship was written by de Carvalho himself in the 1970s (*A construção da ordem & Teatro de sombras*). See also W. Santos, *Ordem burguesa e liberalism politico*, and Graham, *Patronage and Politics in Nineteenth-Century Brazil*. Since this book was published, several works on citizenship in Brazil in the 1820s and 1830s have been published, including, among others: H. Mattos, *Escravidão e cidadania no Brasil monárquico*; Ribeiro, *A liberdade em construção*; Slemian, *Sob o império das leis*; Pereira, *Ao soberano congresso*.

42. Marshall, *Citizenship and Social Class*, 18.

43. *Anais do Parlamento Brasileiro*, session of June 26, 1846. In this speech, Rebouças insists that it makes no difference whether a person was born enslaved or free in order to become a member of the National Guard.

44. *O Brasileiro Pardo* (Rio de Janeiro), no. 1, October 21, 1833; Aviso 211 do Ministério da Justiça de 8 de agosto de 1835; Aviso 28 do Ministério da Justiça de 9 de fevereiro de 1838. See also J. Castro, *A milícia cidadã*, 137.

45. In *O Bahiano* on May 26, 1829, Rebouças complains against the imprisonment of Captain João Marcelino dos Santos, which was carried out with no written order. The Viscount of Camamu, José Egídio Gordilho de Barbuda, was born in 1787; some references state that he was born in Rio Grande do Sul, others that he was born in Portugal. In any case, he arrived in Bahia in 1810 as the "tenente da legião de caçadores" (lieutenant of the legion of hunters). In 1817 he participated in the repression of the Pernambuco rebellion in Alagoas; he sided with Pedro I during the independence movement and until 1825 was the *governador de armas* (Commander in Arms) of the province of Bahia. From 1825 to 1827 he was president of the province of Rio Grande do Sul and, having already been awarded the title of viscount, he returned to Bahia as the president of the province in 1828. He was mur-

dered on February 28, 1830. On Rebouças's arrest and the Viscount of Camamu, see Silva, "A duras e pesadas penas," notes 14, 23–25.

46. Rebouças obtained 72 votes of the 188 electors who decided the deputies to the Legislative General Assembly on December 18, 1828; Francisco Gê Acaiaba de Montezuma obtained 79 votes. "Acta da eleição para Deputado no Colégio Eleitoral da Cidade," *O Bahiano*, December 20, 1828.

47. Kraay, *Days of National Festivity in Rio de Janeiro, Brazil, 1823–1889*, 60–67.

48. On the conflicts that followed in Bahia on April 4, after the Noite das Garrafadas, see D. Silva, "Na trilha das 'garrafadas': A abdicação de D. Pedro I e a afirmação da identidade nacional brasileira na Bahia." We don't know much about Carolina Pinto and her parents. Her mother died a few months after the marriage between Carolina and Antonio Pereira Rebouças on October 13, 1831. Her father was a "merchant" in Salvador, and left the capital during the independence conflicts and went to Cachoeira. Antonio Rebouças, "Graças Honoríficas," April 16, 1862, Arquivo Nacional. On Rebouças's participation in the conflicts in Bahia right after his marriage, see "Notas políticas de Antonio Pereira Rebouças," December 29, 1868, Seção Manuscritos, Biblioteca Nacional, I-3, 24/59; "Biografia," n.d., I-3/24/61. Antonio Rebouças, *Recordações da vida patriótica*, vol. 1.

49. Discussions on the conflicts and deportation of the Portuguese of the Conselho da Província in which Rebouças participated are in "Ata da Sessão do Conselho Provincial sobre os artigos estabelecidos pelos comandantes da força armada e povo," April 5, 1831, Seção de Manuscritos, Biblioteca Nacional, II-33, 33/32; "Ata da sessão ordinária do Conselho Provincial da Bahia em que se tratou da saída dos portugueses da provincial, pelos acontecimentos verificados no Rio de 14 d 15 de abril de 1831," Seção de Manuscritos, Biblioteca Nacional, II-33/33/7. The latter specifies the resolution to expel some Portuguese "in order to maintain quiet and tranquility, and also all the Portuguese monks, and the Portuguese who deserted the troops" as well as the "street vendors known for disturbing the public peace." It was also forbidden for unmarried Portuguese who were not traders, farmers, or day laborers to enter into Salvador unless they had been vouched for by Brazilian citizens. Rebouças was against this last measure; as he later wrote, "even [when it requires] the sacrifice of my own security in moments of greater popular revolt." Antonio Rebouças, "Graças Honoríficas."

50. Antonio Rebouças, "Biografia," n.d., Biblioteca Nacional, Seção de Manuscritos, I-3, 24/61.

51. I wasn't able to find the article itself, but Rebouças refers to it in *Anais do Parlamento Brasileiro*, session of June 25, 1832.

52. This was said by Carneiro da Cunha, at the session of July 26, 1830. *Anais do Parlamento Brasileiro*.

53. During the Islamic and medieval periods, a small number of Moors lived as slaves on the Iberian Peninsula. From the sixteenth to the eighteenth century, more than a million people remained enslaved there. Their presence was codified in Portuguese law in the three editions of the Ordenações. See Stanziani, "Slavery, Debt and Bondage"; Peabody and Grinberg, *Slavery, Freedom and the Law in the Atlantic World*.

54. Fischer, Grinberg, and Mattos, "Law, Silence and Racialized Inequalities," 132–34.

55. *Anais do Parlamento Brasileiro*, session of May 14, 1830, 144.

56. That specific paragraph was quoted fifteen times in the thirty-four freedom lawsuits that occurred between 1806 and 1832. About the freedom lawsuits in Brazil, see Grinberg, "Manumission, Gender and the Law."

57. Freedom lawsuit number 4, box 3, 688, September 7, 1827, São João d'El Rey. The lawsuit ends by reaffirming the enslavement of Felizarda Bernarda. (Pages are not numbered.)

58. Freedom lawsuit number 4, box 3, 688, September 7, 1827, São João d'El Rey.

59. Koster, *Travels in Brazil*, 404–6. Anthropologist Manuela Carneiro da Cunha corrects Koster, saying that the practice of *peculio* was not legal until 1871 (when it was legalized in the Law of the Free Womb of September 28, 1871, that, among other things, legalized savings earned by slaves) and that Koster doesn't seem to have differentiated between customary and positive law. Cunha, "Silences of the Law." On the *peculio* (personal savings), see also Chalhoub, *Visões da liberdade*, 108; Peabody and Grinberg, *Slavery, Freedom and the Law in the Atlantic World*.

60. Antonio Rebouças, *Recordações da vida parlamentar*, vol. 1, p. 3.

Chapter 4

1. Paquetá is an island in Guanabara Bay where Feijó lived.

2. José Bonifacio had been the tutor of the Emperor, but at this point was being persecuted by those in government.

3. Carta de José Bonifácio de Andrada e Silva, April 7, 1835, Biblioteca Nacional, Seção de Manuscritos, I-3/24/32. Other requests for help made to Rebouças can be found in the same section of manuscripts in the National Library in various letters from politicians and friends, I-3/23/24.

4. Antonio Pereira Rebouças, *Recordações da vida parlamentar*, vol. 1, pp. 85–86.

5. Although the Chamber of Deputies authorized the removal of José Bonifácio from the position of tutor of the Emperor, the proposal was rejected in the Senate by one vote. Barman, *Brazil*, 173.

6. Schwarcz, *The Emperor's Beard*, chap. 3.

7. See, for instance, letters from Martim Francisco Ribeiro de Andrada e Silva to Antonio Pereira Rebouças, July 2, 1840, Seção de Manuscritos, Biblioteca Nacional, I-3/24/33; I-3/24/35; I-3/24/36. His friendship with the Andradas was well known: in a tribute to Rebouças published after his death in the *Revista do Instituto Histórico e Geográfico Brasileiro*, a whole paragraph addresses his dedication to the Andradas, "who knew how to respond with greatness to the affection that so worthy and helpful an ally bestowed on them." "Proposta de um voto de pesar pelo falecimento do Conselheiro Antonio Pereira Rebouças," 544.

8. Even though the Brazilian Drama Conservatory was officially created only in 1843, Rebouças's first review is dated November 7, 1841. Rebouças probably reviewed the play at the request of the chief of police, who had the task of approving all theatrical performances that would play in Rio, and the text was then filed with other

reviews in the archive of the Brazilian Drama Conservatory in the National Library. The review of *Isabel, the Orphan from Paraná* is from June 21, 1858. On the Brazilian Drama Conservatory, see J. Souza, *O teatro no Brasil*, 309–19.

9. "Biografia de Antonio Pereira Rebouças," n.d., Coleção Antonio Pereira Rebouças, Seção de Manuscritos, Biblioteca Nacional, I-3/24/61.

10. "Proposta de um voto de pesar pelo falecimento do Conselheiro Antonio Pereira Rebouças," 544.

11. Letter from Diogo Antonio Feijó to Antonio Pereira Rebouças, Vitória, November 15, 1842, Seção de Manuscritos, Biblioteca Nacional, I-3/23/20.

12. Gonçalves Martins, "Simples e breve exposição de motivos sobre a Sabinada," 59–60.

13. Gonçalves Martins, 59–60.

14. Rebouças was not elected to the National Assembly in 1834, but had a position at the Provincial Assembly of Bahia at that time.

15. In 1837, for example, Caetano Silvestre da Silva wrote from Maceió, in the state of Alagoas, to Rebouças asking him to intercede with the Minister of Justice, "his close friend," to help him obtain a position as a judge in the Court of Appeals in Bahia. A few years later, Antonio Simões da Silva made a similar request, knowing that "Rebouças has a close relationship with the Minister of the Empire." Seção de Manuscritos, Biblioteca Nacional, I-3/24/24; I-3/24/26; I-3/24/31 (letters from Caetano Silvestre da Silva) and I-3/24/20; I-3/24/21 (letters from Antonio Simões da Silva). On the politics of patronage in Brazil, see Graham, *Patronage and Politics in Nineteenth-Century Brazil*.

16. Carta do Visconde de Jequitinhonha (Montezuma) a Rebouças, May 26, 1835, Seção de Manuscritos, Biblioteca Nacional, I-3/23/35.

17. Carta de Antonio Paulino Limpo de Abreu about his nomination to the Ministry of Justice, Rio de Janeiro, August 24, 1840, Seção de Manuscritos, Biblioteca Nacional, I-3/23/1.

18. "Biografia de Antonio Pereira Rebouças," n.d., Coleção Antonio Pereira Rebouças, Seção de Manuscritos, Biblioteca Nacional, I-3/24/61.

19. On the role of the Bahians in nineteenth-century national politics, see Mattoso, *Bahia século XIX*.

20. Francisco Gonçalves Martins (1807–1872), born in Santo Amaro, Portugal, was the son of Colonel Raymundo Gonçalves Martins. After studying for some years in Coimbra, he became involved in political movements supporting the Queen of Portugal, Dona Maria II (1819–1853), and immigrated to Spain. He returned to Brazil in 1830. Even though he did not finish his degree, he received a bachelor's degree for having fought in the academic battalion of the university. In addition to being chief of police, he was a judge in Bahia, and retired as a member of the Supreme Court of Justice. Blake, *Dicionário bio-bibliográfico brasileiro*. See also P. Souza, *A Sabinada*, 49–52.

21. Rebouças wrote a response to Francisco Gonçalves Martins's account of Bahian politics in the 1830s, in particular his reports about Sabinada. Most likely he delivered his text as a speech in the Provincial Assembly before publishing it as a small book, *Ao Sr. Chefe de Polícia Gonçalves, responde o Rebouças*. In addition to

criticizing how Gonçalves Martins handled the safety of citizens during the revolts of 1832, 1835, and 1837, Rebouças also reported that when he moved to Rio, after helping Gonçalves Martins be appointed to formal positions, he saw that he was "very ambitious and hungry for advancement and power." Two letters from Gonçalves Martins to Rebouças from July 1831 substantiate the connections between the two men: July 15 and July 22, 1831, Seção de Manuscritos, Biblioteca Nacional, I-3/23/58 and I-3/23/39.

22. Rebouças held the position of deputy in 1837 and was elected again in 1841. The Chamber was dissolved in 1842, and Rebouças was elected again at the next election in 1843. Antonio Rebouças, *Recordações da vida parlamentar*, vol. 2.

23. André Rebouças was born on January 13, 1838, and his brother Antonio Pereira Rebouças Filho on June 13, 1839.

24. The Malê revolt was an important slave revolt in Brazil that was organized by Muslim Africans (referred to as *malês*) and took place on January 24, 1835. The uprising was severely repressed by the authorities, and many Africans were deported; of those who escaped, many moved to other cities, such as Rio de Janeiro and São Luís do Maranhão, seeking refuge. For more on the rebellion, see Reis, *Slave Rebellion in Brazil*.

25. Antonio Pereira Rebouças, *Ao Sr. Chefe de Polícia Gonçalves, responde o Rebouças*.

26. In addition to the information in *Ao Sr. Chefe de Polícia*, this story is based on Reis, *Slave Rebellion in Brazil*, 73–83.

27. Antonio Rebouças, *Ao Sr. Chefe de Polícia*.

28. Antonio Rebouças, 86.

29. Antonio Rebouças, 37.

30. *Anais do Parlamento Brasileiro*, session of April 27, 1843 (emphasis added).

31. The Sabinada revolt (November 17, 1837, to March 16, 1838) was named after its leader, the black doctor Francisco Sabino Alvares da Rocha Vieira, a radical liberal. Even though the revolt did not advocate the abolition of slavery, many poor blacks and mulattoes who sought to extend their political rights supported the uprising. Grinberg, "A Sabinada e a politização da cor na década de 1830."

32. "Graças Honoríficas" in "Pasta Antonio Pereira Rebouças," April 16, 1862, Arquivo Nacional. The friendship between Rebouças and Vasconcelos is evident in a letter written by Vasconcelos to Rebouças in 1837, in which he shares his political fears and emphasizes his trust in Rebouças: "I trust you very much. . . . I very much want you to tell me your thoughts about the administration of justice, outlining any idea that you have. . . . Your friend, and thank you, Bernardo Pereira de Vasconcelos." Letter of November 14, 1837, Seção de Manuscritos, Biblioteca Nacional, I-3/24/29.

33. Antonio Rebouças, *Recordações da vida patriótica*, 101.

34. Kraay, "'As Terrifying as Unexpected.'" See also Reis, *Slave Rebellion in Brazil*, and P. Souza, *A Sabinada*, 165–68.

35. Kraay argues that since 1831, with the first military reforms, Bahian officials had begun to express their dissatisfaction with the policy of the capital. In 1835, 60 percent of Salvador's military men signed a petition complaining about the lack

of promotions since 1824, the low wages, and the creation of the National Guard, a "monstrous organization." Kraay, "'As Terrifying as Unexpected,'" 508–13. In a study of another social revolt, the Balaiada, Matthias R. Assunção also finds evidence of popular discontent related to the military and military recruitment preceding the revolt. Assunção, "Elite Politics and Popular Rebellion in the Construction of Post-Colonial Order."

36. Antonio Rebouças, *Recordações da vida patriótica*, 103.

37. *Anais do Parlamento Brasileiro*, session of April 27, 1843.

38. P. Souza, *A Sabinada*, 49; Antonio Rebouças, *Ao Sr. Chefe da Polícia*.

39. On the crimes, see P. Souza, *A Sabinada*.

40. Paulo Cesar Souza estimates that nearly 5,000 individuals were arrested, wounded, or killed during the attack on Salvador, which would total 7.7 percent of the city's population. During the five-month siege of the city, the rebels were left without flour and had serious difficulties in providing basic food to the population. Information on the basic conditions of survival and Governor Barreto Pedroso's hesitations in initiating an attack can be found in "A Sabinada nas Cartas de Barreto Pedroso a Rebouças."

41. At that time, Rebouças had already expressed concerns about the education of his children, and chose engineering as a profession for his two sons: "I will use all possible means to form the Hearts of my Sons well, but when it comes to their choice of profession, I will watch over them in their inclination or vocation; because I am persuaded that the Shoemaker, the Mason, the Blacksmith, the Carpenter, the Tailor, or any other mechanical Artist, with intelligence, skill, and good comportment, is more worthy of esteem and consideration in a well-established Civil Society than the fallacy of the Magistrate fallacy, who, with no knowledge or decorum, is harmful to Justice, subversive to the Homeland, and a constant public calamity." Antonio Rebouças, *Ao Sr. Chefe de Polícia*.

42. Antonio Rebouças, *Recordações da vida patriótica*, 104–5. See also "O bem que fez e o mal que evitou: Notas políticas de Antonio Pereira Rebouças," December 29, 1868, Seção de Manuscritos, Biblioteca Nacional, I-3/24/59.

43. On judicial reform and the views of Nabuco de Araújo, see Nabuco, *Um estadista do Império*, vol. 1, pp. 182–97. See also Flory, *Judge and Jury in Imperial Brazil, 1808–1871*.

44. Letter from Marquês de Olinda, November 16, 1837. See also letter from Maciel Monteiro, December 31, 1837, in which he reiterates his confidence in Rebouças's loyalty, mainly regarding the pacification of Salvador. Seção de Manuscritos, Biblioteca Nacional, I-3/23/62, I-3/23/29.

45. *Anais do Parlamento Brasileiro*, session of May 13, 1843.

46. In 1833, a prison clerk described Sabino as being of "medium height, rounded head, large, broad forehead with a scar across it, thick eyebrows, brown curly hair, large blue eyes, a rather broad nose, thin lips, a full beard and small sideburns, and a scar on the side of the lower left chin." P. Souza, *A Sabinada*, 46. Luiz Viana Filho described him as having thin lips, "blue eyes, very vivid, contrasting with curly brown hair and broad nose, which betray black ancestry." See Viana Filho, *A Sabinada*, 67.

47. Rebouças had the complete works of Voltaire and Montesquieu in the original. See the will of Carolina Pinto Rebouças, file 693, box 4029, 1865, Arquivo Nacional.

48. Although the leaders of the Sabinada were not seeking to abolish slavery, in January 1838 they created a battalion of freedmen in which any slave could enlist to address the issue of soldiers who refused to fight alongside the many slaves who had volunteered. The recruitment of slaves provided compensation to the masters, and Africans were excluded from taking part. Kraay, "'As Terrifying as Unexpected,'" 517–18.

49. Kraay, 517–18.

50. Kraay, 516–17. In a letter to Rebouças, Barreto Pedroso also mentions the large number of slaves recruited to join the revolt: "The forces of Pernambuco have five hundred men, and Sergipe one hundred. They are great people, but you know the rebels have the blacks, who are vigorous fighters." "A Sabinada nas cartas de Barreto Pedroso a Rebouças," 214.

51. *Novo Diário da Bahia*, December 26, 1837, 2.

52. *Novo Diário da Bahia*, 2. Thank you to Hendrik Kraay for pointing out this document.

53. F. W. O. Morton, "The Conservative Revolution of Independence: Economy, Society and Politics in Bahia, 1790–1840," cited in Kraay, "'As Terrifying as Unexpected,'" 517.

54. *Novo Diário da Bahia*, December 26, 1837, 3.

55. See the "Speech of the Throne" of May 1838, in which the regent Araújo Lima describes the internal conditions of the country in encouraging terms, advocating the end of anarchy and republicanism in Brazil. *Falas do trono desde o ano de 1823 até o ano de 1889*, 187.

56. *Anais do Parlamento Brasileiro*, session of May 18, 1838.

57. Flory, "Race and Social Control in Independent Brazil."

58. Flory, 213, note 37. For Wanderley's quote, see *Anais do Parlamento Brasileiro*, session of 1846, vol. 2, p. 571.

Chapter 5

1. The "Coimbra generation," as they were called at the time, came to power between the 1820s and the 1840s and included notable figures such as the politician Honorius Hermeto Carneiro Leão (1801–1856), future Marquis of Parana, and the diplomat and historian Francisco Adolfo de Varnhagen (1816–1878). On the Coimbra generation, see J. Carvalho, *A construção da ordem*; I. Mattos, *O tempo saquarema*, 125; José Honório Rodrigues, *Teoria da história do Brasil*, vol. 1, p. 398. For a critique of this use of the notion of generation, see Attias-Donfut, "La notion de génération."

2. Bernardo de Souza Franco (1805–1875), future Viscount de Souza Franco, became Minister of the Treasury (1857–1858) and a senator. See Blake, *Dicionário biobibliográfico brasileiro*. J. Macedo, *Anno biográfico brasileiro*; I. Silva, *Dicionário bibliográfico português*, vol. 1, p. 385; J. Carvalho, *A construção da ordem*, 374.

3. These law schools in Brazil became an important space of sociability and political identity throughout the nineteenth century. See J. Carvalho, *A construção da ordem*.

4. Nabuco, *Um estadista do Império*, vol. 1, pp. 74–75.

5. Nabuco, vol. 1, pp. 74–75.

6. Joaquim Nabuco (1849–1910), son of politician José Thomas Nabuco de Araújo, and a politician, abolitionist, diplomat, and historian, was one of the most important figures of the late nineteenth century in Brazil. His main works are *Um estadista do Império* and *Abolitionism: The Brazilian Antislavery Struggle*, edited and translated by Robert Conrad (University of Illinois Press, 1977). See Bethell and Carvalho, *Joaquim Nabuco*; Salles, *Joaquim Nabuco*; Alonso, *Joaquim Nabuco*.

7. Nabuco, *Um estadista do Império*, vol. 1, p. 74.

8. After the political maneuvers of the liberals that resulted in Pedro II taking the throne at only fifteen years old, an episode commonly referred to as the coup d'état of 1840, the liberals organized the first cabinet of the reign of the new emperor; although it lasted only eight months (July 24, 1840–March 23, 1841), the liberals managed to be victorious in the next elections to the Legislative Assembly. The next cabinet, which was conservative, dissolved the House in May 1841, two days before the official start of that session. The prerogative of the Moderating Power to dissolve the Chamber when the political scenario was unfavorable was considered an outrage by several liberals at the time. Iglésias, "Minas Gerais," 405–6. On the liberal revolts of 1842, see I. Mattos, *O tempo saquarema*, 104–9; J. Carvalho, *A construção da ordem*, 188–205; Needell, *The Party of Order*, 104–18. For a good analysis of the dynamics of party politics in the Second Brazilian Reign, see Ferraz, "A dinâmica política do Império."

9. Letter from Montezuma to Rebouças, March 14, 1842, Seção de Manuscritos, Biblioteca Nacional, I-3/23/29. See also his letter dated October 30, 1842, I-3/23/40.

10. Nabuco, *Um estadista do Império*, vol. 1, p. 122.

11. Letter from Paulino José Soares de Souza, Viscount of Uruguay, to Rebouças, Rio de Janeiro, October 3, 1842, Seção de Manuscritos, Biblioteca Nacional, I-3/24/46.

12. Torres, *O Conselho de Estado*, 98.

13. I. Mattos, *O tempo saquarema*, 142–56. Based on his interpretation of Gramsci, Mattos develops the concept of a "projeto de direção para o Império" (project of direction for the Empire), a conservative political project led by landowners, slave owners, politicians, and bureaucrats to restrain social movements and control the political order.

14. I. Mattos, *O tempo saquarema*, 114. Mattos's concept of an "imperial master class" (classe senhorial) is based on the Gramscian view of class and refers to the political power of planters as a "form of national dominant class." Salles, "Passive Revolution and the Politics of Second Slavery in the Brazilian Empire."

15. Marcus Carvalho and Câmara, "A insurreição praieira"; Needell, *The Party of Order*, chap. 4.

16. Urbano Sabino Pessoa de Mello defended these ideas in April 1843. *Anais do Parlamento Brasileiro*, session of April 27, 1843.

17. The Ministério da Conciliação (Ministry of Conciliation) was formed in 1853 to help put a stop to the conflicts between the Liberal and Conservative parties and to create conditions of governability. Needell, *The Party of Order*, 168.

18. During the term of the Olinda-Souza Franco cabinet, between 1857 and 1858, Souza Franco authorized the issue of the currency not only by Banco do Brasil, but also by Banco Comercial e Agrícola, Bank of the Province of Rio Grande do Sul, Bank of the Province of Pernambuco, Banco Rural e Hipotecário, and Bank of the Province of Bahia. Nabuco, *Um estadista do Império*, vol. 1, pp. 379–80. On Souza Franco's ideas about the financial system, see his books: *Os bancos do Brasil; Discursos pronunciados na Câmara; A situação econômica e financeira do Brasil*.

19. On paternalism, see Antonio Rebouças, *Recordações da vida parlamentar*, vol. 2, p. 18; on banking freedom, see Franco, *História do Banco do Brasil*, 250.

20. *Anais do Parlamento Brasileiro*, sessions of May 22, 1840, and June 9, 1845.

21. *Anais do Parlamento Brasileiro*, session of September 2, 1837. On the liberal argument in favor of tax increases rather than repression against traffickers, see J. Carvalho, *A construção da ordem e Teatro de Sombras*, 279. On the end of the slave trade to Brazil, see Bethell, *The Abolition of the Brazilian Slave Trade*; Mamigonian, *Africanos livres*.

22. *Anais do Parlamento Brasileiro*, session of September 11, 1837.

23. *Anais do Parlamento Brasileiro*, session of June 6, 1846, pp 295–96.

24. *Anais do Parlamento Brasileiro*, session of June 6, 1846, pp. 295–96.

25. *Anais do Parlamento Brasileiro*, session of June 6, 1846, pp. 295–96. On the Portuguese laws, see Ana Cristina Nogueira da Silva and Keila Grinberg, "Soil Free from Slaves: Slave Law in Late 18th–Early 19th Century Portugal," in Peabody and Grinberg, *Slavery, Freedom and the Law in the Atlantic World*.

26. *Anais do Parlamento Brasileiro*, session of September 11, 1830, p. 496.

27. *Anais do Parlamento Brasileiro*, session of September 11, 1830, p. 496. I. Mattos, *O tempo saquarema*, 115. Rebouças was very familiar with Bentham's work, as evidenced by the presence of two works of Bentham in his library (which, in 1865, contained 2,008 volumes). Bentham's sentence is taken from Jeremy Bentham, *Principles of the Civil Code*, part 1, chap. 6, article 1.

28. He is referring to the Conservative Party, dominated by the slave dealers.

29. Letter from Martim Francisco Ribeiro de Andrade e Silva to Rebouças, April 6, 1841, Seção de Manuscritos, Biblioteca Nacional, I-3/24/39; also in a letter to Rebouças, Simões da Silva attributes his defeat in the elections to "African smugglers." Letter from Antonio Simões da Silva to Rebouças, February 13, 1841, I-3/24/21.

30. I. Mattos, *O tempo saquarema*, 220–23. On the slave trade and politics, see Florentino, *Em costas negras*, 224. See also Parron, *A política da escravidão*; Marquese, Parron, and Berbel, *Slavery and Politics*, chaps. 3 and 4.

31. J. Carvalho, *A construção da ordem*, 188.

32. Antonio Rebouças, *Recordações da vida parlamentar*, vol. 2, pp. 28–29.

33. *Anais do Parlamento Brasileiro*, session of April 27, 1843.

34. H. Mattos, *Escravidão e cidadania*, 33–35.

35. Blackburn, *The Overthrow of Colonial Slavery*; Sinha, *The Slave's Cause*, 55.

36. H. Mattos, *Escravidão e cidadania*, 12. Ira Berlin, *Many Thousands Gone*, 358–65. Cooper, Holt, and Scott, *Beyond Slavery*.

37. Ira Berlin, *Generations of Captivity*, chap. 3; Sinha, *The Slave's Cause*, chap. 5.

38. Antonio Rebouças, *Recordações da vida parlamentar*, vol. 2, pp. 525–26.

39. Rebouças, vol. 2, pp. 527.

40. Rebouças, vol. 2, pp. 537.

41. Rebouças, vol. 2, pp. 549–50.

42. Rebouças, vol. 2, p. 551.

43. Isaiah Berlin, *Liberty*, 166–217.

44. Flory, "Race and Social Control in Independent Brazil," 214.

45. *Anais do Parlamento Brasileiro*, session of June 26, 1846. It is interesting that Rebouças was asserting that anyone who had at least 400 réis of income—including the freedmen whose entry into the National Guard he was defending—would also own two slaves. This was most likely true. It is well known that one of the first steps taken by freedmen to ascend socially was to buy slaves, not only because they marked the distinction between the former and current life and were perhaps a protection from possible re-enslavement, but also because it was impossible to conceive of obtaining certain services any other way.

46. Resende, *Minhas Recordações*, 176.

Chapter 6

1. Antonio Rebouças, *Petição dirigida*.

2. Rebouças, *Petição dirigida*, 1. For statistics about lawyers in nineteenth-century Rio, see Coelho, *As profissões imperiais*, 90–91.

3. Coelho, *As profissões imperiais*, 151–91.

4. A receipt was received by Eusébio de Queiróz Matoso for the amount of 325 réis paid for the rental of the house at 64 Matacavalos Street during the months of November and December 1846 and January 1847; a letter from Eusébio de Queiróz Matoso to Rebouças includes a receipt for the payment of the quarter ending in July 1848. Seção de Manuscritos, Biblioteca Nacional, I-3/23/14 and I-3/23/15. André Rebouças also references this in *Diário e notas autobiográficas*, 13.

5. This information was taken from the will of Carolina Pinto Rebouças, file 693, Box 4029, 1865, Arquivo Nacional, Rio de Janeiro.

6. Antonio Rebouças, *Petição dirigida*, 4–9.

7. "Carta de habilitação para o exercício da advocacia," Antonio Pereira Rebouças, Seção de Manuscritos, Biblioteca Nacional, I-3/24/56.

8. Information about his books dates back to 1865, the year of his wife's death.

9. The Council of State had ten lawyers who were responsible for petitioning cases and advising Council members. Pimenta Bueno, *Direito publico*, 285–86. Unfortunately, I have never found the internal documents from the Council of State, where presumably the opinions written by the lawyers and the advice to the counselors would be held.

10. Antonio Rebouças, *Aos poderes*.

11. Antonio Rebouças, *Exposição.*

12. See, for example, "Parecer de advogados sobre uma consulta" and "Parecer jurídico," Seção de Manuscritos, Biblioteca Nacional; and "Consulta acerca de estar ou não sujeito a pena o raptor que contrai matrimônio com a raptada logo após perpetrar o crime," lata 386, pasta 5, Instituto Histórico e Geografico Brasileiro.

13. João Rodrigues, *Consultas jurídicas.*

14. All people legally considered "indigent" (including enslaved people, indigenous people, and orphans, for example) had the right to a public defender assigned by a judge. Telles, *Digesto portugues,* 195–96. See also Ordenações Filipinas, book 3, title 41, paragraphs 8 and 9.

15. Civil registries only came to exist after 1871, when it was also made mandatory to register slaves (Law 2040, September 28, 1871).

16. The burden of proof, as in any civil proceeding in Brazil, lies with the plaintiff. In this case, therefore, it would be up to the master to prove ownership of the slave, and not to the enslaved to prove that he is free, as the lawyer of the opposing party himself argues. Gilissen, *Introdução histórica ao direito,* 711–21. Case number 5849, box 3684 (1857), Corte de Apelação, Arquivo Nacional.

17. Case number 11.990, box 3679 (1862), Corte de Apelação, Arquivo Nacional.

18. When a freedom lawsuit began, the person whose slavery was in question was released from the master's control, and the judge appointed a "keeper," who was in charge of the person for the duration of the trial.

19. Case number 8367, box 3690 (1858), Corte de Apelação, Arquivo Nacional.

20. Rocha, *Instituições de direito civil português,* 350.

21. Moncada, "O 'Tempo' e o 'Trastempo.'"

22. Telles, *Digesto portugues,* 86–87.

23. Case number 6641, box 3683, Corte de Apelação, Arquivo Nacional.

24. The Atlantic slave trade to Brazil was prohibited first in 1831 in response to conditions by the British to recognize Brazilian independence, but there was opposition from Brazilian slave dealers and slave owners, and the law was continuously disregarded over the years, creating a space for a strong illegal slave trade, with a state willing to look the other way. A second law was passed in 1850, responding again to British pressure. Bethell, *The Abolition of the Brazilian Slave Trade;* Mamigonian, *Africanos livres.*

25. Case number 6641, box 3683, Corte de Apelação, Arquivo Nacional.

26. Case number 6641, box 3683.

27. Arnaud, *Les origines doctrinales.*

28. Pimenta Bueno, *Direito publico,* 419.

29. Constitution of the Brazilian Empire, Article 179, paragraph 22.

30. Article 544 of the Napoleonic Code. See *Napoleonic Code or the French Civil Code,* 150. See also Arnaud, *Les origines doctrinales,* 179. On how the concept of property changed from the influence of the Universal Declaration of the Rights of Man and of the Citizen, see Kaiser, "Property, Sovereignty."

31. On that occasion, the French Constituent Assembly eliminated "dominant feudalism" without indemnity. But the landlord's rights based on feudal prerogative were only officially abolished, also without compensation, on August 25, 1792. On

July 17, 1793, the French Convention declared that "all feudal titles, registrations, judgments, and decisions concerning suppressed rights should be sent to local agents in three months to be burned." Kaiser, "Property, Sovereignty," 333–34.

32. Arnaud, *Les origins doctrinales*, 194.

33. Arnaud, 194.

34. On the transformation of concepts of property and contract into common law in the eighteenth and nineteenth centuries, see Scheiber, *The State and Freedom of Contract*.

35. On the efforts to regulate property in Portugal in the eighteenth and nineteenth centuries, see the notes on Antonio Manuel Hespanha in Gilissen, *Introdução histórica ao direito*, 651.

36. Gilissen, 648. See also Hespanha, "Sobre a prática dogmática dos juízes oitocentistas," in *A história do direito*.

37. Case number 6641, box 3683, Corte de Apelação, Arquivo Nacional.

38. Rocha, *Instituições de direito civil português*, 356; Telles, *Digesto portugues*, 95.

39. Paula Batista, *Compendio de theoria e prática*.

40. After this decision, Domingos Andrade Figueira appealed once again, requesting that the case be reviewed by the Supreme Court. The document on the case ends here (sheets are missing), but it is most likely that the request was denied.

41. Caetano Alberto Soares (1790–1867), a native of Madeira, was a lawyer, a liberal congressman in Portugal in 1828, and also a member of the Brazilian Historical and Geographical Institute and president of the Institute of Brazilian Lawyers. He was known for his 1845 work *Memória para melhorar a sorte dos nossos escravos*. See the will of Caetano Alberto Soares, Arquivo Nacional, Coleção de Documentos Biográficos, Seção de Manuscritos, Biblioteca Nacional. For a critical view of Caetano Alberto Soares's trajectory, see Pena, *Pajens da casa imperial*, chap. 2.

42. Augusto Teixeira de Freitas (Cachoeira, Bahia, 1816–Rio de Janeiro, 1883) is known as one of the most important jurists in the Brazilian Empire, responsible for an initial draft of the civil code, *Consolidação das leis civis* (1857). On his life and career, see Pena, *Pajens da casa imperial*, and Meira, *Teixeira de Freitas*.

43. Soares, "Direito civil," 27–28. Caetano Alberto Soares posed the question during the session of October 8, 1857.

44. Soares, 28–30.

45. On the debate between Caetano Alberto Soares and Teixeira de Freitas, in which Perdigão Malheiro also participated, and the controversy surrounding the resignation of Teixeira de Freitas, see Pena, "Um romanista"; Meira, *Teixeira de Freitas*, chaps. 6 and 9; Nequete, *O escravo na jurisprudência brasileira*, chap. 11; Dutra, *Literatura jurídica*, 64–70.

46. Malheiro, *A escravidão no Brasil*, 50; Chalhoub, *Visões da liberdade*, 128–30.

47. Malheiro, *Escravidão no Brasil*. A similar definition is found in the manual of Antonio José Rodrigues de Oliveira, in which manumission is defined as "a gift that the master of a slave makes to him of his natural freedom." Oliveira, *Conselheiro fiel*, 91.

48. Case number 6229, box 3691, Corte de Apelação, Arquivo Nacional.

49. Ordenações Filipinas (1603) (book 4, title 11, paragraph 4). In the edition compiled by Almeida, see the notes on this title. C. Almeida, *Ordenações Filipinas*, 285–87.

50. This ordinance cites the maximum amount allowed for a gift without insinuation as 300 cruzados for the husband and 150 for the wife. According to Almeida, this value was tripled in the permit of December 16, 1814, and this remained the reference for fixing the value until the end of the nineteenth century. C. Almeida, *Ordenações Filipinas*, 861.

51. Case number 6621, box 3683, Corte de Apelação, Arquivo Nacional.

52. Inventory of Carolina Pinto Rebouças, 1865, box 4029, number 693, Arquivo Nacional.

53. Kaiser, "Property, Sovereignty," 326.

54. A. Silva, *Coleção da Legislação Portuguesa (1750–1762)*, 200; on the enslavement of indigenous people, see Monteiro, *Negros da terra*.

55. On the historiography of Brazilian slavery, see Hebrard, "Slavery in Brazil"; Reis and Klein, "Slavery in Brazil."

56. Machado de Assis, "Bons Dias," May 11, 1888, in Chalhoub, *Visões da liberdade*, 105. See also Schwarz, *A Master on the Periphery*, 99.

Chapter 7

1. Guimarães, *O Coruja*, 85.

2. Guimarães, 80.

3. H. Mattos, *Das cores do silêncio*, 212.

4. Chalhoub, *Visões da liberdade*, 173. See also by Chalhoub: "Slaves, Freedmen and the Politics of Freedom in Brazil" and "The Precariousness of Freedom in a Slave Society."

5. Chalhoub, *Visões da liberdade*, 104–8.

6. Chalhoub, 104–8.

7. N. Silva, *História do direito português*. See also Grinberg, "Interpretação e direito natural."

8. Candido Mendes de Almeida, "Introdução às Ordenações Filipinas," in Lara, *Ordenações Filipinas: Livro V*, 29–35.

9. Pereira, *O pensamento político*.

10. Robespierre took this idea from a passage in Montesquieu, where he claims to see in the judges "the mouth that pronounces the word of the law." "O espírito das leis, XI, 6," in Gilissen, *Introdução histórica ao direito*, 505.

11. Machado, *Tomás Antônio Gonzaga e o direito natural*, 81. M. Santos, "O século XVIII e o absolutismo português," in *Portugal no século XVIII*. Falcon, *A época pombalina*.

12. On educational reform in the Pombaline period, see A. Almeida, "A república das letras."

13. Arno Wehling and Maria José Wehling, "Cultura jurídica e julgados do Tribunal da Relação do Rio de Janeiro: A invocação da Boa Razão e o uso da doutrina. Uma amostragem," in M. Silva, *Cultura portuguesa*.

14. Imperial Constitution of 1824, title VI (on Judicial Power), Articles 151 and 164; Regulamento das Relações do Império do Brasil, Article 9, in Primeiro Livro para Registro de Decretos da Regência em nome do Imperador, códice IJ74, Arquivo Nacional, Rio de Janeiro. On the continuities between legal training in Coimbra and in Brazil, see J. Carvalho, *A construção da ordem*, 66.

15. Here I use the concept of the relative autonomy of lawyers and judges as conceptualized by Pierre Bourdieu. For him, the definition of law as a legal field would imply the perception of the specificity of the logic of law, which would produce a relatively independent universe of external pressures. Bourdieu, *Language and Symbolic Power*, 211.

16. Duarte, *A ordem privada*, and Faoro, *Os donos do poder*. Fernando Uricoechea's examination of the National Guard and José Murilo de Carvalho's analysis of the political elite were both part of this historiographical trend. Uricoechea, *O Minotauro imperial*, and J. Carvalho, *A construção da ordem*. Later, Sérgio Adorno wrote about the issue in *Os aprendizes do poder*, on the liberalism of law graduates in Brazil in the nineteenth century, as did, more recently, Edmundo Campos Coelho, who in *As profissões imperiais* analyzes the period of regulation of these three activities, which became professions between the end of the nineteenth century and the middle of the twentieth.

17. J. Carvalho, *A construção da ordem*, 18.

18. J. Carvalho, 55.

19. I first had access to these files while doing research that resulted in my first book, *Liberata*.

20. Azevedo, *O direito dos escravos*.

21. As we will see, not many of these attornies could be considered abolitionists, even among lawyers working on cases of appeal. See freedom lawsuits number 4065, file 1737 (1858); number 9067, box 3690 (1859); number 12126, box 3694, and number 12162, box 3690 (both from 1867).

22. See Grinberg, "The Two Enslavements of Rufina" and "Illegal Enslavement, International Relations, and International Law on the Southern Border of Brazil."

23. Coelho, *As profissões imperiais*, 92.

24. Case number 9552, box 3694 (1860), Corte de Apelação, Arquivo Nacional.

25. One of the obligations of the lawyer is "to offer his patronage free of charge to minors, the poor, and the miserable who appear helpless in front of Justice." Ramalho, *Prática civil e comum*, 17. According to the Ordenação Filipina, book 3, title 5, paragraphs 3 to 5, it had already been defined that orphans, widows, or "other indigent persons" would have the privilege to obtain guardians in court when necessary. By the Notice of January 25, 1843, it was stated that the "indigent" included the poor, captives, prisoners serving a sentence, the mentally ill, the mendicant religious, and so on. See Grinberg, *Liberata*, 63–70. Edmundo Campos Coelho raises the possibility that most of the attorneys assigned to represent enslaved persons in a lower court were untrained individuals who were primarily in charge of administrative issues concerning the court. Coelho, *As profissões imperiais*, 91.

26. Case number 6697, box 3683, Serro (1841), Corte de Apelação, Arquivo Nacional.

27. For biographical information on Domingos Martins de Faria, see the Manuscripts section of the National Library, box 732, file 45, and box 1001, file 8; Arquivo Nacional: Decretos Honoríficos, box 787, doc. 57; Registro Geral das Mercês, codex 137; Entrada de Estrangeiros: Passaportes, codices 377 and 422; Juízo de Ausentes (Processo de Arrecadação), no. 1084, box 517, 1865. Faria still owed 128,500 réis to the landlord, who had paid for Faria's medical appointments and medicine. The Order of Christ was a religious and military order created in Portugal in 1319. After Brazil's independence, it became the Imperial Ordem de Nosso Senhor Jesus Cristo, an honorific order; the titles of the orders were given in recognition of services rendered to the nation. Pang, *In Pursuit of Honor and Power*.

28. Biblioteca Nacional, Sessão de Manuscritos, docs. C 378,12 and C 872,50; "Graças Honoríficas," Miguel Borges de Castro Azevedo e Mello, Arquivo Nacional.

29. "Graças Honoríficas," Miguel Borges de Castro Azevedo e Mello, Arquivo Nacional.

30. Cipriano Barata (1762–1838) was a liberal doctor and journalist who participated in the Conjuração Bahiana in 1798 and the Pernambucan Revolution of 1817. He was also a representative of Brazil in Portugal in 1821. Elected as a representative of Bahia to the National Assembly in 1823, he refused to participate in the discussions on the Constitution because he thought there was not enough space for a free discussion. Barata, *Defesa do bacharel*. According to Paulo Garcia, Barata was not the actual author of the *Defesa*. Garcia, *Cipriano Barata*, 81–103. See also Morel, *Cipriano Barata*.

31. Juízo de Ausentes–Processo de Arrecadação: Domingos Martins de Faria: box 517, no. 1084, 1865; Manoel Francisco Rodrigues Pereira Galvão, box 592, no. 6128, 1844. Arquivo Nacional.

32. J. Carvalho, *A construção da ordem*.

33. *Anais do Parlamento Brasileiro*, session of September 6, 1843.

34. Coelho, *As profissões imperiais*, 92.

35. Nabuco, *Um estadista do Império*, vol. 2, p. 1007.

36. *Juiz de fora* referred to a municipal judge (*de fora* meaning from outside, not from the area); he served also as a president of the municipal town council. Flory, *Judge and Jury in Imperial Brazil*, 33.

37. On the professional life of Bernardo de Souza Franco, see Blake, *Dicionário bio-bibliográfico brasileiro*. Biblioteca Nacional, Seção de Manuscritos, doc. C12,4; Instituto Histórico e Geográfico Brasileiro (IHGB), envelope 34, box 634; Ministros da Fazenda 1822–1972. On Antonio Ferreira Lima, see in the National Archives, Segundo Ofício de Notas, vol. 20, p. 274 (1816); Patentes Militares-Alferes, box 1 (1813); códice 652 (1819–1820), p. 34; Decretos Honoríficos (Ordem de Cristo), box 787, doc. 1 (1824); Registro Geral das Mercês, coleção 137; Entrada de Estrangeiros, coleção 381, vol. 7 (1835–1836), p. 7v and vol. 4, p. 11; Mesa do Desembargo do Paço (1823), box 166, docs. 128 and 137; case number 1008, box 56 (1832); codex 544, vol. 21, pp. 62-116; Biblioteca Nacional, Seção de Manuscritos, docs. C-552-13, C-777-13, C-285-13, C733-56, C809-22. On Joaquim Thomaz Nabuco de Araújo, in addition to the already cited *Um estadista do Império*, see Egas, *Galeria dos Presidentes de São Paulo*; Inventário no. 2108, box 4174 (1850), Arquivo Nacional; Biblioteca Nacional,

Seção de Manuscritos, C906-13, C1018-98; C412-34; C1018-85; C1065-36. On Urbano Sabino Pessoa de Mello, see Coleção Sabino de Mello, IHGB; processo de penhora no 3269, file 2322 (1867), Juízo dos Feitos da Fazenda; processo cível no 3498, file 851 (1859), Juízo da Segunda Vara Cível; civil process no 3560, file 851 (1859), Juízo da Segunda Vara Cível, all at the National Archives.

38. J. Carvalho, *A construção da ordem.*

39. Pena, *Pajens da casa imperial*, chap. 2.

40. *Revista do Instituto dos Advogados Brasileiros* 30, vol. 2 (1867).

41. Urbano Sabino Pessoa de Mello (1811–1870), born in Pernambuco, graduated in law from the Faculty of Olinda. He was also a professor of philosophy and geometry at the Seminary of Olinda, and served as a judge in various places in Pernambuco and Rio Grande do Norte. He was a deputy representing Pernambuco in several sessions of the President's Assembly of the Institute of Brazilian Lawyers, an officer of the Order of the Rose, a member of the Historical and Geographical Institute of Brazil, and a collaborator of the institute's journal. He published *Apreciação da revolta praieira de Pernambuco in 1849* (Rio de Janeiro, 1849) in response to a book by Jerônimo Martiniano Figueira de Mello, *Crônica da rebelião praieira em 1848 e 1849.* On Pessoa de Mello, see Fonseca, *Manifesto politico*, and Blake, *Dicionário bio-bibliográfico brasileiro.*

42. Nabuco, *Um estadista do Império*, vol. 1, p. 697.

43. Soares, *Memória para melhorar.*

44. Cited in Nabuco, *Um estadista do Império*, vol. 1, p. 697.

45. Pena, *Pajens da casa imperial*, 43–49.

46. H. Mattos, *Das cores do silêncio*, 199–200.

Chapter 8

1. Antonio Rebouças, *Observações à Consolidação das leis civis*, 174.

2. Antonio Pereira Rebouças "Observações do Advogado Antonio Pereira Rebouças à primeira edição da *Consolidação das leis civis* do dr. Augusto Teixeira de Freitas," in Antonio Rebouças, *Observações à Consolidação das leis civis*, 173–75.

3. Augusto Teixeira de Freitas, "Satisfação em tempo," *O Mercantil*, no. 168 (June 20, 1859), cited in Meira, *Teixeira de Freitas*, 182–83.

4. Antonio Rebouças, *Observações à Consolidação das leis civis*, 272.

5. Rebouças, 274.

6. Pena, *Pajens da casa imperial*, 52.

7. Manoel Alvaro de Souza Sá Vianna, "Augusto Teixeira de Freitas, traços biográficos," 1905, cited in Pena, *Pajens da casa imperial*, 54.

8. "Relatório da Comissão Incumbida de Rever as *Consolidações das leis civis*," in Meira, *Teixeira de Freitas*, 105.

9. Letter from Augusto Teixeira de Freitas to José Thomaz Nabuco de Araújo, June 1854, cited in Meira, *Teixeira de Freitas*, 98.

10. "Contrato para coligir e classificar toda a legislação pátria e consolidar a civil," cited in Meira, *Teixeira de Freitas*, 101.

11. Francisco Ignacio Carvalho de Moreira, "Da revisão geral e codificação das leis civis e do processo no Brasil." This passage is a quotation from the opening speech at the Institute of Brazilian Lawyers given by Francisco Acaiaba Gê de Montezuma, "Discurso recitado pelo sr. Conselheiro Montezuma na sessão de instalação do Instituto dos Advogados em 7 de setembro de 1843." Both are reproduced in *Revista do Instituto dos Advogados Brasileiros*, years I and II, 1862, 1863, facsimile edition, special number, year XI (1977): 113 and 149, respectively.

12. Moreira, "Da revisão geral e codificação das leis," 152.

13. The appointment of Teixeira de Freitas to elaborate on the civil code was decided upon the promulgation of Decree 2318 of December 22, 1858. "Providência sobre a Confecção e Organização do Código Civil do Império."

14. "Relatório da Comissão Incumbida de Rever as *Consolidações das leis civis*," in Meira, *Teixeira de Freitas*, 105–8.

15. A. Freitas, *Consolidação das leis civis*, Article 37. The "Código Negro" (Black Code) was never compiled. According to Eduardo Pena, this would have been a "black code in the footnotes," since, in 1865, maintaining the decision not to insert anything relative to slavery in the main body of the text, there are only references in explanatory notes. Pena, "Um romanista," 36–37.

16. A. Freitas, *Consolidações das leis civis*, note 10, Article 38.

17. Freitas, note 10, Article 38.

18. Antonio Rebouças, *Observações à Consolidações das leis civis*, 22–23.

19. A. Freitas, *Consolidação das leis civis*, note 41 to Article 63, p. 71. In a note to Article 586, Freitas also considered that among the goods donated or left in a will with the clause of never being alienated were the slaves, who, in this case, could never be released. With an argument based on the same ordering, Rebouças also opposed this interpretation.

20. At least four such cases reached the Court of Appeals by 1859: box 3683, number 544 (1829); file 197, number 1329 (1834); box 3690, number 4524 (1851); box 3684, number 8501 (1859), Arquivo Nacional, Rio de Janeiro.

21. See case number 1484, box 3680 (1844), Arquivo Nacional.

22. Pena, *Pajens da casa imperial*, chap. 1.

23. A. Freitas, *Consolidação das leis civis*.

24. Freitas, note 2 to Article 411, in Antonio Rebouças, *Observações às Consolidações das leis civis*, 226.

25. Antonio Rebouças, 98–100.

26. A. Freitas, *Consolidação das leis civis*, 286–87.

27. A. Freitas, 286–87.

28. A. Freitas, 286–87.

29. Freitas, note to Article 421, in Antonio Rebouças, *Observações às Conoslidações das leis civis*, 158.

30. Antonio Rebouças, 200.

31. Rebouças, 201.

32. A. Freitas, *Consolidação das leis civis*, 74.

33. Loureiro, *Instituições de direito civil brasileiro*.

34. Ribas, *Curso de direito civil brasileiro*, note 3, pp. 28–29.

35. Malheiro, *A escravidão no Brasil*, vol. 1, p. 133. Perdigão Malheiro had already addressed the same theme in a speech at the Institute of Brazilian Lawyers: "Illegitimidade da propriedade constituida sobre o escravo.—Natureza de tal propriedade.—Justiça e conveniencia da abolição da escravidão; em que termos." *Revista do Instituto da Ordem dos Advogados Brasileiros* 3, no. 2 (July–September 1863): 131–52.

36. On the crime of reducing a free person to slavery, see Mamigonian and Grinberg, "Le crime de réduction à l'esclavage."

37. André Rebouças, *Diário e notas autobiográficas*, 283.

38. See Mattos, *Das cores do silêncio*, especially part II.

39. "O Sr. Conselheiro Rebouças," *O Novo Mundo: Periódico Ilustrado do Progresso da Edade* 5, no. 53 (February 22, 1875). New York.

40. Among the posthumous tributes to Rebouças, see "Proposta de um voto de pesar pelo falecimento do conselheiro Antonio Pereira Rebouças."

41. In 1867, André Rebouças wrote in his diary: "By nightfall, I had finished the biographical notes dictated by my father." André Rebouças, *Diário e notas autobiográficas*, 155.

Conclusion

1. After going back and forth with the commission that was formed to review his outline and revisions, Teixeira de Freitas wrote a letter to the government in 1867, stating, "There is deep disharmony between my current thinking on these matters and the views of the Imperial Government." "These matters" were the content of the civil code. Teixeira de Freitas wanted the code to address civil and commercial law, which would supersede the commercial code promulgated in 1850. The government, in turn, wanted the civil code to address only those aspects of civil law not included in the commercial code. After this, the lawyer officially disengaged himself from the task of elaborating the code. See Meira, *Teixeira de Freitas*, 368–87.

2. On Nabuco de Araújo's involvement in writing the civil code, see Nabuco, *Um estadista do Império*, vol. 2, pp. 1062–75.

3. This is the argument, for example, of Coelho Rodrigues, *Projeto código civil*.

4. The best analysis of the supposed mental illness of Teixeira de Freitas is by Eduardo Spiller Pena, who also considers how various authors saw signs of mental illness in Freitas's behavior. Pena, *Pajens da casa imperial*.

5. The controversy on the subject between Rebouças and Teixeira de Freitas was only closed by the latter, albeit reluctantly, after the promulgation of the law of 1871, as seen in his responses to Rebouças's observations published in the third edition of *Consolidação das leis civis*, 72–74.

6. Nabuco de Araújo, at the time, emphasized the problems of establishing a system in which children would be free and their parents enslaved. See, for example, the letter he wrote to the Sociedade Democrática Constitucional Limeirense (Limeirense Constitutional Democratic Society), in which he pointed out the drawbacks of no provision being made for those who would remain enslaved until the final abolition. Nabuco de Araújo, *O centro liberal*, 117–22. His son Joaquim Nabuco was also

one of those who pointed out inadequacies in the law of 1871. See Nabuco, *O aboli-cionismo*.

7. Speech delivered in the Senate on September 26, 1871, two days before the law was issued. Nabuco, *Um estadista do Império*, vol. 2, p. 840.

8. Nabuco, vol. 1, p. 845.

9. The Commercial Code of 1850 was taken as a legal code so "comprehensive, governing almost all relations of civil life related to obligations and contracts," that for many a civil code wasn't even necessary. Mercadante, *A consciência conserva-dora*. Pedro Dutra also makes this argument in his book, *Literatura jurídica no Im-pério*.

10. Caulfield, *In Defense of Honor*, especially chap. 1. See also Halpérin, *L'impossible code civil*.

11. Speeches by Nabuco de Araújo in the Senate on June 11 and 13, 1873, in Na-buco, *Um estadista do Império*, vol. 2, pp. 968–73.

12. In a letter to João Lins Vieira Cansanção de Sinimbu in 1877, Nabuco argues that these two propositions come "to be reserved for the Civil Code." Nabuco, *Um estadista no Império*, vol. 2, p. 974.

13. The Padroado was a system created by the Catholic Church and the kings of Spain and Portugal in which they represented the interests of the Church in the new domains of the Americas. In that sense, the kings had the power to represent the Pope, and had the duties to build, organize, and manage churches in their territory.

14. Schafer, *Slavery*, 19–25 and 220–37.

15. Teixeira de Freitas, *Código civil*, 23, note to Article 21.

16. Ira Berlin, *Many Thousands Gone*, 325–26.

17. Cooper, Holt, and Scott, *Beyond Slavery*, 14.

Bibliography

Adorno, Sérgio. *Os aprendizes do poder: o bacharelismo liberal na política brasileira*. Rio de Janeiro: Paz e Terra, 1988.

Alden, Dauril. "The Population of Brazil in the Late Eighteenth Century: A Preliminary Study." *Hispanic American Historical Review* 43, no. 2 (May 1963): 173–205.

Almeida, Anita Correia Lima de. "A república das letras na corte da América portuguesa: A reforma dos estudos menores no Rio de Janeiro setecentista." Master's thesis, Federal University of Rio de Janeiro, 1995.

Almeida, Candido Mendes de, ed. *Ordenações Filipinas*. Books 4 and 5. Reproduction of an edition from 1870. Lisbon: Calouste Gulbenkian, 1985.

Alonso, Angela. *Flores, votos e balas: o movimento abolicionista brasileiro (1868–1888)*. São Paulo: Companhia das Letras, 2015.

——. *Joaquim Nabuco: os salões e as ruas*. São Paulo: Companhia das Letras, 2007.

Anais do Parlamento Brasileiro: Assembleia Constituinte 1823, Rio de Janeiro: Typographia Imperial Instituto Artístico, 1874.

Anais do Parlamento Brasileiro 1846, facsimile ed. Brasília: Câmara dos Deputados, 1982.

Andrews, G. Reid. *Afro-Latin America, 1800–2000*. Oxford: Oxford University Press, 2004.

Arnaud, André-Jean. *Les origines doctrinales du Code Civil français*. Paris: Librairie générale de droit et jurisprudence, 1969.

Assunção, Matthias R. "Elite Politics and Popular Rebellion in the Construction of Post-Colonial Order: The Case of Maranhão, Brazil (1820–1841)." *Journal of Latin American Studies* 31 (1999): 1–38.

Attias-Donfut, Claude. "La notion de génération—usages sociaux et concept sociologique." *L'homme et la Société* 90 (1988): 36–50.

Azevedo, Elciene. *O direito dos escravos: Lutas jurídicas e abolicionismo na província de São Paulo*. Campinas: Editora da Unicamp, 2010.

Barata, Cipriano. *Defesa do bacharel Cipriano José Barata contra as falsas acusações da devassa tirada em Pernambuco em novembro e dezembro de 1824*. Rio de Janeiro: Typographia do Diário, 1825.

Barman, Roderick. *Brazil: The Forging of a Nation, 1798–1852*. Stanford: Stanford University Press, 1988.

Basile, Marcello. "O laboratório da nação: A era regencial (1831–1840)." In *O Brasil imperial*, vol. 3, *1831–1870*, edited by Keila Grinberg and Ricardo Salles. Rio de Janeiro: Civilização Brasileira, 2009.

Berlin, Ira. *Generations of Captivity: A History of African American Slaves.* Cambridge, MA: Harvard University Press, 2003.

———. *Many Thousands Gone: The First Two Centuries of Slavery in North America.* Cambridge, MA: Harvard University Press, 2000.

———. *Slaves without Masters: The Free Negro in the Antebellum South.* New York: New Press, 1975.

Berlin, Ira, Barbara J. Fields, Steven F. Miller, Joseph P. Reidy, and Leslie S. Rowland. *Slaves No More: Three Essays on Emancipation and the Civil War.* New York: Cambridge University Press, 1992.

Berlin, Isaiah. *Liberty: Incorporating Four Essays on Liberty.* Edited by Henry Hardy. Oxford: Oxford University Press, 2002.

Bethell, Leslie. *The Abolition of the Brazilian Slave Trade: Britain, Brazil and the Slave Trade Question.* Cambridge: Cambridge University Press, 1970.

Bethell, Leslie, and José Murilo de Carvalho, eds. *Joaquim Nabuco, British Abolitionists and the End of Slavery in Brazil: Correspondence, 1880–1905.* London: University of London, 2009.

Bevilácqua, Clóvis. "Instituições e costumes jurídicos dos indígenas brasileiros ao tempo da conquista." *Revista Contemporânea* 1, no. 1 (1894).

Blackburn, Robin. *The Overthrow of Colonial Slavery, 1776–1848.* New York: Verso, 1988.

Blaj, Ilana. "Questões a respeito do movimento baiano de 1798." In *História e utopias: Textos apresentados no XVII Simpósio Nacional de História,* edited by Ilana Blaj and John Monteiro. São Paulo: ANPUH, 1996.

Blake, Vitorino Alves Sacramento. *Dicionário bio-bibliográfico brasileiro.* Rio de Janeiro: Typographia Nacional e Imprensa Nacional, 1883–1902.

Blanchard, Peter. *Under the Flags of Freedom: Slave Soldiers and the Wars of Independence in Spanish South America.* Pittsburgh: University of Pittsburgh Press, 2008.

Bosi, Alfred. *Brazil and the Dialectic of Colonization.* Translated by Robert Patrick Newcomb. Urbana: University of Illinois Press, 2015.

Bourdieu, Pierre. *Language and Symbolic Power.* Cambridge, MA: Harvard University Press, 1999.

Brana-Shute, Rosemary, and Randy Sparks, eds. *Paths to Freedom: Manumission in the Atlantic World.* Columbia: University of South Carolina Press, 2009.

Bulmer, Martin, and Anthony M. Rees, eds. *Citizenship Today: The Contemporary Relevance of T. H. Marshall.* London: UCL Press, 1996.

Caenegem, R. C. *Uma introdução histórica ao direito privado.* São Paulo: Martins Fontes, 1995.

Carneiro, Maria Luiza Tucci. *Preconceito racial em Portugal e Brasil colônia.* São Paulo: Brasiliense, 1983.

Carvalho, José Murilo de. *A construção da ordem e Teatro de sombras.* Rio de Janeiro: Civilização Brasileira, 1980.

———, ed. *Bernardo Pereira de Vasconcelos.* São Paulo: Editora 34, 1999.

———. *Cidadania no Brasil: o longo caminho.* Rio de Janeiro: Civilização Brasileira, 2001.

———. "Cidadania: tipos e percursos." *Revista Estudos Históricos* 18 (1996): 337–59.

———. *Desenvolvimiento de la ciudadanía en Brasil*. Mexico City: Fondo de Cultura Económica, 1995.

———. "Dimensiones de la ciudadanía en el Brasil del siglo XIX." In *Ciudadanía política y formación de las naciones e cidadania no Brasil: O longo caminho*, edited by Hilda Sábato. Rio de Janeiro: Civilização Brasileira, 2001.

———. *Pontos e bordados: Ensaios de história e política*. Belo Horizonte: UFMG, 1998.

Carvalho, José Murilo de, and Adriana Campos, eds. *Perspectivas da cidadania no Brasil império*. Rio de Janeiro: Civilização Brasileira, 2011.

Carvalho, José Murilo de, and Lucia Maria Bastos Pereira das Neves, eds. *Repensando o Brasil do oitocentos: cidadania, política e liberdade*. Rio de Janeiro: Civilização Brasileira, 2009.

Carvalho, Marcus, and Bruno A. D. Câmara. "A insurreição praieira." *Almanack Brasiliense* 8 (November 2008): 5–38.

Carvalho, Maria Alice Rezende de. *O quinto século: André Rebouças e a construção do Brasil*. Rio de Janeiro: Revan/IUPERJ, 1998.

Castilho, Celso. *Slave Emancipation and Transformations in Brazilian Political Citizenship*. Pittsburgh: University of Pittsburgh Press, 2016.

Castro, Jeanne Berrance de. *A milícia cidadã: a Guarda Nacional de 1831 a 1850*. São Paulo: Companhia Editora Nacional, 1977.

Castro, Paulo Pereira. "A experiência republicana, 1831–1840." In *História geral da civilização brasileira*, vol. 2, edited by Sergio Buarque de Holanda. São Paulo: DIFEL, 1964.

Caulfield, Sueann. *In Defense of Honor: Sexual Morality, Modernity, and Nation in Early-Twentieth-Century Brazil*. Durham, NC: Duke University Press, 2000.

Chalhoub, Sidney. "The Precariousness of Freedom in a Slave Society (Brazil in the Nineteenth Century)." *International Review of Social History* 56 (December 2011): 405–39.

———. "Slaves, Freedmen and the Politics of Freedom in Brazil: The Experience of Blacks in the City of Rio." *Slavery and Abolition* 10, no. 3 (1989). https://doi.org /10.1080/01440398908574992.

———. *Visões da liberdade*. São Paulo: Companhia das Letras, 1990.

Coelho, Edmundo Campos. *As profissões imperiais: medicina, engenharia e advocacia no Rio de Janeiro*. Rio de Janeiro: Record, 1999.

Coelho Rodrigues, Antonio. *Projeto do código civil brasileiro*. Rio de Janeiro: Imprensa Nacional, 1893.

Conrad, Robert. *Children of God's Fire: A Documentary History of Black Slavery in Brazil*. Princeton, NJ: Princeton University Press, 1983.

Constant, Benjamin. *Cours de politique constitutionelle*. Brussels: Société Belge de Librairie, Imprimerie et Papeterie, 1837.

Cooper, Frederick, Thomas C. Holt, and Rebecca Scott. *Beyond Slavery: Explorations of Race, Labor, and Citizenship in Postemancipation Societies*. Chapel Hill: University of North Carolina Press, 2000.

Correia, Figueiredo. *Pontes de Miranda, o jurisconsulto do século*. Brasília: Câmara dos Deputados, 1980.

Costa, Emilia Viotti da. *Crowns of Glory, Tears of Blood: The Demerara Slave Rebellion of 1823*. Oxford: Oxford University Press, 1994.

Cunha, Manuela Carneiro da. "Silences of the Law: Customary Law and Positive Law on the Manumission of Slaves in 19th Century Brazil." *History and Anthropology* 1 (1985): 427–43.

Dantas, Mariana. *Black Townsmen: Urban Slavery and Freedom in the Eighteenth-Century Americas*. New York: Palgrave Macmillan, 2008.

Drescher, Seymour. *Capitalism and Antislavery: British Mobilization in Comparative Perspective*. New York: Oxford University Press, 1987.

Duarte, Nestor. *A ordem privada e a organização política nacional*. São Paulo: Companhia Editora Nacional, 1966.

Dutra, Pedro. *Literatura jurídica no Império*. Rio de Janeiro: Topbooks, 1992.

Egas, Eugênio. *Galeria dos presidentes de São Paulo: período monárquico 1822–1889*. São Paulo: Seção de Obras do "Estado de São Paulo," 1926.

Egerton, Douglas. *He Shall Go Out Free: The Lives of Denmark Vesey*. Lanham, MD: Rowman and Littlefield, 2004.

Falas do trono desde o ano de 1823 até o ano de 1889. Brasília: Instituto Nacional do Livro, 1977.

Falcon, Francisco José Calazans. *A época pombalina*. São Paulo: Ática, 1982.

Faoro, Raymundo. *Os donos do poder: Formação do patronato político brasileiro*. 2 vols. Porto Alegre: Globo, 1979.

Fede, Andrew. *Roadblocks to Freedom: Slavery and Manumission in the United States South*. New Orleans: Quid Pro, 2012.

Ferraz, Sergio Eduardo. "A dinâmica política do Império: instabilidades, gabinete e Câmara dos Deputados (1840–1889)." *Revista de Sociologia e Política* 25, no. 62 (June 2017): 63–91.

Ferrer, Ada. *Insurgent Cuba: Race, Nation and Revolution, 1868–1898*. Chapel Hill: University of North Carolina Press, 1999.

Finley, Moses. *Ancient Slavery and Modern Ideology*. New York: Viking Penguin, 1980.

Fischer, Brodwyn, Keila Grinberg, and Hebe Mattos. "Law, Silence and Racialized Inequalities in the History of Afro-Brazil." In *Afro-Latin American Studies: An Introduction*, edited by Alejandro de la Fuente and George Reid Andrews. Cambridge: Cambridge University Press, 2018.

Fitzsimmons, Michael P. "The National Assembly and the Invention of Citizenship." In *The French Revolution and the Meaning of Citizenship*, edited by Renée Waldinger, Philip Dawson, and Isser Woloch. Westport, CT: Greenwood Press, 1993.

Florentino, Manolo. *Em costas negras: uma história do tráfico atlântico de escravos entre a Africa e o Rio de Janeiro (séculos XVIII e XIX)*. Rio de Janeiro: Arquivo Nacional, 1995.

Floriano, Raul. *Ex-presidentes do Instituto dos Advogados Brasileiros, desde Montezuma*. Rio de Janeiro: Falcao, 1987.

Flory, Thomas. *Judge and Jury in Imperial Brazil, 1808–1871*. Austin: University of Texas Press, 1981.

———. "Race and Social Control in Independent Brazil." *Journal of Latin American Studies* 9, no. 2 (1977): 199–244.

Foner, Eric. *Reconstruction: America's Unfinished Revolution—1863–1877*. New York: Harper and Row, 1989.

———. *The Story of American Freedom*. New York: W. W. Norton, 1999.

Fonseca, Antonio Borges da. *Manifesto politico—apontamentos de minha vida politica e da vida politica do dr. Urbano Sabino Pessoa de Mello*. Recife: Typ. Commercial de G. H. de Mira, 1867.

Fonseca, Martinho da. *Aditamentos ao Dicionario bibliographico portugues de Inocencio Francisco da Silva*. Coimbra: Imprensa da Universidade, 1927.

Franco, Afonso Arinos de Melo. *História do Banco do Brasil (primeira fase: 1808–1835)*. 4 vols. Brasília: Artenova, 1973.

Freire, Felisbelo. *História de Sergipe*. Book 3. Petrópolis: Vozes, 1977.

Freitas, Augusto Teixeira de. *Consolidação das leis civis*. 3rd ed. Rio de Janeiro: Garnier, 1986.

Freitas, Judy Bieber. "Slavery and Social Life: Attempts to Reduce Free People to Slavery in the Sertão Mineiro, Brazil, 1850–1871." *Journal of Latin American Studies* 26, no. 3 (1994): 597–619.

Garcia, Paulo. *Cipriano Barata ou a liberdade acima de tudo*. Rio de Janeiro: Topbooks, 1997.

Geggus, David. "Slavery, War and Revolution in the Greater Caribbean, 1789–1815." In *A Turbulent Time: The French Revolution and the Greater Caribbean*, edited by David Gaspar and David Geggus. Bloomington: Indiana University Press, 1997.

Genovese, Eugene. *From Rebellion to Revolution: Afro-American Slave Revolts in the Making of the Modern World*. New York: Vintage Books, 1981.

Gilissen, John. *Introdução histórica ao direito*. Lisbon: Fundação Calouste Gulbenkian, 1988.

Gilroy, Paul. *The Black Atlantic: Modernity and Double Consciousness*. Cambridge, MA: Harvard University Press, 1995.

Godoi, Rodrigo Camargo de. *Um editor no Império: Francisco de Paula Brito (1809–1861)*. São Paulo: Edusp, 2016.

Goyard-Fabre, Simone. *Pufendorf et le droit naturel*. Paris: Presses Universitaires de France, 1994.

Graham, Richard. "Ciudadanía y jerarquia en el Brasil esclavista." In *Ciudadanía política y formación de las naciones: Perspectivas históricas de América Latina*, edited by Hilda Sábato. Mexico City: Fondo de Cultura Económica, 1999.

———. *Patronage and Politics in Nineteenth-Century Brazil*. Stanford: Stanford University Press, 1990.

Greene, Jack P. *All Men Are Created Equal: Some Reflections on the Character of the American Revolution*. Oxford: Clarendon Press, 1976.

Grinberg, Keila. "A Sabinada e a politização da cor na década de 1830." In *O Brasil imperial*, vol. 2, edited by Keila Grinberg and Ricardo Salles. Rio de Janeiro: Civilização Brasileira, 2009.

———. "Illegal Enslavement, International Relations, and International Law on the Southern Border of Brazil." *Law and History Review* 35:1 (January 2017).

———. "Interpretação e direito natural: análise do Tratado de Direito Natural de Tomás Antonio Gonzaga." *Revista de História Regional* 2 (Summer 1997): 43–68.

———. *Liberata: a lei da ambiguidade; as ações de liberdade da Corte de Apelação do Rio de Janeiro (1808–1888)*. Rio de Janeiro: Relume Dumará, 1994.

———. "Manumission, Gender and the Law in Nineteenth-Century Brazil: Liberata's Legal Suit for Freedom." In *Paths to Freedom: Manumission in the Atlantic World*, edited by Randy Sparks and Rosemary Brana-Shute. Columbia: University of South Carolina Press, 2009.

———. "Re-enslavement, Rights and Justice in Nineteenth-Century Brazil." In *Translating the Americas*, vol. 1 (2013). http://dx.doi.org/10.3998/lacs.12338892 .0001.006.

———. "The Two Enslavements of Rufina: Slavery and International Relations on the Southern Border of Nineteenth-Century Brazil." *Hispanic American Historical Review* 96 (2016): 259–90.

Grinberg, Keila, and Sue Peabody, eds. *Free Soil in the Atlantic World*. New York: Routledge, 2015.

Guimarães, Bernardo. *O Coruja*. In "O bacharel de direito no século XIX: herói ou anti-herói?," by Eliane Botelho Junqueira. *Luso-Brazilian Review* 34, no. 1 (1997).

Halpérin, Jean-Louis. *L'impossible code civil*. Paris: Presses Universitaires de France, 1992.

Harris, Leslie. *In the Shadow of Slavery: African Americans in New York City, 1626–1863*. Chicago: University of Chicago Press, 2003.

Hazard, Paul. *El pensamiento europeo en el siglo XVIII*. Madrid: Alianza Editorial, 1991.

Hebrard, Jean. "Slavery in Brazil: Brazilian Scholars in the Key Interpretive Debates." *Translating the Americas* 1 (2013). DOI: http://dx.doi.org/10.3998 /lacs.12338892.0001.002.

Helg, Aline. *Our Rightful Share: The Afro-Cuban Struggle for Equality, 1886–1912*. Chapel Hill: University of North Carolina Press, 1995.

Hespanha, Antonio Manuel. *A história do direito na história social*. Lisbon: Livros Horizonte, 1978.

———. *Panorama histórico da cultura jurídica européia*. Lisbon: Publicações Europa-América, 1997.

Heywood, Linda. *Njinga of Angola: Africa's Warrior Queen*. Cambridge, MA: Harvard University Press, 2017.

Higgins, Kathleen J. *"Licentious Liberty" in a Brazilian Gold-Mining Region: Slavery, Gender, and Social Control in Eighteenth-Century Sabará, Minas Gerais*. University Park: Pennsylvania State University Press, 1999.

Hirschman, Albert O. *The Rhetoric of Reaction: Perversity, Futility, Jeopardy*. Cambridge, MA: Belknap Press of Harvard University Press, 1991.

Hobsbawm, Eric. *The Age of Revolution, 1789–1848*. New York: Vintage, 1996.

Holanda, Sergio Buarque de. "Prefácio." In Jeanne Terrance de Castro, *A milícia cidadã: a Guarda Nacional de 1831 a 1850*. São Paulo: Companhia Editora Nacional, 1979.

Holt, Thomas C. *The Problem of Freedom: Race, Labor and Politics in Jamaica and Britain, 1832–1938*. Baltimore: Johns Hopkins University Press, 1992.

Hunefeldt, Christine. *Paying the Price of Freedom: Family and Labor among Lima's Slaves*. Berkeley: University of California Press, 1995.

Iglésias, Francisco. "Minas Gerais." In *História geral da civilização brasileira*, edited by Sergio Buarque de Holanda. 3 vols. São Paulo: Difel, 1976.

Jancsó, István. "Adendo à discussão da abrangência social da Inconfidência Bahiana de 1798." In *História e utopias: Textos apresentados no XVII Simpósio Nacional de História*, edited by Ilana Blaj and John Monteiro. São Paulo: ANPUH, 1996.

———. *Na Bahia, contra o Império*. São Paulo: Hucitec, 1996.

Johnson, Lyman L. "Manumission in Colonial Buenos Aires, 1776–1810." *Hispanic American Historical Review* 59, no. 2 (May 1979): 258–79.

Kaiser, Thomas E. "Property, Sovereignty, the Declaration of the Rights of Man, and the Tradition of French Jurisprudence." In *The French Idea of Freedom: The Old Regime and the Declaration of Rights of 1789*, edited by Dale Van Kley, 300–339. Stanford: Stanford University Press, 1994.

Karasch, Mary. *Slave Life in Rio de Janeiro, 1808–1850*. Princeton, NJ: Princeton University Press, 1987.

Kent, Sherman. *The Election of 1827 in France*. Cambridge, MA: Harvard University Press, 1975.

Knight, Franklin. "The American Revolution and the Caribbean." In *Slavery and Freedom in the Age of American Revolution*, edited by Ira Berlin and Ronald Hoffman, 237–61. Charlottesville: University of Virginia Press, 1983.

Koster, Henry. *Travels in Brazil*. London: Longman, 1816.

Kraay, Hendrik. "Arming Slaves in Brazil from the Seventeenth Century to the Nineteenth Century." In *Arming Slaves: From Classical Times to the Modern Age*, edited by Christopher Leslie Brown and Philip D. Morgan, 146–79. New Haven, CT: Yale University Press, 2006.

———. "'As Terrifying as Unexpected': The Bahian Sabinada, 1837–1838." *Hispanic American Historical Review* 72, no. 4 (1992): 510–27.

———. *Days of National Festivity in Rio de Janeiro, Brazil, 1823–1889*. Stanford: Stanford University Press, 2013.

———. *Race, State, and Armed Forces in Independence-Era Brazil: Bahia, 1790s–1840s*. Stanford: Stanford University Press, 2002.

Landers, Jane. *Against the Odds: Free Blacks in the Slave Societies of the Americas*. New York: Routledge, 1996.

Lara, Sílvia, ed. *Ordenações Filipinas: Livro V*. São Paulo: Companhia das Letras, 1999.

Leme, Ernesto de Morais. *À sombra das arcadas: edição comemorativa do sesquicentenário da Faculdade de Direito de São Paulo, 1827–1977*. São Paulo: Revista dos Tribunais, 1979.

Loureiro, Lourenço Trigo de. *Instituições de direito civil brasileiro*. Rio de Janeiro: Garnier, 1872.

Macedo, Joaquim Manuel de. *Anno biográfico brasileiro*. 2 vols. Rio de Janeiro: Typographia Litografica do Imperial Instituto Artístico, 1876.

Macedo, Silvio de. *Pontes de Miranda e a universalidade de sua mensagem cultural*. Rio de Janeiro: Forense, 1982.

Machado, Lourival Gomes. *Tomás Antônio Gonzaga e o direito natural*. São Paulo: Martins, 1968.

Malheiro, Agostinho Marques Perdigão. *A escravidão no Brasil—ensaio histórico, jurídico, social*. 2 vols. Petrópolis: Vozes/INL, 1976 (1866).

Mamigonian, Beatriz Galotti. *Africanos livres: A abolição do tráfico de escravos no Brasil*. São Paulo: Companhia das Letras, 2017.

Mamigonian, Beatriz, and Keila Grinberg. "Le crime de réduction à l'esclavage dans le Brésil du XIXe siècle." In "Esclavage Contemporain," edited by Rebecca Scott and Jean Hébrard, special issue, *Brésil(s). Sciences humaines et sociales* 11 (May 2017).

Marquese, Rafael, Tâmis Parron, and Márcia Berbel. *Slavery and Politics: Brazil and Cuba, 1790–1850*. Translated by Leonardo Marques. Albuquerque: University of New Mexico Press, 2016.

Marshall, T. H. *Citizenship and Social Class and Other Essays*. Cambridge: Cambridge University Press, 1950.

Martins, Francisco Gonçalves. "Simples e breve exposição de motivos sobre a Sabinada." In *Ao Sr. Chefe de Polícia Gonçalves, responde o Rebouças*, by Antonio Pereira Rebouças. Bahia: Tipographia de Manuel Antonio da Silva Serva, 1838.

Marx, Anthony W. "Contested Citizenship: The Dynamics of Racial Identity and Social Movements." In "Citizenship, Identity and Social History," edited by Charles Tilly. *International Review of Social History* 40, Supplement 3 (1995): 159–83.

Mattos, Hebe. *Das cores do silêncio: Os significados da liberdade no Sudeste escravista—Brasil séc. XIX*. Rio de Janeiro: Nova Fronteira, 1998.

———. *Escravidão e cidadania no Brasil monárquico*. Rio de Janeiro: Jorge Zahar, 2001.

———. "Prefácio." In *Além da escravidão: investigações sobre raça, trabalho e cidadania em sociedades pós-emancipação*, edited by Frederick Cooper, Thomas C. Holt, and Rebecca Scott. Rio de Janeiro: Civilização Brasileira, 2005.

Mattos, Hebe, and Keila Grinberg. "Lapidário de si: Antonio Pereira Rebouças e a escrita de si." In *Escrita de si, escrita da história*, edited by Angela de Castro Gomes. Rio de Janeiro: Fundação Getúlio Vargas, 2004.

Mattos, Hebe, and Ana Lugão Rios. *Memórias do cativeiro: família, trabalho e cidadania no pós-abolição*. Rio de Janeiro: Civilização Brasileira, 2005.

Mattos, Ilmar R. de. *O tempo saquarema*. São Paulo: Hucitec, 1990.

Mattoso, Katia. "A propósito das cartas de alforria: Bahia, 1779–1850." *Anais de História* 4 (1972): 23–52.

————. *Bahia século XIX*. Rio de Janeiro: Nova Fronteira, 1992.

Maxwell, Kenneth. "The Generation of the 1790s and the Idea of Luso-Brazilian Empire." In *Colonial Roots of Modern Brazil*, edited by Dauril Alden. Berkeley: University of California Press, 1973.

————. *Pombal, Paradox of Enlightenment*. Cambridge: Cambridge University Press, 1995.

Mbembe, Achille. *Critique of Black Reason*. Durham, NC: Duke University Press, 2017.

Meira, Sílvio. *Clóvis Bevilácqua: sua vida. Sua obra*. Fortaleza: Edições Universidade Federal do Ceará, 1990.

————. *Teixeira de Freitas, o jurisconsulto do Império: vida e obra*. Rio de Janeiro: Livraria José Olympio/Brasília: Instituto Nacional do Livro, 1979.

Mendonça, Joseli. *Entre a mão e os anéis: a lei dos sexagenários e os caminhos da abolição no Brasil*. Campinas: Editora da Unicamp, 1999.

Mercadante, Paulo. *A consciência conservadora no Brasil*. Rio de Janeiro: Editora Saga, 1965.

Miki, Yuko. *Frontiers of Citizenship: A Black and Indigenous History of Postcolonial Brazil*. Cambridge: Cambridge University Press, 2017.

Moncada, Luís Cabral de. "O 'Tempo' e o 'Trastempo' nos costumes municipais portugueses." *Estudos de História do Direito* 2 (1949): 1–54.

Monteiro, John. *Negros da terra: índios e bandeirantes nas origens de São Paulo*. São Paulo: Companhia das Letras, 1995.

Moreira, Francisco Ignácio Carvalho de. "Da revisão geral e codificação das leis civis e do processo no Brasil." *Revista do Instituto dos Advogados Brasileiros*, years I and II (1862, 1863). Edição fac-similar, no. especial, ano XI, 1977.

Morel, Marco, ed. *Cipriano Barata: a sentinela da liberdade e outros escritos (1821–1835)*. São Paulo: EDUSP, 2009.

Mott, Luiz. "A revolução dos negros do Haiti e o Brasil." *História: Questões e Debates* 3, no. 4 (1982): 55–63.

————. "Brancos, pardos, pretos e Índios em Sergipe, 1825–1830." *Anais de História* 6 (1974): 139–74.

————. "Pardos e pretos em Sergipe, 1774–1851." *Revista do Instituto de Estudos Brasileiros* 18 (1976): 7–37.

————. "Violência e repressão em Sergipe: notícia das revoltas escravas (século XIX)." *Mensário do Arquivo Nacional* 11, no. 5 (1980): 3–21.

Motta, Marcia. *Nas fronteiras do poder: conflitos de terra e direito agrário no Brasil de meados do século XIX*. Niterói: Eduff, 2008.

Nabuco, Joaquim. *O abolicionismo*. Petrópolis: Vozes, 1977.

————. *Um estadista do Império: Nabuco de Araújo; sua vida, suas opiniões, sua época*. 3 vols. Rio de Janeiro: H. Garnier, 1899.

Nabuco de Araújo, José Thomaz. *O centro liberal*. Brasília: Senado Federal, 1979.

Napoleonic Code or the French Civil Code. London: William Benning Bookseller, 1827.

Needell, Jeffrey. *The Party of Order: The Conservatives, the State and Slavery in the Brazilian Monarchy, 1831–1871*. Stanford: Stanford University Press, 2006.

Nequete, Lenine. *O escravo na jurisprudência brasileira: magistratura e ideologia no Segundo Reinado*. Porto Alegre: Revista dos Tribunais, 1988.

Nishida, Mieko. "Manumission and Ethnicity in Urban Slavery: Salvador, Brazil, 1808–1888." *Hispanic American Historical Review* 73, no. 3 (1993): 361–91.

———. *Slavery and Identity: Ethnicity, Gender, and Race in Salvador, Brazil, 1808–1888*. Bloomington: Indiana University Press, 2003.

Nogueira, José Luís de Almeida. *Tradições e reminiscências da Academia de São Paulo*. 5 vols. São Paulo: Saraiva, 1977.

Nunes, Maria Thetis. *História de Sergipe, a partir de 1820*. Rio de Janeiro: Cátedra/ Brasília: Instituto Nacional do Livro, 1978.

———. *Sergipe no processo de independência do Brasil*. Aracajú: Cadernos da UFS, Universidade Federal de Sergipe, 1973.

Oliveira, Antonio J. R. *Conselheiro fiel do povo ou coleção de formulas*. Rio de Janeiro: H. Laemmert, 1884.

Pang, Eul-Soo. *In Pursuit of Honor and Power: Noblemen of the Southern Cross in Nineteenth-Century Brazil*. Tuscaloosa: University of Alabama Press, 1988.

Parron, Tamis. *A política da escravidão no Império do Brasil, 1826–1865*. Rio de Janeiro: Civilização Brasileira, 2011.

Paula Batista, Francisco de. *Compêndio de teoria e prática do processo civil*. Rio de Janeiro: Russell, 2002.

Peabody, Sue, and Keila Grinberg. *Slavery, Freedom and the Law in the Atlantic World*. New York: Bedford Books, 2007.

Pena, Eduardo Spiller. *Pajens da casa imperial: jurisconsultos, escravidão e a lei de 1871*. Campinas: Editora da Unicamp, 2001.

———. "Um romanista entre a escravidão e a liberdade." *Afro-Asia* 18 (1996): 33–75.

Pereira, José Esteves. *O pensamento político em Portugal no século XVIII: Antonio Ribeiro dos Santos*. Lisbon: Imprensa Nacional/Casa da Moeda, 1983.

Pereira, Vantuil. *Ao soberano congresso: direitos do cidadão na formação do estado imperial brasileiro (1822–1831)*. São Paulo: Alameda, 2010.

Philips, Christopher. *Freedom's Port: The African American Community of Baltimore, 1790–1860*. Champaign: University of Illinois Press, 1997.

Pimenta Bueno, José Antonio. *Direito público brasileiro e analyse da constituição do Império*. Rio de Janeiro: Typographia Imperial de J. Villeneuve, 1857.

Pinto, Ana Flavia Magalhães, and Sidney Chalhoub, eds. *Pensadores negros— pensadoras negras, Brasil, séculos XIX e XX*. Rio de Janeiro: MC&G Editorial; Belo Horizonte: Editora Fino Traço, 2016.

Pontes de Miranda. *Fontes e evolução do direito civil brasileiro*. Rio de Janeiro: Forense, 1981 (1928).

———. *O sistema de ciência positiva do direito*. 4 vols. São Paulo: Bookseller, 2005.

———. *Tratado de direito privado*. São Paulo: Bookseller, 2013.

"Proposta de um voto de pesar pelo falecimento do Conselheiro Antonio Pereira Rebouças." *Revista do Instituto Histórico e Geográfico Brasileiro* 43, no. 2 (1880): 540–47.

Quarles, Benjamin. "The Revolutionary War as a Black Declaration of Independence." In *Slavery and Freedom in the Age of American Revolution*, edited by Ira Berlin and Ronald Hoffman, 283–301. Charlottesville: University of Virginia Press, 1983.

Quintas, Amaro. "A agitação republicana no Nordeste." In *História geral da civilização brasileira*, edited by Sergio Buarque de Holanda. Vol 3. São Paulo: DIFEL, 1976.

Ramalho, Joaquim Ignácio. *Prática civil e comum*. São Paulo: Typographia Imparcial de Joaquim Roberto de Azevedo Marques, 1861.

Rasmussen, Daniel. *American Uprising: The Untold Story of America's Largest Slave Revolt*. New York: Harper Perennial, 2012.

Rebouças, André. *Apontamentos para a biografia do Engenheiro Antonio Pereira Rebouças Filho*. Rio de Janeiro: Tipografia Nacional, 1874.

———. *Diário e notas autobiográficas: texto escolhido e anotado por Ana Flora e José Ignácio Veríssimo*. Rio de Janeiro: Livraria José Olympio, 1938.

Rebouças, Antonio Pereira. *Aos poderes politicos e aos brasileiros em geral*. Rio de Janeiro: Laemmert, 1867.

———. *Ao Sr. Chefe de Polícia, responde o Rebouças*. Bahia: Typographia de Manoel Antonio da Silva Serva, 1838.

———. *Exposição por parte do visconde da Torre de Garcia d'Ávila à Assembléia Geral Legislativa do Império*. Rio de Janeiro: Typografia Brasiliense de F. M. Ferreira, 1851.

———. *Observações do advogado Antonio Pereira Rebouças à Consolidação das Leis Civis do dr. Augusto Teixeira de Freitas*. Rio de Janeiro: Typographia do Correio Mercantil de M. Barreto, Filhos e Octaviano, 1859.

———. "O Cavalo de Mazzepa." *Revista Mensal do Ensaio Philosophico Paulistano*, series 5a, no. 6 (São Paulo) (September 30, 1855).

———. *Petição dirigida aos srs. Representantes da nação brasileira para ser reconhecido habilitado para exercer quaisquer empregos para os quais se hão por habilitados os bacharéis formados como se carta de formatura tivesse*. Rio de Janeiro: Tipografia do Brasil, 1847.

———. *Recordações da vida parlamentar do advogado Antonio Pereira Rebouças: moral, jurisprudência, política e liberdade constitucional*. Vols. 1 and 2. Rio de Janeiro: Laemmert, 1870.

———. *Recordações da vida patriótica do advogado Rebouças*. Rio de Janeiro: Typographia G. Leuzinger & Filhos, 1879.

———. *Requerimento dirigido ao imperador D. Pedro I*. Rio de Janeiro: Typographia Nacional, 1823.

Rebouças, Manoel Mauricio. *Tratado sobre educação doméstica e pública em harmonia com a ordem do desenvolvimento orgânico dos sexos desde a gestação até a emancipação civil e política*. Bahia: Typographia de Antonio Olavo da França Guerra, 1859.

Reis, João José. *Death Is a Festival: Funeral Rites and Rebellion in Nineteenth-Century Brazil*. Chapel Hill: University of North Carolina Press, 2003.

―――. *Slave Rebellion in Brazil: The Muslim Uprising of 1835 in Bahia.* Baltimore: Johns Hopkins University Press, 1995.

Reis, João José, and Herbert Klein. "Slavery in Brazil." In *The Oxford Handbook of Latin American History,* edited by José Moya. DOI: 10.1093/oxfordhb/9780195166217.013.0007.

Resende, Francisco de Paula F. *Minhas recordações.* São Paulo: Editora Itatiaia, 1988.

Ribas, Antonio Joaquim. *Curso de direito civil brasileiro—parte geral.* Rio de Janeiro: Laemmert, 1865.

Ribeiro, Gladys Sabina. *A liberdade em construção: identidade nacional e conflitos antilusitanos no Preimeira Reinado.* Rio de Janeiro: FAPERJ/Relume Dumará, 2002.

Ricci, Magda. *Assombrações de um padre regente: Diogo Antonio Feijó, 1784–1843.* Campinas: Editora da Unicamp, 2002.

Robertson, David. *Denmark Vesey: The Buried Story of America's Largest Slave Rebellion and the Man Who Led It.* New York: Vintage, 2000.

Rocha, Manuel Antonio Coelho da. *Instituições de direito civil português.* 7th ed. (1852). Lisbon: Livraria Clássica Editora, 1907.

Roche, Maurice. "Citizenship, Social Theory, and Social Change." *Theory and Society* 16, no. 3 (May 1987): 363–99.

Rodrigues, João José. *Consultas jurídicas ou coleção de propostas sobre questões de direito civil, comercial, criminal, administrativo e eclesiástico respondidas pelos Primeiros Jurisconsultos Brasileiros.* 2 vols. Rio de Janeiro: Laemmert, 1873.

Rodrigues, José Honório. *A Assembléia Constituinte de 1823.* Petropolis: Vozes, 1974.

―――. *Teoria da história do Brasil.* 2 vols. São Paulo: Companhia Editora Nacional, 1975.

"A Sabinada nas Cartas de Barreto Pedroso a Rebouças." *Anais da Biblioteca Nacional* 88 (1968): 207–18.

Salles, Ricardo. *Joaquim Nabuco: um pensador do Império.* Rio de Janeiro: Topbooks, 2002.

―――. "Passive Revolution and the Politics of Second Slavery in the Brazilian Empire." In *The Politics of Second Slavery,* edited by Dale Tomich. New York: State University of New York Press, 2017.

Santos, Maria Helena Carvalho dos. *Portugal no século XVIII–de D. João V à Revolução francesa: comunicações apresentadas ao Congresso Internacional da Sociedade Portuguesa de Estudos do século XVIII.* Lisbon: Editora Universitária, 1991.

Santos, Wanderley Guilherme dos. *Ordem burguesa e liberalismo político.* São Paulo: Duas Cidades, 1978.

Schafer, Judith Kelleher. *Becoming Free, Remaining Free: Manumission and Enslavement in New Orleans, 1846–1862.* Baton Rouge: Louisiana State University Press, 2003.

―――. *Slavery, the Civil Law and the Supreme Court of Louisiana.* Baton Rouge: Louisiana State University Press, 1997.

Scheiber, Harry N., ed. *The State and Freedom of Contract.* Stanford: Stanford University Press, 1998.

Schulz, Kirsten. *Tropical Versailles: Empire, Monarchy and the Portuguese Royal Court in Rio de Janeiro, 1808–1821.* New York: Routledge, 2001.

Schwarcz, Lilia Moritz. *The Emperor's Beard: Dom Pedro II and His Tropical Monarchy in Brazil.* New York: Hill and Wang, 2003.

——. *O espetáculo das raças: cientistas, instituições e questão racial no Brasil—1870–1930.* São Paulo: Companhia das Letras, 1993.

Schwartz, Stuart. "Cantos and Quilombos: A Hausa Rebellion in Bahia, 1814." In *Slaves, Subjects and Subversives: Blacks in Colonial Latin America,* edited by Jane Landers and Barry Robinson. Albuquerque: University of New Mexico Press, 2006.

——. "The Manumission of Slaves in Colonial Brazil: Bahia, 1684–1745." *Hispanic American Historical Review* 54, no. 4 (November 1974): 603–35.

——. *Sugar Plantations in the Formation of Brazilian Society: Bahia, 1550–1835.* Cambridge: Cambridge University Press, 1985.

Schwarz, Roberto. *A Master on the Periphery of Capitalism: Machado de Assis.* Durham, NC: Duke University Press, 2011.

——. "Misplaced Ideas: Literature and Society in Nineteenth-Century Brazil." In *Misplaced Ideas: Essays on Brazilian Culture.* London: Verso, 1992.

Scott, Rebecca. "Fault Lines, Color Lines, and Party Lines: Race, Labor and Collective Action in Louisiana and Cuba, 1862–1912." In *Beyond Slavery: Explorations of Race, Labor, and Citizenship in Postemancipation Societies,* edited by Frederick Cooper, Thomas C. Holt, and Rebecca Scott. Chapel Hill: University of North Carolina Press, 2000.

Sewell, William H., Jr., "Le Citoyen/la Citoyenne: Activity, Passivity and the Revolutionary Concept of Citizenship." In *The French Revolution and the Creation of Modern Political Culture,* edited by Colin Lucas. Oxford: Pergamon Press, 1988.

Sharp, William. "Manumission, Libres, and Black Resistance: The Colombian Chocó, 1680–1810." In *Slavery and Race Relations in Latin America,* edited by Robert Brent Toplin, 89–111. Westport, CT: Greenwood Press, 1974.

Silva, Antonio Delgado da. "Coleção da Legislação Portuguesa (1750–1762)." *Revista do Instituto Histórico e Geográfico Brasileiro* 165, no. 424 (July/September 2004).

Silva, Daniel Afonso da. "A duras e pesadas penas: imprensa, identidade e nacionalidade no Brasil imperial." *Topoi* 10, no. 19 (July–December 2009): 55–69.

——. "Na trilha das 'garrafadas': a abdicação de D. Pedro I e a afirmação da identidade nacional brasileira na Bahia." *Analise Social* 47, no. 203 (2012): 268–97.

Silva, Innocencio Francisco da. *Dicionário bibliográfico português.* 23 vols. Lisbon: Imprensa Nacional/Casa da Moeda, 1973.

Silva, Justino Adriano Farias da. *Pequeno opúsculo sobre a vida e obra de Pontes de Miranda.* Porto Alegre: EST, 1981.

Silva, Maria Beatriz Nizza da, ed. *Cultura portuguesa na Terra de Santa Cruz.* Lisbon: Editorial Estampa, 1995.

Silva, Nuno Espinosa Gomes da. *História do direito português.* Lisbon: FCG, 1985.

Singham, Shanti M. "Jews, Blacks, Women, and the Declaration of the Rights of Man." In *The French Idea of Freedom: The Old Regime and the Declaration of Rights of 1789*, edited by Dale Van Kley, 115–53. Stanford: Stanford University Press, 1994.

Sinha, Manisha. *The Slave's Cause: A History of Abolition*. New Haven, CT: Yale University Press, 2016.

Slemian, Andrea. *Sob o império das leis: constituição e unidade nacional na formação do Brasil*. São Paulo: Hucitec, 2009.

Soares, Caetano Alberto. "Direito civil—questões de liberdade—Se escravos libertos em testamento com obrigação de servir tiverem filhos enquanto durar este ônus, eles são livres—etc." *Revista do Instituto dos Advogados Brasileiros* (1977) (originally published in 1862 and 1863).

———. *Memória para melhorar a sorte dos nossos escravos, lida na sessão geral do Instituto dos Advogados Brasileiros, no dia 7 de setembro de 1845*. Rio de Janeiro: Typographia de Paula Brito, 1847.

Sobrinho, J. F. *Dicionário bio-bibliográfico brasileiro*. Vol. 1, Rio de Janeiro: Irmãos Pongetti, 1937. Vol. 2, Rio de Janeiro: Ministério de Educação e Saúde, 1940.

Souza, Antonio Loureiro de. *Bahianos ilustres*. Salvador: Ibrasa, 1979.

Souza, Iara Lis Franco Schiavinatto Carvalho. *Pátria coroada: o Brasil como corpo político autônomo (1780–1831)*. São Paulo: UNESP, 1999.

Souza, J. Galante de. *O teatro no Brasil*. Vol. 1, *Evolução do teatro no Brasil*. Rio de Janeiro: MEC/INL, 1960.

Souza, Otávio Tarquínio. *Bernardo Pereira de Vasconcelos*. Belo Horizonte: Itatiaia/São Paulo: EDUSP, 1988.

———. *Diogo Antonio Feijó*. Rio de Janeiro: Livraria José Olympio, 1942.

———. *História dos fundadores do Império do Brasil*. Rio de Janeiro: José Olympio, 1957.

Souza, Paulo Cesar. *A Sabinada: a revolta separatista da Bahia, 1837*. São Paulo: Brasiliense, 1987.

Souza Franco, Bernardo. "A situação econômica e financeira do Brasil." *Bibliotheca Brasileira*, vol. 1:1 and 2 (1863).

———. *Discursos pronunciados na Câmara dos Deputados na sessão de 1851 da nona legislatura da assembléia geral*. Rio de Janeiro: Tipographia Nacional, 1851.

———. *Os bancos do Brazil, sua história, defeitos da organização atual e reforma do sistema bancário*. Rio de Janeiro: Tipographia Nacional, 1848.

Spitzer, Leo. *Lives in Between: The Experience of Marginality in a Century of Assimilation*. Cambridge: Cambridge University Press, 1989.

Stanziani, Alessandro. "Slavery, Debt and Bondage: The Mediterranean and the Eurasia Connection from the Fifteenth to Eighteenth Century." In *Debt and Slavery in the Mediterranean and Atlantic World*, edited by Gwyn Campbell and Alessandro Stanziani. London: Pickering and Chatto, 2013.

Taunay, Affonso. *Grandes vultos da independência do Brasil*. São Paulo: Companhia Melhoramentos, 1922.

Tavares, Luis Henrique Dias. *A independência do Brasil na Bahia*. Rio de Janeiro: Civilização Brasileira/Brasília: Instituto Nacional do Livro, 1982.

Teixeira, Antonio Ribeiro da Liz. *Curso de direito civil portugues; ou Commentario às Instituições do sr. Paschoal José de Mello Freire sobre o mesmo direito. . . .* 2 vols. Coimbra: Imprensa da Universidade, 1848.

Teixeira de Freitas, Augusto. *Código civil: Esboço.* Rio de Janeiro: Ministério da Justiça e Negócios Interiores, 1952.

Telles, José Homem Correia. *Digesto português, ou Tratado dos modos de adquirir a propriedade, de a gozar e administrar, e de a transferir por derradeira vontade; para servir de subsídio ao novo código civil.* Coimbra: Imprensa da Universidade, 1846.

Tomich, Dale, and Rafael Marquese. "O Vale do Paraíba escravista e a formação do mercado mundial do café no século XIX." In *O Brasil imperial*, vol. 2, edited by Keila Grinberg and Ricardo Salles. Rio de Janeiro: Civilização Brasileira, 2009.

Torres, João Camillo de Oliveira. *O Conselho de Estado.* Rio de Janeiro: Edições GRD, 1965.

Turner, Bryan S. "Outline of a Theory of Citizenship." *Sociology* 24, no. 2 (May 1990): 189–217.

Uricoechea, Fernando. *O minotauro imperial: a burocratização do Estado patrimonial brasileiro no século XIX.* São Paulo: Difel, 1978.

Valladão, Alfredo. *Da aclamação à maioridade, 1822–1840.* Rio de Janeiro: Companhia Editora Nacional, 1939.

Vampré, Spencer. *Memórias para a história da Academia de São Paulo.* Brasília: INL, 1977.

Veiga, Gláucio. *História das idéias da Faculdade de Direito do Recife.* Recife: Universitária, 1980.

Velloso-Rabello, A. *Aperçu des sources historiques du droit brésilien.* Brussels: Imprimerie F. Van Buggenhoudt, 1911.

Venâncio Filho, Alberto. *Das arcadas ao bacharelismo.* São Paulo: Perspectiva, 1977.

——. *Francisco Gê Acaiaba de Montezuma, Visconde de Jequitinhonha, 1º presidente do Instituto dos Advogados Brasileiros.* Rio de Janeiro: IAB, 1984.

Veríssimo, Ignácio José. *André Rebouças através de sua autobiografia.* Rio de Janeiro: José Olympio, 1939.

Viana Filho, Luiz. *A Sabinada (a República bahiana de 1837).* Rio de Janeiro: José Olympio, 1938.

Vilhena, Luís dos Santos. *Recopilação de notícias soteropolitanas e brasílicas contidas em XX cartas, ano de 1802.* Salvador: Imprensa Oficial do Estado da Bahia, 1921.

Weber, Max. *Economy and Society.* 2 vols. Berkeley: University of California Press, 2013.

White, Shane. *Somewhat More Independent: The End of Slavery in New York City, 1770–1810.* Athens: University of Georgia Press, 1991.

Whitman, Stephen. *The Price of Freedom: Slavery and Manumission in Baltimore and Early National Maryland.* Lexington: University Press of Kentucky, 1997.

Index

Note: Information in figures and tables is indicated by *f* and *t*.

9 781469 652771